THE COWBOY PRESIDENT

THE AMERICAN WEST AND THE MAKING OF THEODORE ROOSEVELT

MICHAEL F. BLAKE

TWODOT®

Guilford, Connecticut
Helena, Montana

To
Nolan and Liam Dame,
my favorite Rough Riders,
and
Terry Shulman,
from Lincoln to TR and beyond.

A · TWODOT® · BOOK

An imprint of Globe Pequot
A registered trademark of Rowman & Littlefield

Distributed by NATIONAL BOOK NETWORK

British Library Cataloguing in Publication Information available
Library of Congress Cataloging-in-Publication Data available

ISBN 978-1-4930-3071-2 (paperback)
ISBN 978-1-4930-3072-9 (e-book)

♾™ The paper used in this publication meets the minimum requirements of American National Standard for Information Sciences—Permanence of Paper for Printed Library Materials, ANSI/NISO Z39.48-1992.

Printed in the United States of America

CONTENTS

It was still the Wild West in those days, the Far West, the West of Owen Wister's stories and Frederic Remington's drawings, the West of the Indian and the buffalo-hunter, the soldier and the cow-puncher . . . It was a land of vast silent spaces, of lonely rivers, and of plains where the wild game stared at the passing horseman.
—*THEODORE ROOSEVELT: AN AUTOBIOGRAPHY,* 1913

PREFACE

HE LED THE ROUGH RIDERS TO GLORY, CHARGING UP SAN JUAN HILL. As police commissioner of New York City, he instituted sweeping changes and fought corruption inside and outside the department. When he was governor, he served the people of the Empire State, not the wishes of the party bosses. As president, he took on J. P. Morgan's railroad trust—and won. He pushed Congress to pass both the Meat Inspection Act and the Pure Food and Drug Act, and he ended a devastating coal strike just before the onset of a harsh winter. He helped Panama gain its independence from Colombia, and started building the canal that would link the Atlantic and Pacific oceans. To end the war between Russia and Japan, he brought them to the table and negotiated a peace treaty. For his efforts, he was the *first* US president to be awarded the Nobel Peace Prize.

In his lifetime, he authored thirty-seven books and hundreds of magazine articles and editorials. As president, he preserved over 230 million acres of unspoiled land for the American public. He was a respected ornithologist, a big-game hunter, and an ardent conservationist. He spoke French and German and read a copy of Tolstoy's *Anna Karenina* while pursuing boat thieves in the Dakotas. He loved boxing, and when he was blinded in one eye from a sparring match, took up judo, earning a third-degree brown belt. A sickly child, he long suffered from asthma and digestive problems, yet endorsed "the strenuous life," partaking in hiking, rowing, swimming, horseback riding, and tennis. He disliked fishing, finding it too sedentary for his taste. An avid reader, he consumed two books a week and rarely went anywhere without a book at his side.

He was the inspiration for the beloved teddy bear.

When he walked into a room, his personal energy was that of a tornado blowing through. He was charismatic, magnetic, forceful, funny, egotistical, and moralistic. His eldest daughter, Alice, once described her father as wanting to be the "bride at every wedding, and the corpse at every funeral."[1] Even his enemies admitted he was a force to be reckoned with, but couldn't help liking him despite his policies.

This was Theodore Roosevelt.

Throughout the years, numerous historians and biographers have highlighted all of these accomplishments and traits, as well as many others. However, lost in many of these texts is how and where Theodore, the reedy dude from New York, became the Theodore Roosevelt who gazes down at us from Mount Rushmore. When did he become the man who was known for saying "Walk softly, but carry a big stick"? Where did his love for the land turn him into an impassioned conservationist? Who inspired him to stand up for and defend the American people?

Historians properly note that Theodore's father was a major influence in his life, but his actions over the course of his sixty years were not entirely dominated by the things his father had taught him. *Something else* had had a profound impact on his life and his actions. It is this entity that most biographers quickly breeze over, when writing about Theodore in the rush to detail his presidential years. In doing so, they do both Theodore's memory and the reader a disservice in overlooking this major influence.

It was the American West.

Granted, his biographers explain how his time in the Dakota Territory helped him to overcome personal grief and strengthened his body. They also mention his dealing with a drunken cowboy and arresting some boat thieves. But Theodore's time in the Dakotas did more than just heal his broken heart and bolster his physique. His time in the West was where the man carved on Mount Rushmore began to take shape—where he learned how to carry a big stick, and when to use it. It was in the West that Theodore learned firsthand about the importance of conservation.

Then there were the people. The men and women who lived in the West influenced and shaped his beliefs by example. Unlike the blue-bloods of Fifth Avenue or the questionable politicians of the New York Assembly, the people of the West were the type of individuals toward whom Theodore easily gravitated. Their integrity, courage, humor, and ability to adapt to harsh conditions resonated with him. They were, in many ways, spiritual allies, and the people of the Western lands were, allegorically, descendants of Daniel Boone and Davy Crockett, two of

Theodore's heroes. The people of the Dakotas had come to the West to start new lives, braving hardships and loneliness. They did not complain when things got tough. The strong survived; the weak perished. Theodore saw in these people a bit of himself. Many had little advance knowledge of how to survive on the prairies or in the mountains, but they learned by doing. When they survived whatever mishaps their mistakes brought them, they counted themselves lucky for having learned a valuable lesson and continued on.

In his lifetime, Theodore would come to know failure. Failure is one of life's bitter lessons that all of us must learn from. He put it in perspective when he stated, "It is hard to fail, but it is worse never to have tried to succeed."[2]

Theodore Roosevelt's proving ground was the American West. Here he would test himself against what Nature had to offer. He loved a good fight, whether it was getting one of his policies enacted in Washington, riding his horse across a swollen river, or chopping down a tree and removing its stump. The tougher, the better. Meeting the challenge was what truly mattered to him, not necessarily the winning. If he failed but had fought an honorable fight, he accepted the outcome with dignity.

The West would shape him, his policies, and, eventually, a nation.

The men and women of the Western lands lived by their own code. This code was not written on a stone tablet, nor taught in a school. They learned it by doing. By living. It was passed on from family to family, cowboy to cowboy. This code was simple yet insightful. Like a cowboy, they were spare and to the point. You took pride in your work. A person's word was their bond. You could be tough, but fair. You knew where to draw the line, and that some things could never be bought. And, most importantly, you rode for the brand.[3]

Theodore Roosevelt came to embody these unspoken commandments while living in the Dakotas. They were part and parcel of his everyday life. One may contend that Theodore was already living many of these edicts before he went west, and there are illustrations to support that theory. However, it wasn't until he was in the West that they truly manifested themselves, cementing his foundation of beliefs. This code of honor would influence many of his decisions throughout his life.

His time in the West was not only an education, but also where he came to restore himself. Whether it was mending a broken heart or simply taking a break from the presidency, Theodore continually returned to the West. The Badlands, Yellowstone, and Yosemite allowed him to reconnect with what mattered most to him and brought him great joy. The wide-open spaces became his sanctuary, where he could lose himself riding alone for days on end.

The most important thing a person must understand about Theodore Roosevelt is that he was a romantic—not only in the sense of romance between a man and a woman, but also toward life itself. Theodore believed deep within his heart the romantic notions of honor and duty, much like the knights in the medieval era, and as found in the adventure novels he consumed as a child. Theodore always had one emotional foot in the romanticism of the era that was quickly passing, clinging to its creed as a guide in the waning years of the "modern" nineteenth century.

He had an ongoing love affair with the West ever since his childhood, when he read about hardy pioneers crossing the plains and the mountains. When he was old enough to visit those areas himself, they ignited a passion within him. Even in the harshest of conditions, he found beauty in the West. It became his adopted home, and he considered himself more of a Westerner than an Easterner. His love of the West is demonstrated not only in his actions, but also in his writing. When he writes about riding in the Badlands in the early hours as the sun is just breaking over the horizon, it's not a picture he is painting for the readers; it is his heart, speaking the truth.

The American West transformed Theodore Roosevelt, and he returned the favor by protecting it and instilling in others the love he had for it.

A YOUNG MAN IN MOTION

I'm inclined to look back at it [childhood] with some wonder that I should have come out of it as well as I have!

AT THE AGE OF TWENTY-FOUR, THEODORE ROOSEVELT WAS HARDLY what anyone would have called "cowboy material"—let alone presidential. He was a beanpole of young man, adorned with glasses and a high voice, and was asthmatic and suffering from digestive problems.[1]

Erudite and highly moralistic, he wasn't the type one would expect to embrace the rough-and-tumble life of the American West. When he came west, the locals of Medora called him "Rosenfelder," "Four Eyes," and "Storm Windows." He didn't help matters by dressing in what he thought was standard cowboy clothing of the day: buckskin shirt and pants (they were *not* made by Brooks Brothers), a silver Bowie knife made by Tiffany, a nickel-plated, engraved Colt pistol, and alligator-hide boots. Locals laughed over his enthusiastic usage of "By Jove!" and "By Godfrey!"

He was definitely different. But, as Theodore once noted, "It is always better to be an original than an imitation." And original he was.

What he lacked physically in his young childhood, he countered with knowledge. A voracious reader all his life (he was known to finish a book within a day or two), young Theodore quickly fell in love with the written word. Theodore once noted that his parents did not compel him to read books, having "the good sense not to try to get me to read anything I did not like, unless it was in the way of study."[2] He was a boy filled with imagination of adventures in the faraway lands of the American West or the dark, unknown jungles of Africa. His health limited his physical activity at times, so Theodore lived vicariously through the heroes he

I

found in books. Daniel Boone and Davy Crockett were two of his childhood favorites, as were the characters in James Fenimore Cooper's trilogy of the American frontier. Heroes larger than life allowed the sickly boy to escape, at least in his imagination, by leading the charge of an army or fighting off Indians attacking a fort. Another author, Mayne Reid, made an important impression on Theodore with his 1853 book, *The Boy Hunters*,[3] sparking Theodore's early interest in natural history.

Unbeknownst to his parents, Theodore was tremendously nearsighted. The young boy had no idea how bad his eyesight was until one day, at the age of thirteen, he realized he could not read a billboard with huge letters. (Jack Willis, a hunter friend from Montana, recalled Theodore could not recognize anyone ten feet away without his glasses.[4]) Relaying this information to his father, he was fitted with a pair of eyeglasses. The optical lenses "literally opened an entirely new world to me. I had no idea how beautiful the world was until I got those spectacles." The incident also imbued Theodore with a "keen sympathy" for children in school who were "often unjustly blamed" for being "obstinate, unambitious, or mentally stupid."[5]

New York City in the 1850s and 1860s was hardly the optimal location for a child with asthma. The city's poor air quality from the heavy use of burning wood and coal (primary sources for fuel and heat) certainly contributed to Theodore's severe bouts, the first striking him at age three. Asthma is a chronic inflammation of the airways, causing shortness of breath, and for an adult, it can be irritating and frustrating. For a child, it is beyond frightening.

Theodore recalled numerous times in his childhood when he would sit up in bed, gasping for air. He remembered how his father would carry him in his arms, walking up and down in his room in an effort to soothe him. Sometimes, when the attacks came at night, Theodore's father would bundle the boy up and take him for a ride in the family carriage, hoping the night air would provide relief. Unlike today, when medication can relieve an asthmatic attack, there was little in the way of treatment to help in Theodore's era. His parents often filled him with coffee or made him smoke a cigar, the latter making him sick, thus breaching his asthma attack.[6]

Fortunately, Theodore's parents could afford the best medical attention that money could buy. The Roosevelt family was part of a small group of wealthy New Yorkers whose forebears dated to 1649, when the area was known as New Amsterdam. (Theodore was the seventh generation of Roosevelts to be born in New York.) Theodore's paternal grandfather, Cornelius Van Schaack Roosevelt, ran the family firm, Roosevelt and Son, which dealt in finance and became a leading plate-glass supplier in the country. Theodore Roosevelt Sr., fifth son of Cornelius, born in 1831, joined the family firm twenty years later. He was placed in charge of the plate-glass division, where he did quite well, until the 1873 financial panic forced the company to divest its plate-glass business to focus solely on banking.

During a trip to Georgia in 1850, Theodore Sr. met Martha ("Mittie") Bulloch, "a sweet, gracious, beautiful Southern woman." Born in Hartford, Connecticut, in 1835, Martha and her family moved to a mansion (dubbed Bulloch Hall) near Roswell, Georgia, four years later. At their plantation, the Bulloch family owned thirty slaves who, by all reports, were treated much like family. (However, that feeling did not stop Martha's half-brother, James, from killing a slave in a fit of anger.) During the Civil War, James served as the Confederacy's chief agent in England, where he purchased ships and outfitted them with cannons and a crew to attack blockades and raid Union commercial ships. (It has been rumored that some of Bulloch's funds may have had a hand in the Lincoln assassination.[7]) In later years, James shared his knowledge of ships and naval fighting with Theodore, which proved useful when he authored his book on the War of 1812 naval actions.

Theodore Sr. and Martha married on December 22, 1853, in Bulloch Hall; after a honeymoon, the couple returned to New York City. They moved into a fashionable five-story brownstone at 28 East Twentieth Street, a gift for the newlyweds from Theodore Sr.'s father. Their first child, Anna (nicknamed "Bamie"), was born in 1855. Theodore Roosevelt Jr. was born on October 27, 1858. (For most of his childhood his family called him "Teddie," a name he disliked as he grew older.) Brother Elliott was born in 1860, and sister Corinne in 1861. Not only was Theodore a sickly child, but his siblings also suffered from ailments. As a baby, Bamie was accidentally dropped, which caused a lifelong spinal problem that forced her to wear a brace. Elliott suffered from headaches (and later epilepsy), while Corinne had to deal with her own bouts of asthma.

Martha Roosevelt was the quintessential Southern belle. She bathed twice a day, her skin was described as "moonlight white," and, in any season, she dressed in white. Having expensive tastes, she decorated her homes with the finest furniture and sculptures. Although she was a loving mother, Martha suffered a setback with the end of the Civil War. Her beloved South was in ruins, her brothers were exiled in London, and her mother died, all at once. She became languid, almost brittle, falling into a childlike capacity that made her unable to handle even basic daily household duties.

By all accounts, the Roosevelt children had a happy relationship with their parents. Theodore adored his father, treasuring every minute he spent with him. Martha, albeit reluctantly, seems to have accepted that Theodore was his father's favorite. As the oldest, Bamie came to help her younger siblings as time went on. Letters between her and Theodore indicate she became his confidante, especially as a young adult. Elliott lived in the shadow of his older brother, burdened with that age-old curse of always trying to be better, but the two boys remained close growing up. Corinne followed along wherever Theodore went.

When the Civil War began in April 1861, it tore families apart—including the Roosevelts. The Bulloch family's loyalty fell to the Confederacy, while Theodore Sr. was a confirmed Lincoln-Union supporter. With Martha awaiting the birth of their fourth child, Theodore Sr. faced a decision that many men, in both the North and the South, were confronting. Martha's brothers had joined the opposition; adding to the tension, her mother and sister were now living with them. For Theodore Sr. to march off and fight against the Confederacy would place tremendous strain on his marriage, not to mention the possibility of his having to fire on one of his in-laws in battle. Therefore, like others who had the financial means, Theodore Sr. paid a bounty and hired a substitute to serve in his place.[8] To help in the war effort, Theodore Sr. sponsored a civilian commission that visited various military camps, urging soldiers to set aside money to send home instead of spending their meager pay with unscrupulous sutlers.

Corinne always believed Theodore was forever disappointed that his father chose *not* to fight for the Union, while his uncles defended the Confederacy. (A teenaged Theodore reportedly said he would have fought for the Union if he had been old enough.) Interestingly, his autobiography omits any mention of his father's choosing not to fight in the Civil War and his work on civilian committees. Theodore's tendency to completely ignore something that was painful to him would become very obvious in two decades. It also explains why he was so fervent in wanting to be part of the Spanish-American War, forming his own group of army volunteers.

In 1865, at the age of seven, Theodore's interest in natural history took hold of him. Passing an outdoor market one day, he spied a dead seal laid out on a slab of wood. The mammal filled "me with every possible feeling of romance and adventure."⁹ He eventually obtained the seal's skull, and with two cousins quickly established the "Roosevelt Museum of Natural History." Two years later, Theodore wrote a detailed thesis (with illustrations) entitled "Natural History of Insects," detailing "their habits from observ-a-tion" of ants, spiders, fireflies, beetles, and dragonflies. He soon found himself mesmerized by birds, reading every book he could, taking profuse notes, and sketching meticulous drawings. Theodore, much to the distaste of the household help and his mother, also took up taxidermy. (None of the Roosevelt children attended school, having private tutors to oversee their educational needs.)

When Theodore turned twelve, his father, concerned that his son was still frail and reedy, told the boy he had to expand his body as he had his mind. Young Theodore took the advice to heart, and with the tenacity he would display in his adult life, began to remake his body. The second-floor piazza was set up with all sorts of athletic equipment, and, very slowly, the exercises began to show results. During a trip to Maine, Theodore learned a humbling lesson. Another asthma attack sent him on his own to Moosehead Lake, where two boys his own age bullied and picked on him unmercifully. Finally standing up to defend himself, the two boys, he wrote later, handled "me so as not to hurt me much," and prevented him from inflicting "any damage." Returning home, he asked to learn the art of boxing, which was taught to him by former prizefighter John Long. Theodore, by his own admission, was a "slow and awkward pupil," but stayed at it. "I can see his rooms now, with colored pictures of the fights between Tom Hyer and Yankee Sullivan, and Heenan and Sayers, and other great events in the annals of the squared circle," he recalled in his autobiography.[10] During his presidency, Theodore was boxing with an army officer one day when he received a hard blow, leaving him blind in his left eye. He never mentioned it, fearing it would result in a backlash against the officer.

Theodore's father planned another European excursion in October 1872, focusing not only on parts of Europe, but also Egypt and the Holy Land. (Their first visit was in 1869–70.) For Theodore, the land of Egypt was filled with adventure. "At eight o'clock we arrived in sight of Alexandria. How I gazed on it! It was Egypt, the land of my dreams. . . . It was a sight to awaken a thousand thoughts, and it did."[11] He rode an Arabian horse he named Grant over the sands. He said the animal was "very swift, pretty and spirited." He found the Jordan River to be, in his eyes, the equivalent of a small creek back home. As the family cruised up the Nile River, Theodore noted in a letter to his aunt Anna (Mittie's sister) that "I think I have never enjoyed myself so much as in this month. There has always been something to do, for we could always fall back upon shooting when everything else fails us. And then we had those splendid and grand old ruins to see, and one of them will stock you with thoughts for a month. The templ[e] that I enjoyed most was Karnak. We saw it by moonlight. I never was impressed by anything so much. To wander among those great columns under the same moon that had looked down on them for thousands of years was awe-inspiring; it gave rise to thoughts of the ineffable, the unutterable; thoughts which you cannot express, which cannot be uttered, which cannot be answered until after The Great Sleep."[12]

It was during this monthlong cruise that Theodore shot his first African bird. "I have had great enjoyment from the shooting here . . . As you are probably aware Father presented me on Christmas with a double barreled breech loading shot gun, which I never move on shore without, excepting on Sundays," he wrote his aunt Anna.[13] It was the beginning of Theodore's fascination with hunting, not to mention mounting his trophies. He associated hunting with manliness; it was a way of proving oneself against nature, a rite of passage into adulthood. The characteristics found in Basil, the hero of Mayne Reid's *The Boy Hunters*, are mirrored in Theodore. For Basil, the chase of the quarry is the biggest thrill, even more so than the actual killing. The danger the chase provides stirs his emotions. It was the same for Theodore, who always found the chase the most exciting part of hunting.

"The chase is among the best of all national pastimes; it cultivates that vigorous manliness for the lack of which in nation, as in the individual, the possession of no other qualities can possibly atone," he wrote in the preface of *The Wilderness Hunter*.[14] Like many events in his life, hunting a wild beast was a test of his ability, to prove to himself that he could do it, and succeed.

Theodore turned fifteen as his family sailed back to America in the fall of 1873. After a year and a half of private tutoring, Theodore passed Harvard's entrance exams and was accepted into the class of 1880. He had designs to major in natural sciences, and his father advised him that if this was his chosen field, he would have to take it seriously. Theodore also understood that if he selected science as a career, he "must abandon all thought of the enjoyment" a moneymaking career could offer, and "find my pleasures elsewhere."[15] At the university, Theodore became disillusioned with their approach to natural sciences, which "utterly ignored the possibilities of the fauna naturalist, the outdoor naturalist and observer of nature." Harvard treated biology as a science of the laboratory and microscope, something that a man with Theodore's energy could not tolerate. He had to be outside, observing and watching nature in its element. For him, working in a laboratory was akin to sitting in a jail cell. "There was a total failure to understand the great variety of kinds of work that could be done by naturalists . . . . My taste was specialized in a totally different direction, and I had no more desire or ability to be a microscopist and section-cutter than to be a mathematician. Accordingly, I abandoned all thought of becoming a scientist."[16]

In his first year, Latin and mathematics proved to be his shortcomings, and he had to make a mad scramble to keep up his grades. His memory was very good (some said it was close to photographic), especially when it was something that interested him, such as poems and the common names of birds. Basically, whatever stimulated his interest, he never forgot.

Harvard students who took a first glance at Theodore that freshman year were left with an odd impression. He wore his sideburns in the muttonchops style; he ran from one class to another (it was considered bad form to run anywhere at the university); he had a high voice, and was oblivious to the others students' loud shenanigans while he studied at the library—not to mention his hobby of conducting taxidermy in his room. However, his personality and growing charisma soon won over his detractors. Theodore became a member of the Delta Kappa Epsilon fraternity, joined the Porcellian Club in his junior year (membership was the highest social honor at the university), and served as the secretary in the Hasty Pudding Club. He was also president of the literary fraternity, Alpha Delta Phi, and vice president of the Natural History Society.

Theodore longed to play football, but not only did his myopic eyesight prevent him, his slight build and lack of coordination also left him on the sidelines of most sports. However, hiking, rowing, and riding horses filled him with great delight. Classmate Richard Welling recalled that he agreed to accompany Theodore ice-skating one afternoon. Welling, having observed his friend's slight build while exercising at the school gymnasium, thought their excursion on the ice would be short-lived. The ice on the pond proved to be very rough, and the wind bitingly harsh. After a few minutes on skates, Welling thought to himself, Theodore would have enough. Instead, the bespectacled skater had a grand time, exclaiming, "Isn't this bully!" Welling wanted to quit, but Theodore showed no signs of letting up. The harder the wind blew, the better Theodore liked it, continually exclaiming how "bully" it was. Only when darkness fell did Theodore call it a day.[17]

Theodore Sr. began experiencing intestinal cramps in late October 1877. His condition worsened in early December, when he collapsed, with doctors believing he had acute peritonitis. Theodore Sr. did his utmost to hide his discomfort from his children—especially Theodore. "I am very uneasy about Father," Theodore wrote to his sister Bamie on December 16. "Does the Doctor think it anything serious? I think that a traveling trip would be the best thing for him; he has always too much work on hand. Thank fortune, my own health is excellent, and so, when I get home, I can with a clear conscience give him a rowing up for not taking better care of himself."[18] Arriving home for the holidays, the son naturally worried over his father's condition, yet on Christmas Day, he noted in his diary that his father was "much better."

Theodore returned to Harvard after the holidays, unaware how dire his father's condition really was. It was not acute peritonitis but a malignant tumor in the bowels that had left him screaming in agony.[19] Late Saturday afternoon, February 9, Theodore received a telegram instructing him to come home immediately. Hopping the overnight train, he arrived in the morning to find his father had passed away shortly before midnight. "I feel that if it were not for the certainty, that as he himself has so often said, 'He is not dead but gone before,' I should almost perish," Theodore wrote in his diary on February 12.[20]

Theodore Sr. left a long shadow for his children to fill. He had been a well-known philanthropist over the years, creating the Roosevelt Hospital, Bellevue Training School for Nurses, and the New York Orthopedic Dispensary for the Deformed and Crippled. He was a heavy donor to the YMCA, and founded the Children's Aid Society, the Society for the Prevention of Cruelty to Animals, the Metropolitan Museum of Art, and the American Museum of Natural History. On Sundays, he would teach in mission schools in the morning, while in the evenings, he served supper at the Newsboys' Lodging-House, which he also helped found. He took urchins off the street and, with the help of his Children's Aid Society, sent them to work and live on farms in the West. An oft-told story described Theodore Sr., with a fixed expression, walking into the offices of a business colleague. Seeing his determined look, they would simply ask, "How much this time, Theodore?"[21]

Theodore's father left him an inheritance of $125,000, which would be paid out annually in the sum of $8,000 per year. While it was a healthy amount for the time, it did not give him complete financial independence, but Theodore splurged, purchasing fine suits and, in his senior year, a horse and buggy.

During the early days of September 1878, he met a man who not only had an impact on his life, but with whom he formed a friendship that lasted until Theodore's death. William Sewall was an authentic woodsman, complete with a full beard. As a boy, he had learned the ways of the woods and was an expert with an ax. A respected logger, he also worked as a guide in the Maine woods. Theodore met him when he traveled to Island Falls for a hunting expedition on the recommendation of his old tutor, Arthur Cutler. Sewall, aware of Theodore's health issues, was doubtful the young man could handle the outdoor rigors, but he was quickly proven wrong.[22] For three weeks, the two men canoed, hiked, fished, swam in lakes and creeks, hunted, and camped. Theodore enjoyed every minute of it.

Sewall took a liking to Theodore almost from the start. He told his nephew, Wilmot Dow, that Theodore was "a different fellow to guide from what I had ever seen." Theodore was always obliging and never complained, even though it was obvious that he did not always seem up to snuff. (Decades later, Theodore admitted that in Sewall's company he would have been ashamed to have complained.) Sewall noted years later that people said Theodore was headstrong and aggressive, but he never found him to be that way except when necessary. "I've always thought that being headstrong and aggressive, on occasion, was a pretty good thing," he commented.[23]

For Theodore, Sewall was just like the frontiersmen he had read about in books—a living, breathing version of Crockett, Boone, and Natty Bumppo combined. (Sewall felt that his nephew, Wilmot, was a much better guide and hunter than he was.) Thirteen years older than Theodore, Sewall became the young man's mentor, showing him the ways of the woods, and also becoming the older brother Theodore never had. In Sewall's words, they "hitched well" from the beginning. Not only was he a gifted woodsman, but he was also well read and, like Theodore, a lover of heroic literature. The two would swap quotes from books as they paddled a canoe or hiked a trail.

In October of that year, Theodore's life took another change. He fell in love.

Alice Lee was a seventeen-year-old beauty from a Boston family. She was tall and energetic, with pale blue eyes framed by golden curls and a smile that many said just radiated. (Because of her intoxicating smile, family and friends nicknamed her "Sunshine.") They met at a party given by a friend and fellow Harvard classmate, Richard Saltonstall. Theodore was immediately smitten. "A very sweet, pretty girl" is how he described her. After spending Thanksgiving in her company, Theodore, in his typical fashion, vowed he would win her heart. It was a venture that would, at times, drive him "nearly crazy," as Alice, although fond of her pursuer, played coy with her true feelings. To distract himself from Alice's just-out-of-reach commitment, Theodore began writing what would become the first of his thirty-seven books, *The Naval War of 1812*, in December 1879.

"I am so happy that I dare not trust in my own happiness," Theodore wrote in his diary on January 20, 1880, regarding Alice's accepting his proposal of marriage.[24] Ten days before their wedding, he wrote to Alice, "Oh my darling, I do so hope and pray I can make you happy. I shall try very hard to be as unselfish and sunny tempered as you are, and I shall save you from every care I can. My own true love, you have made my happiness almost too great; and I feel I can do so little for you in return."[25]

They were married on his twenty-second birthday, October 27, 1880, at Brookline Unitarian Church. Spending a brief two-week honeymoon in Oyster Bay, New York, the newlyweds moved into the Roosevelt family home on Fifty-Seventh Street, occupying the third floor. The couple's official honeymoon began in May 1881, when they traveled to Ireland, England, France, Germany, Holland, and Switzerland. During their stay in the latter country, Theodore climbed the famous Matterhorn in two days. Ironically, just before he graduated from Harvard, a doctor examined him and found he had an irregular heartbeat. The physician advised his young patient to eliminate any strenuous activities. Typically, Theodore ignored the warning.

In June 1880, Theodore ranked number 21 out of 177 students at his graduation from Harvard. That fall he enrolled at Columbia Law School, but the practice of law lost its appeal for Theodore, who felt the teachings in the textbooks and classroom were "against justice." Examining his prospects, he felt limited. He enjoyed writing, but it could not sustain him and his wife. He had some interest in politics, but it wasn't the type of career a well-raised, cultured young man entered. The well-to-do regarded politics as a job for "lower types," such as saloon owners and laborers, although the wealthy did not hesitate to throw cash at a candidate that benefited their own interests. The profession of politics was a hard, often bruising, engagement—much like life in the West. Parties were run by an organization, not gentlemen. The term *political machine* was used to describe the groups that ran the Democratic and Republican parties. Tammany Hall was one of those political organizations, controlling the Democratic ticket in New York City. Such organizations would deliver votes for a chosen candidate in return for favors, such as lucrative city contracts, ignoring certain criminal acts, or creating a job as a favor. To reciprocate, the chosen candidate was assured of winning handily, plus receiving monetary favors.

The headquarters of the Twenty-First District of the Republican Party Association was situated above a saloon on Fifty-Ninth Street. They called it Morton Hall, which catered to businessmen and professionals, albeit a different caste than one would find on Fifth Avenue. It became the church of Theodore's political baptism.

Joseph Murray was one of those lower-society people the well-to-do ignored—unless they needed a political favor. A refugee from the Irish famine, Murray had fought in the Union Army, and later was recruited by Tammany Hall to help deliver votes for certain candidates. Murray, a street fighter, was not one to shy away from a confrontation in order to get a man elected. The power brokers in Tammany Hall had promised Murray many things for his help but never delivered. That was their mistake. Offended by their failure to keep the promises made to him, Murray switched to the Republican Party and made use of the same tactics he had used to help the Democrats. The result was that the Republicans won heavily in the next election, much to the dismay of Tammany Hall. Always on the lookout for a new candidate who would serve the Republican Party (and his own efforts), Murray soon settled on Theodore. When he suggested that the young man run for the State Assembly on the Republican ticket, Theodore jumped at the idea.

At the age of twenty-three, Theodore Roosevelt entered the political arena.

Because Theodore was a complete unknown on the ticket, Murray quickly went to work securing endorsements to vouch for his ability.

Murray obtained Joseph Choate and Elihu Root, of the Fifth Avenue population, to sing Theodore's praises.[26] "Having been nominated as a candidate for member of the Assembly for this District, I would esteem it a compliment if you honor me with your vote and personal influence on Election day," Theodore wrote in a letter distributed to voters of the Twenty-First Assembly District.[27]

That was only half of the work that needed to be done. Saloon owners were very important in getting the word out to vote for a certain candidate. Theodore's first visit to a saloon showed his handlers he was very much his own man. Reportedly, Murray and another associate took Theodore to press the flesh in saloons within the district. One saloon owner complained to Theodore that, at $200 a year, liquor licenses were too high. If the candidate was elected, the owner expected him to treat liquor interests fairly. Theodore replied that he intended to treat *all* interests fairly— adding that he believed all liquor license fees should be doubled! Murray and his colleague quickly hustled their candidate out of the saloon.[28] It was Theodore's *only* visit to a saloon during his campaign.

On November 5, 1881, Theodore defeated his Democratic opponent with a majority of 2,200 votes, twice the typical Republican returns. "As far as I can judge the next House will contain a rare set of scoundrels," he wrote fellow assemblyman William O'Neill, "and we Republicans will be in such a hopeless minority that I do not see very clearly what we can accomplish, even in checking bad legislation. But at least we will do our best."[29]

The youngest member of the New York State Assembly arrived in Albany on January 2, 1882. A *New York Times* correspondent recounted his first meeting with the new assemblyman, noting that he had "a good, honest laugh . . . his teeth seemed to be all over his face. He was genial, emphatic, earnest, but green as grass." Another reporter, for the *New York Sun*, noted that despite the cold weather, Theodore wore "an expansive smile" in place of an overcoat. However, not all were impressed with him. His high-pitched voice, glasses, and his first name (which many felt was as ridiculous as Algernon, Seymour, or Percy) added to his difficulty in being taken seriously as an elected official. "What on earth will New York send us next?" a *New York Tribune* reporter wailed.[30]

It wasn't only the news reporters who looked disdainfully at Theodore. His colleagues often mocked him, referring to him as "college boy," "dude," or "society man." Theodore was equally critical of his brethren, based on their actions, ethics, and intelligence—or lack of them. The Democrats were quick to earn his abhorrence, noting that the chairman of the Committee on Affairs of Cities "adds a great deal of stupidity" to his position, while another politician was "either dumb or an idiot—probably both." Nor did he spare chastising members of his own party, observing that one Republican's intelligence was "equal to an average balloon."[31]

Assemblymen William O'Neill and Mike Costello were two men Theodore not only liked but with whom he shared similar political views. O'Neill, a Republican from upstate, was a strong admirer, as was Theodore, of Alexander Hamilton and Abraham Lincoln. Costello, an Irish Tammany Hall Democrat, was more of an independent than a politician who towed the party line. "He and I worked hand in hand with equal indifference to our local machines," Theodore said of his association with Costello.[32]

Jay Gould, one of the most reviled of the nineteenth-century "robber barons," was known for his tactics in driving a specific market up or down at will. On September 29, 1869, he was the major influence which caused the "Black Friday" collapse of the gold market, when the premium over face value on a gold Double Eagle fell 27 percent. While he managed to make a small profit from the panic, he eventually lost it all in ensuing lawsuits. In 1882, Gould owned controlling interests in four major railroads (including Union Pacific and Missouri Pacific), as well as nearly 15 percent of all railroad tracks in the United States. He also maintained controlling interest in Western Union, which gave him bragging rights in that he could quickly learn what his competitors were doing. Having recently acquired the *New York World* newspaper, Gould set his sights on the elevated trains in New York City. Using his newspaper, Gould floated rumors about Manhattan Elevated, one of the major carriers. The tactic worked, ultimately driving down the company's stock price; then, with his typical modus operandi, Gould swept in and bought controlling interest of the company. Once that was done, Manhattan Elevated's stock price doubled, and Gould raised fares. To make certain that he would not have to pay a heavy tax burden, he used his connections in the State Assembly and Tammany Hall to amend a completely unrelated bill, inserting a clause that would remit one-third of the taxes paid by elevated lines. The amended bill would be included during the eleventh-hour end of the Assembly session, where it would easily pass in the confusion and be overlooked by the press.[33]

Costello and Roosevelt made it a habit of checking bills to "find out what the authors really had in mind." They discovered this addition, which technically made it a new bill and open to discussion. However, the "Black Horse Cavalry" moved to see that the amended proposal was quickly passed. ("The Black Horse Cavalry" was the nickname of party hacks that loyally did the bidding of the party machine.) When Costello and Theodore stepped out of the chamber, the speaker pro tem jumped into action, ordering the bill to be read and voted on. Costello quickly returned and launched into a filibuster, despite the continuing slams of the speaker's gavel and his declarations that the assemblyman was out of order. Finally, as the sergeant at arms dragged Costello out of the chamber, Theodore rose up to continue the filibuster, which erupted into a maelstrom. Slamming his gavel and yelling "Out of order!" to no avail, the speaker declared the bill passed and sent it on to the governor. Newspapers reported the entire mess, as well as what the amended bill actually contained, unleashing a public uproar. With all the negative press and opinion the amended bill attracted, Governor Grover Cleveland refused to sign it. Theodore called the whole incident "the most openly crooked measure" during his time in the Assembly. (For his heroic actions, Mike Costello was repaid by Tammany Hall with defeat in the next election.)

Theodore's first book, *The Naval War of 1812*, was released in May of 1883. Reviews were generally positive, and his work served as a textbook in many colleges. Probably the highest praise for his book came from the Navy Department, which ordered every ship's library to carry a copy. For nearly a century, *The Naval War of 1812* stood as the definitive work in its field.

Clark's Tavern, located on West Twenty-Third Street, held its annual dinner for the New York Free Trade Club on May 28, 1883. As one of many speakers, Theodore spoke out against possessive tariffs in the

United States, which was well received by those in attendance. One of the attendees was Henry Gorringe, a lieutenant commander in the US Navy, who had recently resigned after a dispute with the secretary of the navy. Gorringe's biggest claim to fame was bringing the obelisk known as Cleopatra's Needle from Alexandria, Egypt, to New York City in 1880.[34]

Gorringe was a man always working an angle. He had tried to raise capital for a shipbuilding company, but failed. Now he was on to a new business opportunity, running a hotel and hunting lodge in the Dakota Territory. The lodge was located in the Badlands along the Little Missouri River, right near the tracks of the Northern Pacific Railroad. Gorringe sought out Theodore, and no doubt their interest in naval dominance sparked a conversation. It soon gave way to discussion of Gorringe's new efforts in the Dakota Territory, with tales of hunting various wild game, including buffalo. The former naval officer may have been sizing up Theodore, as he did others, as a potential investor for his operation. He offered to escort him on a hunting trip.

Theodore was hooked, and quickly made plans to go west.

THE BADLANDS

I grow very fond of this place, and it certainly has a desolate, grim beauty of its own, that has a curious fascination for me.

DURING A MILITARY CAMPAIGN AGAINST THE SIOUX IN 1864, US ARMY brigadier general Alfred Sully described the Badlands in the eastern Dakota Territory as "hell with the fires out . . . grand, dismal and majestic."[1] French trappers who roamed the area in the 1820s and 1830s labeled it *Mauvais Terres*. To the Spanish it was known as *Malpaís*, while the Sioux called it *Mako Shika*. No matter the language, it all meant the same thing—the "Bad Lands."[2] (Located in the western end of North Dakota, it should not to be confused with the Badlands National Park in South Dakota.)

It is a harsh land. Unforgiving. Blistering hot in the summer. Bone-chillingly cold in the winter, when temperatures can dive well below zero. One does not conquer this land. No human bests this environment. The most one can do is adapt to it and live with it. Theodore once described the Badlands as "so fantastically broken in form and so bizarre in color as to seem hardly properly to belong to this earth."[3]

No words can adequately portray this forlorn, bleak, windswept terrain, with its odd formations and colorful landscapes. Yet there is a seductive beauty to the land. "I heartily enjoy this life, with its perfect freedom . . . and there are few sensations I prefer to that of galloping over these rolling limitless prairies, rifle in hand, or winding my way among the barren, fantastic and grimly picturesque deserts of the so-called Bad Lands," Theodore wrote to his friend Henry Cabot Lodge.[4] The Badlands cast an intoxicating hold on anyone who visits, including Theodore, who felt that "the desolate, grim beauty" held a "curious fascination" for him.

The landscape of the Badlands one visits today was millions of years in the making.

A scant sixty-five million years ago (just after the extinction of the dinosaurs), the western half of North America began to buckle, twist, and fold to create what is now the Rocky Mountains. Sediments (such as sand, silt, and mud) were carried from the eastern slopes by ancient rivers, ultimately depositing in layers in what is now the Badlands of North Dakota. At the same time, erupting volcanoes sent out huge clouds of ash. (Many of these volcanoes were located in present-day South Dakota, Montana, and Idaho, as well as elsewhere in western North America.) Carried by the wind and rivers, the ash deposited itself into standing water in present-day North Dakota. As time went on, the sediments from the mountains turned into sandstone, siltstone, and mudstone layers, while the tiers of ash transformed into bentonite clay.

With the beginning of the Pliocene Epoch (roughly five to two and a half million years ago), natural erosion began, as rivers drifted through the wide valleys of the plains of the western Dakotas and eastern Montana. Many of these rivers changed their courses, although, at the end of the epoch (about 2 million years ago), one of these rivers existed in nearly the identical location of the current Little Missouri River.[5] This era also experienced three glacier periods, the last one being 640,000 years ago. One of these massive continental ice sheets made its way from what is now Canada, reaching as far south as the North Unit boundary of Theodore Roosevelt National Park. Boulders carried by that massive ice sheet still remain in one area of the park's northern unit, ripped out by the glacier from Canadian bedrock four hundred miles north.[6] Because of this ice blockage, rivers flowing north were suddenly forced into forming a new course that moved east and south. The Little Missouri River's new path (which still moved north before being diverted eastward) was steeper, giving it a faster flow that allowed the river to carve into the land. Torrential downpours followed by dry periods made quick work of the soft sedimentary rocks and began to create the unique, colorful landscape that exists today.[7]

Scientific evidence reveals that much of this area was once part of a flat, swampy area with rivers. Trees found in this area included sequoia, bald cypress, and magnolia, and their leaves and branches fell into the still waters of the swamps and eventually built up a heavy layer of vegetation called peat. Pressure from sediments overlying the peat caused it to compress, which eventually led to a chemical change that turned the peat into a soft, woody-textured coal known as *lignite*, the lowest, poorest grade of coal. The areas that had lignite would often catch fire and burn for years; these were known as burning coal veins.[8] The majority of coal veins self-ignite, hidden from view underground, while the few visible burning veins emit smoke from the ground, accompanied by a strong sulfur odor. (An exposed burning vein will burn off any nearby trees or sagebrush.) The overlying sediments are literally baked into a natural brick known as *scoria*, which is much more resistant to erosion than the soft sedimentary rock.

Two of the odder formations found within this area are called hoodoos and cannonballs. *Hoodoos* are composed of a soft sedimentary rock at its base capped with a harder stone (such as well-cemented sandstone, limestone, or basalt) that resists erosion. They take on a unique form when water wears away the softer underlying layer, leaving the resistant layer cap to act as an umbrella for the base. Eventually water erodes and destroys the soft layer, causing the cap to fall off.[9] *Cannonballs* are formed by the deposits of a mineral around a core, which can form in any shape but generally take on a round appearance; hence, the name. (Visitors to the North Unit of Theodore Roosevelt National Park find a concentration of cannonballs, while the South Unit has the majority of hoodoos.)

As the centuries went on, numerous animals found the area a comfortable refuge, either on a temporary or permanent basis. Buffalo, elk, white-tailed and mule deer, pronghorns, and prairie dogs were attracted to the grasses populating the area, which provided an ample food source. The river and its small tributaries allowed cottonwood trees to thrive, offering not just another food source but also shelter from the heat and cold. The water thoroughfare served as a habitat for almost 186 species of birds that either called the area home or used it as a migration stop. Long before these creatures, dinosaurs had populated the Badlands; although numerous fossils have been uncovered, nothing compares to the 1999 discovery of a dinosaur mummy, named "Dakota" by the scientists, in the Hell Creek Formation.[10] This rare find, which wasn't officially announced until 2007, provided not only bones but also fossilized soft tissue (i.e., skin, tendons, and ligaments).

Few humans chose to live in this area. The land is covered with bentonite clay that is hard to navigate when dry and impassable when it rains. Other than the Little Missouri River and the subsequent creeks, most water in the area, when it was found, had a strong alkaline content. Indications of humans inhabiting the western Badlands date to only 5,500 to 500 BC. It is possible humans might have inhabited the area earlier, but any supporting evidence would have been lost to erosion. The Historic Period (AD 1742–1880s) offers richer evidence that the Badlands were used, if not permanently inhabited, by humans. The Mandan and Hidatsa tribes hunted in the area, as did the Crow, Blackfeet, Gros Ventre, Chippewa, Cree, and Sioux.[11] There is no record of when the first European explorers sighted the Badlands, although many believe Jean Baptiste LePage may hold that distinction. In 1804, LePage came down the Little Missouri River to meet with the Lewis and Clark Expedition at their winter camp, Fort Mandan. Historians surmise that he would have seen some, if not all, of the area. The increase in fur trapping, as well as steamboat travel, on the Missouri by the mid-1830s makes it very likely that trappers scouted and hunted in the Badlands area.

◆

The Northern Pacific Railroad Act of 1864 was intended to link the Great Lakes to Puget Sound of the Pacific. Construction, which was plagued by several problems, did not begin until 1870. The first significant difficulty, aside from the underestimated cost of construction, was that the proposed railroad tracks would run across land that had been given to the Sioux under the Treaty of Fort Laramie. This 1868 treaty gave a large swath of land (roughly the western portion of the state of South Dakota) to the Sioux, forbidding any non-Indians from entering the area—except the US government.

Between the arrival of the Iron Horse and the discovery of gold in the Black Hills (including a town named Deadwood), the stage was set for a deadly confrontation between the tribes of the Great Plains and the US Army. Until the "Indian problem" was eliminated, the Northern Pacific Railroad could not advance safely over the contested land. Victory against the US Army at the Little Bighorn on June 25, 1876, ultimately led to the defeat of the Great Plains tribes. (Lt. Col. George Custer and his Seventh Cavalry, heading to their destiny, passed through the Badlands, making camp five miles south of present-day Medora.) After the Little Bighorn defeat, the military launched an aggressive and unrelenting campaign known as the Great Sioux War of 1876, which eventually forced Sioux, Cheyenne, and other tribes onto reservations.

Then there was the American buffalo.*

The buffalo's ancestors had migrated to North American from Siberia, across the Bering land bridge, more than 600,000 years ago, making their way into Canada and the United States.[12] The buffalo we know today evolved from its relatives roughly 10,000 to 5,000 years ago. The majority of these herds, in what is referred to as "primitive North America" (circa AD 1500), ranged from Alberta and Saskatchewan in the north to central Texas in the South, the Rocky Mountains in the West, and the Mississippi River in the East. (Some were found as distant as California, northern Mexico, and even parts of Florida.) It is estimated that, during this primitive period, thirty million buffalo ranged across the North American continent. By 1885, the population was down to nearly a thousand.[13]

While many people believe the near extermination of buffalo began with the opening of the transcontinental railroad, numerous herds had already seen their population decrease as far back as the 1830s and 1840s. Part of their decline was due to hunting by the mountain men and Great Plains tribes. The mountain men's first choice of fur was beaver, but as the demand for those pelts began to fade, they turned to the buffalo. Long before the various Great Plains tribes hunted by horseback, hunters would chase a herd on foot, shaking blankets and yelling, forcing them in the direction of a cliff or cut-bank. (This hunting tactic is known as a "buffalo jump.") The animals would plummet over the precipice, bouncing and slamming into the rocks as they tumbled. Those that were not killed

---

* For years, the terms *buffalo* and *bison* have been used interchangeably in describing these beasts. For the sake of clarity, I have chosen to use *buffalo* to refer to the animal.

in the fall were disabled, usually breaking their legs, leaving the hunters to finish off their prey with spears and arrows. As far back as Lewis and Clark's 1803 expedition, many bones and skulls were found as silent testimony to the Indians' hunting tactics.[14] Today, many buffalo jump sites are proving to be a treasure for archaeologists. Another reason for the decline in the buffalo herds was from various parasites such as ticks, botflies, and mites. Some of these parasites would be inhaled by the buffalo as it foraged for grass, often occupying nasal passages and working their way into the lungs. Bacteria which led to pneumonia were another fatal cause of death. In 1887, pneumonia wiped out the entire buffalo herd of Buffalo Bill's Wild West Show in New York City.[15]

However, the advancement of the transcontinental railroad was the final step in the decimation of the buffalo herds on the Southern Plains. Buffalo heads became fashionable as decorative items, often mounted in train stations, Eastern office buildings, and the mansions of the wealthy. The winter hides were popular as rugs or coats. Advancements in tanning buffalo hides in the East and in Europe meant even the summer hides (which lacked any heavy hair) could be used for various products, including belts and boots.

Descending onto the Southern Plains like locusts, buffalo hunters came armed with their deadly Sharps .50 caliber rifle, a weapon that with one shot could bring down a mighty male bull weighing two thousand pounds. The Sharps, which cost $125 in 1871, was a large-bore rifle with a barrel length of thirty inches. The lever-action weapon had great long-range accuracy, firing one cartridge at a time. It was said to be one of—if not *the*—most powerful black-powder cartridges ever produced. A hunter would sit, or lie, a distance away from the herd, usually staying downwind, as buffalo would scatter when they smelled something they perceived as dangerous. The boom from the hunter's rifle sounded a lot like a clap of thunder, something that did not necessarily upset a buffalo herd. Oblivious to the danger surrounding them, they continued to graze, heedless of the slaughter that was about to begin.

At first, hunters killed for a buffalo's coat and the decorative head. Dismantling the hide and head was left to men called "skinners." It was a thankless, bloody, smelly, and time-consuming job accomplished under a baking sun. As skinners made their way from one dead body to another, the stench grew fouler because the carcasses were simply left to rot in the sun. (This did not count the buffalo that were shot but staggered away to die and were never skinned.) Once the hides were stripped from the body, they would be staked out in the sun to dry, then stacked in a wagon. In 1872, a buffalo hide sold for $3. (Today, a buffalo hide can cost from $800 to over $1,500.) The sun-bleached bones of a buffalo were also found to be useful when they were ground up and used as fertilizer.

It wasn't the public clamoring for the hides and heads that led to the slaughter of the buffalo. A set of circumstances combined nearly simultaneously to spell their destruction. Writing about the slaughter, Theodore noted that it went on "with appalling rapidity and thoroughness."[16]

The first circumstance was a military maneuver. In fighting a war, the quickest way to subdue an opponent is to cut his line of supply. The shaggy beasts were a vital source of survival for the Great Plains tribes. Aside from the meat they provided, hides, especially the winter coats, provided warmth as blankets and robes, as well as covers for a tepee. The animal's sinews served as bowstrings, and were used for sewing, while bones became cooking utensils, hide scrapers, and weapons. Hooves proved to make a useful glue, while the bladder functioned as a short-term water pouch. General Philip Sheridan realized that destroying the buffalo herds was the quickest way to solve the "Indian problem." Thus, Sheridan approved the wholesale slaughter of the shaggy beasts.

The second circumstance was the railroad industry. It was not uncommon for a train to sit on the tracks for hours, if not a whole day, waiting for a huge herd to pass. Also, a buffalo herd was quite capable of derailing an engine and other cars if the locomotive was unable to stop in time. During the harsh winters, buffalo sought shelter in the cuts formed by the grade of the tracks that wound through hills and mountains, which could delay a train for days.

There was also money to be made. The transcontinental railroad made a hefty profit shipping buffalo hides, heads, and bones to market, not to mention offering hunters from the East and Europe the opportunity to shoot at a herd from the safety of a passing train traveling along the Southern Plains. These fearless hunters banged away from the security of a train window, leaving dead and wounded animals in the engine's wake. They were not even skinned for the hides or the meat; it was done solely for the thrill of killing from a passing train.

Lincoln Lang, traveling on the train from Dickinson to Little Missouri with his father, recalled how a group of hunters threw open the windows after spotting a small, bedraggled herd of buffalo along the track. As the train approached, the buffalo "made off up an open draw, at their characteristic bobbing gait" while the hunters were "bombarding them."[17] Lang's father asked the train conductor to at least stop and pick up the dead animals, but the request was denied.

Buffalo also incurred the wrath of the telegraph company—the third set of circumstances effective in their demise. In the summer, buffalo shed their winter coats, thereby losing protection from the constant attack of flies. A buffalo usually seeks the solace of a tree to scratch his back and sides for relief, but on the Plains, where no tree can be found, a telegraph pole becomes a worthy substitute. No telegraph pole can withstand the force of a buffalo in need of a scratch. Consequently, poles would be pushed down, severing the telegraph line. Eliminating the buffalo from the area solved the telegraph company's quandary.

By 1878, the buffalo herds of the Southern Plains had been completely eliminated.

Hunters now turned their attention to the Northern Plains herd, and the endless slaughter continued. In 1881, a Montana supplier shipped 250,000 buffalo hides back east. Two years later, he sent only ten.[18] In the summer of 1883, the US government hired a band of Sioux to kill a herd of five thousand buffalo along the Northern Pacific Railroad in order to prevent train wrecks. Later that season, the manager of the Standing Rock Indian Agency had tribal members kill another ten thousand buffalo.[19] By the time Theodore arrived in Dakota Territory in September 1883, the once-massive buffalo herds had been reduced to a small group of stragglers, finding refuge from the large-bore rifles in the various coulees of the Badlands. (A band of twenty-three buffalo managed to survive in Yellowstone National Park during the decimating hunt of the Northern Plains herd.) Aside from the tribes of the Great Plains, few people concerned themselves with the eradication of the buffalo. Money was to be made in killing them, and once the Plains were free of them, another moneymaking venture moved in—cattle.

◆

Unlike the buffalo's migration to North America, cattle were imported, first by the Spaniards in 1521.[20] Cattle arrived on the East Coast of North America in 1611 at Jamestown, Virginia, and more stock arrived by the mid-1600s from England, Sweden, Denmark, and the Netherlands. These herds also grew quickly in size, roaming freely over the land.[21] As the Spanish moved north, they brought with them a large herd of cattle that quickly spread out across what is now Texas. As early as 1842, Texas cattle were being driven to Shreveport and New Orleans and sent north via ships. During the Mexican-American War, Texan Edward Piper drove a herd to Ohio, while other Texans moved cattle overland to San Francisco during the California Gold Rush.[22] Once the Civil War ended in 1865, the men of Texas returned to find that much of the cattle they had left unattended had grown by leaps and bounds. The Easterners were clamoring for beef, offering $40 to $50 a head. The opening of the 345-acre Chicago Union Stock Yards on Christmas Day, 1865, baptized the Illinois city as the center for cattle business.

Texans had plenty of cattle. The transcontinental railroad being built across the Plains could ship the beef to Eastern markets. The cattle drive was born.[23]

Jesse Chisholm had made his way up and down a faint trail from roughly central Texas to Wichita, Kansas, as early as 1865.[24] The Chisholm Trail (1867–1882) became one of the best-known cattle trails in the West, making its way north from the Nueces River in Texas through Indian Country (now Oklahoma), where it originally drifted northeast to the towns of Wichita and Abilene. The trail could also branch off toward the future cow towns of Ellsworth (north) or Dodge City (northwest). Each time the railroad made a significant advance in laying tracks, a new cow town was born. Each one of these new towns enabled thousands of cattle to be shipped to Chicago meat markets for processing.[25]

The cattle of choice was longhorn. Tough, rangy animals that sported long legs and even longer horns (many extending to seven or eight feet), they thrived in the arid climate and, despite being occasionally ill-tempered, were born for the long drives.[26] The breed was resistant to disease and easily subsisted on the minimal vegetation of the Texas plains.

Driving cattle required men, horses, and supplies. A cattle owner could, barring any calamities on the trail, earn a hefty profit from beef buyers when all went well. The drive itself, however, offered numerous difficulties, from lack of water to interference from Indians, foul weather, and one of the most dreaded events—stampede. Timing was everything in getting a herd to market. Push them too fast, they dropped weight, which meant less money. Bring your herd up too slowly and you risked having competing cattle outfits sell their stock at the best price. Leaving too soon could mean the grass your herd would need to feed on wouldn't be mature enough, while a later departure meant the good grass would already be consumed.

Indians were another headache. They could steal some of your stock or demand a toll for crossing their reservation. The toll usually came in the form of handing over a certain number of cows. Experienced cattle owners picked up wandering mavericks (unbranded cattle) to serve as a possible toll a tribe may demand. Others chose to take a different direction, avoiding Indian land, although that could mean days without access to water. Water was essential for a successful cattle drive. Without an adequate supply, a herd could be finished before reaching the railhead. From the beginning of the cattle drives, most cattlemen followed established trails that were near major rivers, as well as tributaries that could keep both cattle and men from going dry.

Depending on the size of the drive (herds numbered as low as 500 to as high as 2,500), the need for men to handle the drive ranged from a dozen to possibly twenty. The trail boss ran the outfit. He was a man of experience, knowing cattle, men, and the land they would cross. Often riding ahead of the herd (usually two or three miles in advance), he would scout the land, as well as search for water and any signs of trouble. To keep a herd in check, a trail boss picked a dominant animal, usually a bull, to become the lead steer. Because of its assertive attitude, the lead steer would keep others in line. Where he led, the rest followed. (The lead steer was often not sold, instead making numerous trips up the trail.) The chuck wagon and the remuda (horse herd) would be ahead and to the right or left of the herd. "Riding point" was given to the more-established riders, along with the lead steer. As the herd snaked out along the trail, "swing" or "flank" riders rode alongside, ready to chase any animal that tried to break from the group. "Riding drag" was the least desirable position, often given to the newer members of the crew. They rode behind the herd, keeping the stragglers moving. Most of these riders became heavily covered in dust, not to mention enduring the various smells courtesy of the cattle. If the weather cooperated, a herd could make fifteen miles on the trail on an average day.

Weather on the Plains in the late spring and early summer was fickle. It could be chilly, then boiling hot—within hours. Rain would tamp down the dust, but the resulting mud made moving a herd dirty at best, dangerous at worst. A thunderstorm could easily spook the cattle, which was the greatest fear of a trail boss and his men. It could happen in broad daylight or in the middle of the night. At night, crew members worked two-hour shifts riding circles in opposite directions around the herd, often softly singing a ballad to calm the sleeping animals. If a stampede began, the one place no rider wanted to be, especially at night, was ahead of cattle running wildly. One slip of a horse's hoof and both rider and horse were finished.

Feeding a crew of cowboys was left to the cook, who typically had a variety of nicknames, such as Cookie, Biscuit Roller, Hash Slinger, Sourdough, Belly Cheater, and Grub Spoiler. If the cattle owner and trail boss were smart, they hired the best available, because a good cook was worth every cent. He would also tend to dental problems, set broken bones, stitch wounds, and even cut hair. He was first up, setting the fire and getting the morning breakfast ready to serve by four in the morning: black coffee (commonly called Arbuckles for the company that sold it), biscuits, beans, meat, and gravy. Once breakfast was served, the cook quickly broke camp and drove the chuck wagon ahead to a spot, chosen by the trail boss, to set up to serve a quick lunch (often beans, biscuits, and coffee), before moving on to the night camp. Every night, he would point the tongue of his wagon to the North Star as a way to guide the herd to their destination.

The chuck wagon was the cook's domain. In it he carried everything he needed for the drive. Often called a "commissary on wheels," it was the creation of cattleman Charles Goodnight. Taking a typical wagon with a canvas top, he added a box at the rear (called a chuck box) that would hold tin dishes, Dutch ovens, a kettle, and the large coffeepot. It also had various drawers that held the cook's staples: coffee, flour, beans, and sugar. A folding board was attached to the bottom of the chuck-box lid that served as a table when cooking a meal. The rest of the wagon would hold the bedrolls for the cowboys and each man's "war bag" (either a canvas or flour bag that held his personal items or extra clothes). Alongside the wagon was one, sometimes two, water barrels. A canvas sling (known as a "bitch" or "caboose") was strung under the wagon to hold dry wood or buffalo chips for future use as firewood. The wagon also carried necessary tools and possibly an extra wagon wheel. (Some cattle drives had an additional wagon, called the hoodlum, which carried the bedrolls and the cowboys' war bags.)

The most important part of a cattle drive, next to the herd, was the cowboy. Most men on a drive were no older than twenty-five, former soldiers from either side of the Civil War. The cowboys, as Theodore noted, "form[ed] a class by themselves." He observed that the cowboys from Texas were "the best at the actual cowboy work . . . fearless riders." They understood the habits of the cattle they watched over, and were "only excelled by the Mexicans" in using a rope.[27] (The word *cowboy* originated in Ireland, circa AD 1000, where boys were hired to herd cows.) A cowboy's clothing and equipment was adapted from those of the *vaqueros* in Mexico, and little has changed in almost two hundred years. The leather chaps (from the word *chaparreras*) protected the rider's legs from the brush, especially the chaparral, as well as keeping his legs warm in winter. A vest, usually with four pockets, carried his pocket watch, tobacco, folding knife, and other items. The hat, especially in the Southwest, had a wide brim to shield his face from the blistering sun. It also doubled as a quick water bucket for his horse. His boots, with high leather necks, boasted a high heel that prevented his boot from slipping through the stirrups. Gloves protected his wrists from rope burns from the lariat he was consistently using. One of the most important features a cowboy wore was a bandana. Made generally from silk, it served multiple purposes, aside from looking stylish. A bandana served as a mask if one was riding drag, as a towel, and as ear cover in winter. It tied down the rider's hat in windy weather and served as a sling for a broken arm or a strainer for muddy water. Most cowboys also carried a sidearm, but left their rifles in the chuck wagon unless the trail boss expected trouble.

Equally important for the cowboy was his Western saddle, an off-shoot of the Mexican saddle. Working a cattle drive, most cowboys carried a minimum of equipment on their horse. The two most important items were a canteen and the ever-present lariat (made out of rawhide, grass, or horsehair), which were tied to the saddle using leather strings. If rain was expected, the cowboy's slicker would be tied onto the back of his saddle. During a single day on the drive, a cowboy would use a minimum of three horses, switching out his first horse at lunch, and then switching out again when riding night herd.

The year 1883 marked the arrival of Texas cattle in the Little Missouri region. Taking the Western Trail from Ogallala, cattlemen swung their herds northwest on what quickly became known as the Texas Trail. A vital reason why Texas cattle arrived on the Northern Plains was the grass ("breast high to the horse"). Unlike the scrubby grass found on the Southern Plains, cattlemen soon learned that their herds gained more weight from grazing on the stem-cured bunch (which offered better nutritional value for the beef), grama, and buffalo grasses. Not only did the grass last during the summer, but cattle could also find enough to survive in the winter by pawing through the snow. This was another circumstance for the elimination of the buffalo: They grazed on the same grass.

The Little Missouri area was a late bloomer in the cattle business mainly because of the clashes with the various Indian tribes and the lack of transportation shipping cattle to market. The defeat of the Great Plains tribes and their relocation to various reservations by 1879–1880 solved one problem: The Northern Pacific's arrival resolved the lack of transportation in the Northern Plains, and opened the door to the cattle industry. When the economic panic of 1873 struck, triggering a six-year depression, many investors in the Northern Pacific Railroad exchanged their stock holdings for land rights along the proposed Dakota Territory route, leading to an influx of cattle investors.[28]

Investing in cattle during the early 1880s became the latest vogue for the rich in the East, and many Europeans, especially after an 1881 report claimed that an investor could realize a 33 percent return on their money. Such potential wealth led to a huge influx of capital from England.[29] Most investors were absentee proprietors, or at best, infrequent visitors, leaving the daily operations to a knowledgeable foreman and the cowboys. While turning a profit from their investment was their main purpose, visiting their holdings in the far West allowed owners to hunt and ride (even though many were dreadful failures in both departments) to impress their equally well-off friends.

The open-range policy was an attractive incentive to invest in the cattle industry because much of the Western lands were not held in private hands, excluding what was owned by the government.[30] Stories of fast profits while feeding cattle on "free grass" were an irresistible lure for investors—especially those who had come to the area first. Fences were virtually nonexistent in the West, although the creation of barbed wire in 1870 was a harbinger of things to come. While the open-range policy had its advantages, it was vulnerable to disaster. A rancher needed roughly thirty to forty acres for each head of cattle he owned for grazing purposes. A rancher with a herd count of 1,500 would need at least sixty thousand acres of grazing land, while an outfit with 2,000 head of cattle required a minimum of eighty thousand acres. By 1884, there were eighteen major cattle outfits operating in the Little Missouri region, most owning between 1,100 and 2,400 head of cattle per operation. (Theodore's two ranches had a total of 3,650 head, which required 146,000 acres.) As big as the area was, it could not properly sustain a large number of cattle outfits without damaging the land. Overgrazing was, and still is, a problem. Too many livestock feeding in a region that cannot support the numbers simply denudes it. This leads to soil erosion, because the grass cannot recover and regrow in adequate time, which seriously impairs the land's future ability to be productive. Areas that experienced overgrazing saw lush grasslands reduced to a desert, even in the Northern Plains, for many years.[31] Investors paid no attention to how many acres were needed for their herds. They saw nothing but profits while living a fantasy as a Western cattle baron. Newspapers hawked the rich grass, mild weather (even claiming Dakota Territory winters were mild!), blue skies, and abundant water. As the Northern Pacific Railroad laid its tracks in the Little Missouri area, newspapers heralded the numerous hunting opportunities that were just a train ride away.

September 1880 saw the arrival of the railroad into the Badlands. Inching its way across the Northern Plains, the railroad required protection for its survey and construction crews from potential Indian attacks. Even though they had been subjugated and removed to reservations, many young men from various tribes felt the need to prove themselves. The crews became easy targets for an attack, and preventing such situations was left to the US Army. A detachment of forty to sixty infantry troops was assigned to protect the railroad construction crew. It was a colorless duty for a soldier, standing on both sides of the construction area in skirmish formation, watching for potential trouble that rarely, if ever, came.[32] The biggest problem was boredom. Standing in the hot sun for hours, looking across the rolling plains or the barren landscape of the Badlands, offered soldiers little satisfaction.

Company B from the Sixth Infantry constructed a cantonment (a military compound) on the western bottomland side of the Little Missouri River, naming it the Badlands Cantonment. The location of the buildings was not a wise choice from the perspective of fighting strategy because the buildings were close to the nearby bluffs, allowing an enemy to fire down onto the compound from high ground. The eleven buildings, arranged around a small parade ground, consisted of company barracks, officers' quarters, administration, hospital (holding nine beds), storehouse, blacksmith, two laundresses' quarters, guardhouse, bakery, and icehouse, plus stables to hold twenty-two horses. To add a sense of comfort to the cantonment, trees were planted for shade, as was a garden.[33]

Whether it was the coming of the railroad, the arrival of cattle, or a sudden mining strike, towns were not far behind, literally blooming overnight to cater to the needs of hardworking men. The Badlands was no different. Aptly named Little Missouri, this town mercurially came to life in September to greet the railroad construction crew. Located on the west side of the river, it hardly challenged the plush establishments of Denver or Tombstone. Little Missouri (nicknamed "Little Misery" by some locals) nevertheless served a purpose, supplying liquor, gambling, and a few "sporting ladies" to relieve the workers and soldiers of their money.

The newly baptized hamlet wasn't much to look at. The small railroad depot was just a rough shack in which to send and receive telegrams, and only a few other buildings dotted the area. "Captain" Moore, who had run the sutler's store at the cantonment, was now the manager of a two-story building known as Pyramid Park Hotel. Moore, an abbreviated, squat man with a white beard and a nose bright red from sampling too much "who-hit-john" (Western slang for liquor), was reportedly a former riverboat captain with the mouth and verbiage to prove it. Hardly the ideal person to offer "friendly" service, his demeanor and appearance matched that of the hotel. The bottom floor held a manager's office with a roughed-out table and benches for feeding guests. The upstairs sleeping quarters weren't much better. A stairway, which had no handrails, led to a large room with fourteen cots lined up in a row, each offering a quilt and a dirty feather pillow. Privacy was not an option. The cost for such luxury was two bits.

Not far from the hotel was Big-Mouthed Bob's Bug-Juice Dispensary, a florid appellation for a saloon if there ever was one. This establishment provided the necessary drinks, gambling, and female company for any man with money in his pocket.

In the spring of 1883, Eugene V. Smalley's *History of the Northern Pacific Railroad* was published. It was the perfect timing a press agent could only dream of, as the railroad would soon link Chicago to the Pacific Ocean. The book, which featured black-and-white photographs of the Little Missouri area, tantalized many an Easterner with dreams of seeing and hunting in the Wild West. Newspapers were extolling the abundant wild game available for hunting (there was no mention of any buffalo), while the recently abandoned cantonment buildings would become a hunting lodge. The Northern Pacific soon published its own brochure promoting travel to the area they called "Pyramid Park"—instead of the Badlands.

Image was everything.

His name was Antoine Amédée Marie Vincent Manca de Vallambrosa.

Tall and dark, with penetrating eyes, black hair, and a mustache with sharply waxed ends, he looked and acted like the aristocrat he was. Most people in the Badlands called him the Marquis de Morès, or simply "the Marquis." He was born to blue-blooded French parents in Paris on June 14, 1858. The oldest of four children, he was proficient in French, Italian, English, and German by age ten.[34] After graduating from Jesuit College in 1876, he enrolled in France's elite military academy in St. Cyr, before entering the cavalry school at Saumur.[35] Commissioned a first lieutenant in 1880, the Marquis joined a regiment of mounted cavalry near the Belgian border, and was then assigned to the Tenth Hussars, where he took part in putting down an uprising in Algiers. Returning to garrison duties, the Marquis resigned in early 1882, mainly due to a lack of military action. It had been reported that during his military tenure he was involved in two duels, killing both opponents.

Returning to Paris, and having reached legal age, he took the title Marquis de Morès et de Montemaggiore. Living lavishly, he invested his money in the Paris securities market, hoping to make a hefty profit. The market was experiencing unparalleled speculation, eventually leading to the burst of the financial bubble, which left the Marquis in debt.[36] While visiting his father (who paid off his debts) in Cannes, he met Medora von Hoffman, daughter of Louis von Hoffman, a wealthy New York banker. They quickly fell in love and married on February 15, 1882. Moving to New York with his wife, the Marquis took a position in his father-in-law's bank.

A visit from his cousin, Count Fitz-James, reawakened the Marquis's desire for adventure. Having returned from a hunting trip in the Badlands, his cousin told tales of numerous animals just waiting for an experienced hunter. It is also likely that the Marquis read newspaper accounts about the Northern Pacific Railroad and the surrounding land being offered to cattle investors. At the same time, he crossed paths with Henry Gorringe, who was busily promoting his planned hunting lodge and expeditions in the Little Missouri area. Gorringe's likely pitch to invest in the area—namely, in his venture—increased the nobleman's desire to explore the possibilities. Like other moneyed men, the Marquis viewed the growing cattle industry as another way to increase his wealth. The Badlands area offered many promising potentials for a business. It was adjacent to the railroad (having the shortest run to Chicago or New York), and an abundance of water, ice (in the winter), and fuel (via lignite coal).

The Marquis quickly seized on the idea of owning a cattle ranch, as well as a slaughterhouse and packing plant, all in one operation. Most cattle were shipped to Chicago, where they were held in feed lots until slaughtered and dressed for markets in the East and West. The Marquis came up with a plan to own refrigerator cars which would ship the dressed beef directly from his plant to various markets, including his own meat shops in New York City. He planned to sell his product three cents a pound cheaper than his competitors, thus increasing his profit.

If nothing else, the Marquis de Morès was not short on confidence.

After discussing his ideas with his wife and father-in-law, the Marquis and his personal secretary, William Van Driesche, left for the Badlands in March 1883. The Marquis originally planned to base his operations out of the hamlet of Little Missouri, but he was not impressed with the area. He and his secretary rented horses and scouted the surrounding land on the eastern side of the Little Missouri River. Lunching on sardines, foie gras, potted meat, cheese, bread, and a bottle of white wine (chilled in the stream), the two men found the land charming, with the deep-sided ravines offering abundant food and winter shelter for the cattle.[37] After several days of scouting, the Marquis chose a portion of land on the eastern side of the river. The six-acre parcel would become the town of Medora, named after his wife. (His land holdings totaled four thousand acres, as well as twelve thousand acres to grow wheat outside of Bismarck.[38])

As he plotted out the new town's site, the Marquis went ahead with building his slaughterhouse, also located on the eastern side of the river, and purchased sixteen thousand cattle. The Marquis also planned to launch a number of other businesses, including a tannery, a fertilizer-manufacturing company, a soap works, and even shoemaking. Many of the locals began to refer to him as the "Crazy Frenchman." Loads of lumber and other building material arrived with each train, as did the craftsmen to build the various places the Marquis envisioned, including his chateau, located on a bluff on the western side of the Little Missouri River.[39] For a brief while, the Marquis and Van Driesche lived in a large white tent on the town property, but he soon required more-respectable quarters, and rented a private railroad car from the Northern Pacific, placing it on a newly built side track.

On May 12, 1883, the Marquis, Herman Haupt Jr., and C. Edgar Haupt incorporated the Northern Pacific Refrigerator Car Company. Ranchers in the surrounding area, and in eastern Montana, were happy to sell their cattle to the Marquis, getting a very handsome price for each head of cattle. The *Mandan Pioneer* was quick to breathlessly promote the Marquis's new venture, stating that his new company "[would] call for 2,500 to 5,000 cattle a month," and "the value of this industry" would provide a market for cattlemen.[40]

Many locals viewed the new resident with a wary eye and deep suspicion. After all, he was a *foreigner*. Despite the fact that many would benefit from the Marquis and his deep pockets, these same people were equally quick to denounce him, especially when he committed the most unpardonable sin—fencing in his land. Ranchers in the Northern Plains were primarily "squatters" on government or railroad land. Few owned the land where they had built their cabins, stables, and other buildings, let alone the vast range their cattle grazed upon. Up to this point, both the government and the railroad had turned a blind eye, realizing that the cattle industry served a useful purpose. Very few ranchers staked a legal claim, other than placing a permanent structure on the land, because the open-range policy promoted an unspoken agreement among ranchers that a certain area was considered their land, even while all cattle could (and did) graze upon it, to the advantage of everyone.

While the Marquis did legally purchase and hold title to his land, his fencing it was a breach of this covenant in the Little Missouri area. His actions, along with his aloof manner, only exacerbated an already-uncomfortable situation. What the Marquis did not understand (or perhaps simply did not care about) was that fencing his land holdings also encumbered a web of trails that had been open to anyone who used it. Fencing such trails meant that riders, who were used to the open range, had to take detours, sometimes going miles out of their way. Cattle herds, which used the trails as shortcuts to the river or water holes, were now forced to take a longer route. Fences also represented the encroachment of civilization, an end to the free, open life many men had embraced for decades. Routes to the river that were blocked by the Marquis's barbed-wire fences were cut. Men working for de Morès would repair the fences, only to find them cut again. It was a never-ending routine. The American West was peppered with numerous range war stories involving the fencing of land by other cattlemen or farmers. It was no different in the growing town of Medora, possibly because of the Machiavellian efforts of Eldridge "Jerry" Paddock.

Paddock, who had been living in the Little Missouri area since the 1860s, worked as a guide for hunters. A man with broad shoulders and a black mustache that was reportedly so long he could tie it under his chin, he was one of the most feared men in the area. He had been arrested twice on murder charges (in both cases he was found not guilty), had been accused of receiving stolen property, and had committed extortion and cattle rustling. Most locals described him as sneaky, conning others to do the dirty work while he reaped the rewards. He was known as a dead shot with a gun and was not hesitant to use it to settle arguments. One man who owed him money had been found, in a questionable manner, to have been "kicked to death by horses." Often described as "cold" and "quiet," Paddock was not one to let an opportunity slip by him. He quickly befriended the Marquis de Morès, working his way into becoming something of a confidant.

Fencing the land led to hard feelings between the Marquis and three hunters—Frank O'Donald, "Dutch" Wannegan, and Riley Luffsey. One of the fences blocked the only way from the hunters' camp to the hamlet of Little Missouri. As many times as the hunters cut the fence, the Marquis repaired it. Hard feelings quickly took root. The three men resented the land being fenced, claiming that it infringed on their rights to go where they pleased. As American citizens, they found this particularly galling because the person fencing the land was a foreigner. Paddock supposedly started spreading a rumor that the Marquis would force the men off the land, certain that the word would reach O'Donald's ears.

It did.

O'Donald told Gregor Lang that whoever tried to jump them would "jump from there right into his grave!"[41] On June 21, 1883, the three men rode into Little Missouri. Drinking copious amounts of *who-hit-John*, the trio soon launched into a tirade about the Marquis and his fences. Over the next few days, they continued to consume ample amounts of liquor, cursing the Marquis, and launched "a perfect reign of terror . . . firing promiscuously" into various buildings.[42] Many heard O'Donald threaten the life of the Marquis, including Paddock, who relayed the threats to his new friend, the Marquis. Paddock also claimed that O'Donald had threatened him and another employee, Dick Moore, if they continued to work for the Frenchman. Adding further fuel to the fire, Paddock stated that O'Donald bragged he would shoot the Marquis "like a dog."[43] With no local law or judicial enforcement in the area, the Marquis left the following morning on the train for Mandan. Hoping to find the local sheriff to swear out a warrant for O'Donald's arrest, the Marquis was disappointed to learn he was out of town on business. He then sought advice from the justice of the peace, Martin Bateman. After explaining the situation, Bateman simply commented that the Marquis should shoot back.[44]

Returning to Medora, the Marquis had dinner at his new home with Van Driesche, Frank Miller, Dick Moore, and Paddock. Soon the house was rocked by gunfire, with the Marquis and his men returning shots. By sunrise, the attackers had left. "Armed Desperadoes Are Making Matters Unpleasantly Lively in Little Missouri" splashed the headline on the front page of Bismarck's *Daily Tribune*. The article went on to note that "Everything points to a desperate state of affairs up there and some startling news may be expected this morning."[45] De Morès sent a telegram to his lawyer in Bismarck, urging him to send Sheriff Harmon and an armed posse "in shortest possible time."

The following day, Deputy Sheriff Henry Harmon and his posse arrived by train. (The posse ranged from three to twenty men, depending on who was telling the story.) Greeted by O'Donald, Wannegan, and Luffsey, rifles at the ready, Deputy Sheriff Harmon announced he had a warrant for O'Donald's arrest, but the man refused to be taken. "I've done nothing to be arrested for, and I won't be taken," O'Donald replied. The three men rode off, and no effort was made by Harmon to follow the men.[46] The Marquis had suspected the three men would refuse to be arrested and ride out of town. Taking the advice from the justice of the peace, the Marquis, Paddock, and Frank Miller chose the likely route the three men would take back to their camp, where the trail and railroad narrowed and curved to the left around steep bluffs opposite the cantonments. As the three men rode along, shots rang out, hitting their horses. Taking cover behind their fallen horses, a gunfight began. At one point, Luffsey raised his head to get a better shot when a bullet struck him at the base of the neck. "Wannegan, oh, Wannegan!" he reportedly cried out before dying.[47] O'Donald was hit in the thigh, while Wannegan had only bullet holes in various areas of his clothing. A coroner's jury ruled that Luffsey died from shots fired by the Marquis, Frank Miller, and Dick Moore. (Paddock, typically, managed not to be seen or implicated by the deputy sheriff.) Warrants were issued for the three men, and they were bound over for a hearing by Justice of the Peace Bateman, the same jurist who had advised the Marquis to shoot at those threatening him. All three men were acquitted of the charges, citing that they fired in self-defense.[48] Two days later, the Marquis, Miller, and Moore were once again arrested on murder charges. After another hearing that lasted twenty-six days, under Judge Daniel Collins, the charges were once again dropped.[49]

The incident provided local newspapers with plenty of material for the summer of 1883. As fall began to descend on the Badlands, one more event filled the pages of the local newspapers. September 8, 1883, marked the completion of the Northern Pacific rail line to Seattle, Washington, with the driving of a golden spike in Gold Creek, Montana Territory. To commemorate the special event, the president of Northern Pacific, Henry Villard, commissioned a locomotive to carry four luxury private cars holding three hundred guests from the East to the ceremonial location, including former president Ulysses S. Grant. The festooned train, with fluttering American flags, passed through the tiny hamlet of Little Missouri on September 7, as the locals waved, shouted, and, in typical Wild West fashion, fired off rounds from their pistols.

Hours later, no newspapers covered the arrival of another person. No locals came to greet him. No one in the Badlands, at that time, was aware of Theodore Roosevelt.

THE DUDE GOES WEST

Life is a great adventure . . . accept it in such a spirit.

THE LOCOMOTIVE MADE ITS WAY THROUGH THE DARKNESS IN THE early-morning hours of September 8, 1883, the passenger cars rocking back and forth rhythmically. Anyone who happened to be awake at three in the morning would have seen nothing outside the windows. With no full moon to illuminate the landscape, the view offered nothing but blackness.

The lamp at the front of the locomotive splashed out in a vain attempt to brighten the tracks ahead, but it hardly pierced the onyx of the evening. The temperature was in the low fifties; the air was cold and crisp. Stars glistened in the sky like diamonds against black velvet. As stunning as the area was in the daytime, night offered a mixture of feelings, making one feel diminutive and peaceful, but with a hint of uneasiness that *something* might be out there. The nighttime silence of the Badlands was absorbed by the vast darkness draping the land.

Slowing as it made its way down the slope and across the bridge that spanned the Little Missouri River, the train eased its way to a stop at the local depot. Unlike most train depots, the one in Little Missouri was devoid of such pleasantries as a waiting platform or porters to handle luggage. The simple rough shack, which handled telegraph messages and little else, was closed up. The waiting platform was nothing but the ground, mixed with sagebrush. Steam hissing from the engine created its own melody as the wheels offered up a massive moan, coming to a halt. The train's lantern did little to illuminate the endless nightfall. Stepping down from one of the passenger cars, the conductor, lantern in hand, waited for a sole passenger.

The slim, bespectacled young man of twenty-five came down the steps carrying his duffel bag, his Sharps .45 caliber rifle, and a double-barreled shotgun. His face was still showing the effects of a serious bout with asthma and of the cholera morbus he had suffered only a few months earlier.[1] The combination of building a new home at Oyster Bay on Long Island and learning his wife was pregnant with their first child had been sufficient stress to trigger another attack.

Waving his lantern to signal the engineer they were clear, the conductor climbed aboard without so much as a glance at the young man. Blowing the whistle, the engineer slowly moved the throttle as the large wheels groaned. The passenger cars, making the familiar sound of clanging and lurching in synchronization, began to roll out.[2] Standing alone in the crisp night air, the young man watched as the train made its way along the tall bluffs, its headlamp shining into the darkness as it picked up speed and disappeared around the bend.

He looked around, discerning the faint outline of a few buildings as the cottonwood trees rustled in the wind. Surmising the two-story structure to be the hamlet's hotel, he picked up his bag and rifles and walked to the building.

Theodore Roosevelt had arrived in the Badlands.

There was no light in any of the hotel's windows. No clerk on duty. Banging on the door, Theodore kept up this noise until he rousted from the arms of Morpheus the manager of the hotel, the always crusty "Captain" Moore. Opening the door, he offered some of the salty verbiage he had learned as a riverboat captain. It wasn't until Theodore showed him his letter of introduction from Henry Gorringe that Moore's tirade subsided and he escorted his guest into the building. For reasons that are lost to history, Gorringe had dropped out of the planned hunting trip, leaving Theodore to travel alone. He had provided the young man with a letter of introduction, as well as alerted his secretary, W. R. Wright, to see to Theodore's needs.

Climbing up the stairs, the manager waved a hand at the only cot available. A few fellow guests may have grumbled their dislike of being awakened, but Theodore paid them no mind. Nor did he look too carefully at the bed or the well-used pillow. Tired from his long trip, Theodore rolled into the blanket and slept.

Breakfast in all Western towns begins early—very early. The fourteen guests at the Pyramid Park Hotel had all the luxuries one could expect out West: one washbasin and one towel for all to share. By the time the guests had made use of the water and towel, it resembled the Missouri River's nickname, "The Big Muddy." After cleaning up, they stampeded down the stairs to the long table and benches, where breakfast would be served. Conversation was minimal, if any at all. Manners did not matter, and a timid soul was apt to wind up with little on his plate. Breakfast in most Western establishments consisted of pancakes, biscuits, bacon, eggs, and an ample amount of coffee. Depending on the location and how civilized the hotel and cook were, steak, fresh fruit, and even preserves could be offered.

With his breakfast consumed, Theodore stepped outside the hotel to see Little Missouri in daylight. What met his eyes that morning were steep slopes and a bottomland that greeted the banks of the Little Missouri River. No doubt it filled him with a romantic feeling of the Wild West he had read about. The landscape enveloped him with wonder. The magnetic beauty of the area, the lyrical sounds of the cottonwood leaves blowing in the wind, the enchanting melody from a meadowlark, and the comforting sound of a babbling river ignited his emotions.

Gorringe's secretary, W. R. Wright ("a wide awake Yankee," as Theodore called him), had had the young man's belongings moved to the company ranch house, where, as Theodore noted in a letter to Alice, he had "a room to myself and am very comfortable." Wright then took him for a horseback ride to show him the landscape. (Gorringe had probably ordered Wright to do this, with hopes of enticing Theodore to invest in his hunting lodge.) Theodore described the land as "a very desolate place, high, barren hills, scantily clad with coarse grass . . . a few stunted cottonwood trees." The washouts, he noted, would deepen into great canyons in some areas, while the steep cliffs, "a most curious formation," were everywhere.[3] He also saw the growing town of Medora, which by the time of his arrival had an assortment of tents dotting the area mixed in with wood-frame buildings in various stages of completion. Slightly west of the town-in-progress was the Marquis's slaughterhouse, a series of buildings with a tall brick chimney, set to open within a few weeks.

Although the horseback tour was entertaining, Theodore was anxious to get started on his hunting trip. Wright introduced Theodore to Frank Moore, the son of the manager of the Pyramid Park Hotel, as someone who might help to locate a guide. Unlike his father, Frank was a genial man willing to help anyone, despite his fondness for the bottle. Frank quickly suggested Joe Ferris, the superintendent of Gorringe's cantonment stables, as a likely candidate.

Joe Ferris was a year older than his potential client. A native of New Brunswick in eastern Canada, he sported a typically long Western mustache on a wide face with strong cheekbones and a nose that gave him a no-nonsense look. He had come west, along with his brother, Sylvane, to find employment. They had taken jobs clearing wheat in the Red River Valley area near Fargo in 1880.[4] It was there that they had crossed paths with Bill Merrifield, a Quebec native, and the three young men struck up a friendship that lasted until their deaths. Learning that the Northern Pacific Railroad was providing free transportation to any passenger willing to work on the frontier, the trio quickly boarded the next train, landing in Little Missouri in the summer of 1881. What they did not realize was that a return trip on the rails would cost five cents a mile, so the three were effectively stranded in this small outpost. They worked as section hands until the jobs were completed, then made arrangements to cut cordwood for the railroad from autumn through the winter of 1882. After that, Joe and Sylvane took jobs at the cantonment stables, while Merrifield hunted game for the railroad.

Joe Ferris took one look at Theodore and flatly refused.

Theodore was just another Eastern dude coming to the West to play frontier hunter, Ferris thought. He sensed the dude wouldn't be able to stand a long hunting trip, and he himself would have to serve not only as guide but as nursemaid. It was not the type of job Ferris wished to take. In addition to being a dude, Theodore's glasses were a negative setback. To Westerners, a man who wore glasses, especially at such a young age, was looked upon as somewhat defective, a cross Theodore had to bear in his younger years. "When I went among strangers," he wrote in his autobiography, "I always had to spend twenty-four hours living down the fact that I wore spectacles, remaining as long as I could judiciously deaf to any side remarks about 'four eyes,' unless it became evident that my being quiet was misconstrued and that it was better to bring matters to a head at once."[5] Whether it was Theodore's persistence, or the money he offered, Joe Ferris finally gave in and agreed to guide the dude to find his buffalo.

Ferris and Moore discussed the best place for a buffalo hunt, especially for a bull, deciding it would be wise to head to Gregor Lang's ranch and start from there. Lang, a friend of Ferris's, would let them bunk at his cabin, a perfect spot to serve as a base. Loading a wagon with provisions, Ferris and Theodore left in the late afternoon, with Ferris hoping to find a buffalo and get rid of his charge in short time. As they crossed the ford near the train trestle, the two men discovered that Theodore's Sharps rifle had a broken hammer. Ferris stopped at the cabin of Eldridge "Jerry" Paddock, who supplied Theodore with a new part, as well as lending him another buffalo rifle.

Over the years, there has been a question about which rifle had the broken part. Hermann Hagedorn claimed that it was a Winchester, but that company never manufactured a buffalo rifle. Prior to his trip, Theodore had written in a letter to Gorringe that he had a .45 Sharps rifle, and in his *Hunting Trips of a Ranchman* (1888), he commented, "When I first came to the plains I had a heavy Sharps rifle . . . and a 50-calibre, double barreled English express [shotgun]."[6] Author Carleton Putnam suggested that the Winchester Hagedorn mentioned may have been Theodore's "faithful old standby," the 1876 Winchester Centennial model (.45-75).[7] It is possible that the hammer, or the firing pin, may have been broken on his Sharps rifle, and that is why Paddock lent him another. There is no documentation that Theodore was carrying his Winchester, and Hagedorn may simply have mistaken the Sharps for a Winchester.

They forded the Little Missouri several times, and as the wagon creaked along, Theodore found himself mesmerized by the landscape. A wide valley would open to them, followed by high buttes close enough to touch. Cottonwood trees lined the riverbank, a sure sign of water for any novice to notice. Seven miles later, the two men arrived at the Chimney Butte ranch run by Joe's brother, Sylvane, and Bill Merrifield. Sylvane was the same age as Theodore; Merrifield, the senior man of the trio, was twenty-eight years old. Although they had a minimal education, the three men were all literate and known for their honesty and forthrightness. Wanting to cash in on the growing cattle business, Sylvane and Merrifield leased land from Hiram B. Wadsworth and W. L. Halley, two ranch owners from Minnesota, and added a few horses and head of cattle in 1882. The two owners made a deal to supply 150 additional cattle; in exchange, the young men would act as superintendents.[8] Sylvane and Merrifield named it the Chimney Butte Ranch, but people in the area called it the Maltese Cross, because of its brand.

Joe introduced Theodore to the other two men, who treated him coolly. They were not impressed, naturally thinking that he was just another dude coming west to play cowboy.

The cabin was a small, one-room shack with three beds, a table, few chairs, and a dirt floor. Behind the cabin was a chicken coop and a horse corral. After dinner, the four men played a card game of "Old Sledge," which started to break the ice. They dropped their cards when the chickens in the coop raised a ruckus over a visiting bobcat. Rushing out the door, they found nothing but a few highly agitated chickens and returned to their card game. During the game, Theodore asked Sylvane and Merrifield if he could have the loan of a saddle horse, because the idea of sitting on the bench seat of a creaking wagon was not his idea of seeing the West. Both Sylvane and Merrifield were unmoved by the dude's pleas and began to get suspicious of his request. They replied they had none to lend him.

"By gosh, he wanted that saddle horse so bad," Joe Ferris later recalled. "We were afraid to let him have it. Why, we didn't know him from Job's off ox. We didn't know but what he'd ride away with it. But, say he wanted that horse so blamed bad, that when he saw we weren't going to let him have it, he offered to buy it for cash."[9] Theodore took ownership of a buckskin mare he called Nell, his first Western horse.

While the trio was somewhat impressed by this dude when he offered to buy the horse, they really began to question their first impression of him when it came to bedding down for the night. Theodore refused to take one of their bunks, happy to roll up in his blankets and sleep on the dirt floor.

As dawn broke over the hills, Joe and Theodore were on their way toward Gregor Lang's ranch. It took them all day and into the early evening, crossing the Little Missouri River at least twenty times, before they reached the shallow Little Cannonball Creek.

Fifty yards from where the creek hooked up with the Little Missouri stood Gregor Lang's ranch. Lang had arrived in Little Missouri with his sixteen-year-old son, Lincoln, that spring on behalf of London capitalist Sir John Pender. Gregor, a Scotsman who had settled in Dublin, Ireland, had knowledge of raising cattle and was a business acquaintance of Pender's. As he had been doing with other potential investors, Henry Gorringe had spoken to Pender about the money to be made in the growing cattle business in the Dakota Territory, especially in his hunting lodge project. Pender was a shrewd businessman, and so asked Lang to go to America, namely the Little Missouri area, and report on Gorringe's proposal.

In New York City, Gorringe met Lang, accompanied by his son, Lincoln, with a cold detachment. He had hoped Pender would arrive with cash in hand to invest, not send an underling to investigate the area. The Langs departed New York in early April for Little Missouri. Quickly assessing that Gorringe's proposal was fraught with headaches, namely "Captain" Moore's questionable accounting practices, Lang advised Pender against entering any business deal. Pender swiftly replied that he would provide the capital for Lang to purchase a ranch and the necessary cattle for their own enterprise.

As the sun was setting behind the hills that September evening, Gregor and Lincoln were about to have dinner when they heard the rumble of the buckboard wagon approaching. Stepping into the doorway, Lincoln made out the beefy build of the driver as Joe Ferris, even before he shouted hello.[10] The rider on the pony was a complete stranger.

"To the rear, sitting on a pony, with a rifle lying across the saddle in front of him, was a second individual of lighter build," Lincoln later wrote. "I could make out he was a young man, who wore large conspicuous-looking glasses, through which I was being regarded with interest by a pair of bright twinkling eyes. Amply supporting them was the expansive grin overspreading his prominent, forceful looking lower face, plainly revealing a set of large white teeth. Smiling teeth, yet withal conveying a strong suggestion of hang-and-rattle, the kind of teeth that are made to hold anything they once close upon."[11]

Gregor Lang stepped through the door and past his son to greet the two men. When introduced by his father to Theodore, Lincoln was greeted by the familiar "*Dee-lighted*," grasping the boy's hand with both of his in a hearty handshake. "I don't know if it was the direct, forceful manner of his speech, his sincere hearty grip, the open friendly gaze with which he regarded me, or something of all combined, that instantly reached for and numbered me among his friends," Lincoln recalled.[12]

Theodore offered a letter of introduction from Gorringe, but Lincoln said no letter was needed, as his father was a good judge of men and took an immediate liking to the dude from the East. The four men sat down to dinner, and both Gregor and Theodore commenced to talk about a vast array of subjects. The fact that Gregor had named his son after his—and Theodore's—favorite president, Abraham Lincoln, was just the starting point. Despite the long train ride and equally long trek to the Lang ranch, Theodore and Gregor Lang talked into the early morning hours, each sharing their interests and opinions. Joe Ferris, oblivious to the never-ending conversation, rolled up in his blankets on the dirt floor and promptly fell asleep. Lincoln was sent to bed, but tried his best to stay up and listen to the conversation between his father and this unique guest. Close to two in the morning, Gregor and Theodore went to sleep. Once again, Theodore refused to take Gregor's bunk, sleeping on the floor in his blankets.

Come dawn, his great adventure to hunt one of the remaining buffalo on the Northern Plains would begin.

HUNTING THE SHAGGY BEAST

By Godfrey, but this is fun!

THEODORE AWOKE TO RAIN ON SEPTEMBER 10. WHILE SOME HUNTERS wouldn't pay much mind to rain, in the Badlands it was messy and downright dangerous. The bentonite clay, when dry, is hard packed and leaves a dust trail by any animal or man crossing it. When it rains, the clay takes on a whole different texture, making any attempt to navigate over it chancy at best, lethal at worse. As the clay absorbs water in a storm, it swells up and becomes a gelatin-like mud that is *very* slippery and can easily cause a man or horse to fall and possibly break a leg. Attempting to walk through this wet clay requires a tremendous amount of extra exertion, which can lead to numerous problems, especially in cold weather.

Joe Ferris urged Theodore to put off the hunting trip for a day until the rain had cleared up, explaining the potential danger. Gregor Lang echoed Ferris's sentiments, but when Theodore made a decision, there was no changing it. He wanted to start the hunt for a buffalo that morning.

Saddling up their horses and riding east from the Lang ranch, Theodore and Ferris set out in a downpour, and the rain never let up that day. As they rode on, both rider and mount acquired layers of the wet clay. Theodore never complained about the weather, although the same probably couldn't be said of Joe, who no doubt wondered what he had gotten himself into, guiding this dude.

There was no sign of buffalo that day, not even on a faraway bluff or valley. The only animals they came across, at too far a distance to make a credible shot, were some mule deer. Later in the day, they came upon a single buck, getting within two hundred feet of it when Theodore fired. He missed the target. Joe swung up his rifle, bringing the buck down.

"By Godfrey!" Theodore exclaimed in disgust, slamming his rifle to the ground. "I'd give anything in the world if I could shoot like that!"[1] Theodore was never a great shot, mainly because of his poor eyesight. He was once asked if he was a good shot. "No," he said, "but I shoot often." Nor did he ever use foul language when angry or frustrated. "By Godfrey!" was about as profane as it got with him.

As evening approached, the two men, covered in mud, returned to Lang's ranch. After eating dinner, Joe wrapped himself in his blankets and quickly fell asleep on the floor. Theodore, on the other hand, was wide awake and bright, and welcomed another long conversation with Gregor, while Lincoln did his best to stay awake and listen. One of the subjects the two men discussed that evening was cattle.

The following morning the rain, showing no sympathy for the two men, continued. Again they rode, despite Ferris's pleas to rest a day, in search of a buffalo. Lincoln Lang noted that as the two men left his father's ranch every morning, Theodore's hope of finding his buffalo that day was reflected in his parting grin. At night, when he returned empty-handed, "the grin was still there, being apparently built in and ineradicable."[2]

Every night after the meal, it was the exhausted Joe Ferris who rolled into his blankets and slept, while Theodore and Gregor Lang talked for hours. The subject of raising cattle came to dominate much of their conversation.

Like clockwork, the rain, Joe's feeble protests to lay up, and returning with nothing at night continued for nearly a week. As Joe would later recall, "Bad luck followed us like a yellow dog follows a drunkard."[3] The nightly conversations between Theodore and Gregor, while the exhausted Joe fell asleep after the evening meal, continued, as well. Lincoln noticed on more than one evening that Joe was on the brink of caving in, but he could not fall down on a tenderfoot dude from New York. "So he was obliged," Lincoln noted, "to keep going while trying to look as if he enjoyed it."[4] Certainly, Joe began to rethink his assessment of his client. He hardly had to serve as a nursemaid.

In a letter to Alice, dated September 14, 1883, Theodore related some of his adventures, including a close encounter with a buffalo.

I have been out a week now, nearly, and though it is a good game country, yet, by Jove, my usual bad luck in hunting has followed. I have had adventures enough at any rate . . . We left the river and after scrambling for some fifteen miles through very broken country, among canyons, washouts and gullies, we at last got out onto the great rolling, grass covered plains where we hoped to find the buffalo. Over these we journeyed nearly all day without seeing a thing till at about four we made out four great buffaloes feeding out in the open.

We brought the ponies up to about half a mile from them, when we left them and began the stalk. The ground was [so] flat that, after going on our hands and knees for some time, we had to crawl for nearly a quarter of a mile on our stomachs like snakes. Finally we got within about a hundred yards of the great beasts, and I took aim for the shoulder of the target. As the rifle cracked the old bull plunged forward on his knees, and I heard the "pack" of the bullet and saw the dust fly from his hide as the ounce ball crashed through his ribs; too far back, unluckily, for the wound did not disable him, and recovering himself he went off after the others, who were covering the ground pretty fast, with their lumbering gallop. We ran back for the ponies and loped along for some seven miles on the trail, and the sun was just setting when we came on them, where they had halted at last.

They were so far from cover, and it was getting so dark, that we did not have time to make a stalk, and made up our minds to run them. As we dashed down the hill they again broke into a run; and the next hour was as exciting as any I ever had spent. The ground was pretty hard, but I went straight as an arrow over the most break neck places, digging the spurs into the pony and gradually closing in on the wounded buffalo, while the others nearly held their own with us. Ferris, better mounted than I was, finally headed the wounded bull; then I ran in, driving my spurs into the flanks of my jaded horse. I fired once but the motion made me miss; and as I urged the horse still closer—for it was very dark—the bull turned to bay and charged me; the lunge of the formidable looking brute frightened my pony, and as he went off he threw up his head and knocked the heavy rifle I was carrying against my head in such force that it gave me a pretty severe cut on the crown, from which the blood flowed over my face and into my eyes so that it blinded me for the moment. The bull charged Ferris and drove him off . . . following him closer than was pleasant for a hundred yards, while it was so dark that he missed his aim. I put one more bullet in him; but my jaded horse played out, being run to a regular standstill; it had become so dark that, after a trial, we found we could not follow on foot; and the infernal beast escaped after all![5]

One thing Theodore omitted in his letter was blundering "into a bed of cactus, and fill[ing] my hands with the spines" while he and Joe were crawling on their stomachs.[6] The two men continued their quixotic adventure.

They eventually came across a small pool of water. ("Such a pool! The water was mere green scum; but it was liquid, and so we had to make it do."[7]) Dinner in their camp consisted of a biscuit, with not even a dried-out twig to make a fire. With no tree or brush to tie their horses, they unsaddled them and picketed the reins to their saddle horns. Exhausted, Theodore and Joe used the saddles as pillows, and rolled up in their blankets.

Shortly before midnight, they were roughly awakened when the saddles were violently yanked out from under them. Jumping to their feet, Theodore and Joe saw the horses "snorting wildly" as they disappeared into the darkness, dragging the saddles behind them. (They later surmised a wolf had spooked their mounts.) Fortunately, the horses were too tired to run far, and the two men caught up to their mounts a half-mile away. Returning to camp, they hobbled the horses and crawled back into their blankets. Around three in the morning, a light rain began to fall, which quickly grew heavier. Within a few minutes they found themselves lying in nearly four inches of water.

"By Godfrey, but this is fun!" Theodore exclaimed.[8]

Joe's comments have been lost to history.

◆

As the dark sky began to grow gray, the rain continued. Theodore and Joe did the best they could to maintain any warmth, a difficult task when one's blankets and clothing were completely soaked. Breakfast consisted of some hard biscuits before saddling up. "We were off, glad to bid good-bye to the inhospitable pool, in whose neighborhood we had spent such a comfortless night," Theodore stated.[9] The search for buffalo continued, and after several miserable, cold hours in the saddle, they spotted something in the distance. "As we rose over a low divide the fog lifted for a few minutes, and we saw several black objects slowly crossing some rolling country ahead of us, and a glance satisfied us they were buffalo," he later wrote.[10]

Quickly tying their horses to some sagebrush, they proceeded to move up on the buffalo, creeping through the wet grass and mud. Despite the rain blowing into their faces, both Theodore and Joe managed to come within a hundred yards of a large cow. Chilled to the bone, clenching his teeth so they wouldn't chatter, Theodore took aim at his long-awaited target and fired.

"To crown my misfortunes, I now made one of those misses which a man to his dying day always looks back upon with wonder and regret," he commented.[11] Theodore estimated that he either overshot his target or, just as he fired, gave a nervous jerk, which pulled his rifle completely off its mark. The gunshot spooked the band of buffalo, which made a hasty departure before he could attempt to reload his weapon with stiff and numb fingers. Theodore and Joe, "in wet, sullen misery," went back for their horses and trudged on. That night the two men camped, without a fire, "in shivering misery."

The following morning the sky was clear of rain and dark clouds. However, the change in the weather did nothing to alter their misfortunes. Joe's horse very nearly had a fateful encounter with a rattlesnake. While riding along a steep bluff, the soil broke free, sending riders and mounts sliding and rolling to the bottom in a tangled heap. Later, Theodore and his horse Nell were galloping through some brush-covered land when his mount stepped into a badger hole, and "turned a regular somersault, sending myself and rifle about twenty feet; but we were not hurt at all."[12] As if these episodes weren't sufficient indication of how bad things were going, later in the day, Theodore and Nell were riding across what appeared to be a hard bed of a creek. The ground gave way under Nell ("like a trap door"); the animal quickly found itself down to its withers in sticky mud. Theodore managed to get off and struggled to the bank, with lasso in hand. Between the two men and with Joe's horse, they pulled Nell free from the mud pit.

"So far the trip had certainly not been a success, although sufficiently varied as regards its incidents," Theodore wryly commented.[13]

Despite the setbacks, Theodore was enjoying himself, and the Western life, immensely. "I am every day and all day long on horseback, scrambling over the almost inconceivably rocky and difficult hills of the 'bad lands,' or galloping at full speed over the rolling prairie or level bottom," he gleefully wrote his wife.[14]

Returning to the Lang ranch, plastered head to toe in mud, chilled to the bone, and hungry, Theodore was quite willing to have his usual evening talk with Gregor Lang. This time he had a definite subject to cover: He wanted to become a cattle rancher.

He asked Gregor to become his partner and manager. Lang regretfully turned him down, citing that he couldn't back out of his contract with Pender. While disappointed with the reply, Theodore not only understood but respected Lang even more. Gregor strongly suggested his new friend talk to Sylvane Ferris and Bill Merrifield.

The next morning, Lincoln was in the saddle on the way to Maltese Cross Ranch with a message for Sylvane and Bill to come to the Lang cabin. During the two days necessary to complete the round-trip, because of rain and a high river, Theodore and Joe were back in the saddle in hopes of finding a buffalo. The evening of the second day they returned to Lang's cabin, empty-handed as usual, but found Sylvane and Bill waiting. After dinner, Theodore and his two potential partners sat on a log outside Gregor's cabin to discuss the proposal. Although both men were very willing to handle cattle for Theodore, they told him it would depend on getting out of their agreement with Wadsworth and Halley. Theodore understood and, to sweeten the deal, said that he would purchase the 150 cattle the two Minnesota men had stocked on the ranch, provided Sylvane and Bill would be released from their duties. Then the conversation turned to the financial logistics required to adequately stock a ranch. Sylvane felt that to do it properly, it would "spoil the looks of forty thousand dollars," but a third of that amount would be enough to start off.[15]

Theodore handed the two men a check for fourteen thousand dollars. Merrifield asked Theodore if he wanted a receipt. "Oh, that's all right," he replied. "If I didn't trust you men, I wouldn't go into business with you." Instead, they shook hands. Both men were amazed. Sylvane later stated that the only security Theodore had for his money "was our honesty."[16]

Fourteen thousand dollars was a significant amount back then. Theodore's state assemblyman salary garnered him only $1,200 a year, and he was just beginning to receive modest royalties from *The Naval War of 1812* book.[17] His expenses were certainly not minor, what with his building a huge home in Oyster Bay, a baby on the way, investing $20,000 as a partner in G. P. Putnam's Sons (which had published his book), and $5,000 in a Wyoming cattle company. (The latter proved to be a failure.) Before his trip to the Badlands, he was seriously considering investing $5,000 in Gorringe's project, until James Roosevelt—his uncle, and head of the Roosevelt and Sons bank—vetoed the idea. James, who oversaw Theodore's finances, was of the opinion that the cattle industry was as risky an investment as a gold mine.[18]

The following morning, September 19, Theodore put off his hunt, much to the relief of Joe Ferris, and spent the day drafting a contract with his new partners. It was decided that Sylvane and Bill would take the next train for Minnesota to see if they could be released from their contract. If they were freed, Theodore instructed them to purchase a few hundred additional head of cattle for the ranch.

On September 20, as Sylvane and Bill left for the Little Missouri train station, Theodore and Joe resumed their hunt for the elusive shaggy beast. The weather was kind to them as they headed west of the Lang ranch, near the upper reaches of the Little Cannonball Creek, just over the Montana Territory line. Suddenly, their horses threw up their heads, sniffing the air with their muzzles pointing toward the head of a gully. Immediately the two men believed their mounts sensed buffalo nearby. (Horses and buffalo share a precarious relationship, at best.) Slipping quietly off their horses, Theodore and Joe snaked their way up the coulee for one hundred yards, where they found fresh tracks. Moments later, peering over a hillock, they found their prey. It was a male bull, no more than fifty yards away, feeding on the grass.

"His glossy fall coat was in fine trim, and shone in the rays of the sun; while his pride of bearing showed him to be in the lusty vigor of his prime . . . he held up his head and cocked his tail in the air," Theodore wrote of the moment in *Hunting Trips of a Ranchman*.[19]

Ferris pointed out a spot on the buffalo, just back of the animal's shoulder, to focus on. If Theodore hit the animal there, Ferris noted, the young man would have his buffalo. The bullet hit the animal at the precise spot, yet the great bull bounded up the ridge and down the other side. Knowing that the shot was fatal, the two men trotted their horses over the ridge, where they found the elusive beast lying dead in a gully. Theodore jumped off his horse and, like a child opening his favorite gift on Christmas morning, did his version of an Indian dance around the fallen prize. He whooped, hollered, and yelled.

Needless to say, this demonstration of joy left Joe a bit perplexed. "I never saw anyone so enthused in my life, and, by golly, I was enthused myself for more reason than one. I was plumb tired out, and, besides he was so eager to shoot his first buffalo that it got into my blood," he later commented.[20]

Ecstatic with his success, Theodore handed Joe a hundred-dollar bill as a way of expressing his thanks. Then the men settled down to the business of skinning the buffalo, removing its head, and taking some of the choice meat cuts. The following day, they returned with the wagon to take the head and skin back to Little Missouri to be mounted and sent home.

"Hurrah!" Theodore boasted in a letter to Alice. "The luck has turned at last. I will bring you home the head of a great buffalo bull." Interestingly, in this letter, he does not mention to Alice the potential deal to own a cattle ranch.[21] Certainly Alice's feelings during this time were mixed, to say the least; pregnant with their first child, her husband had left her with her parents to go on a hunting trip. Theodore realized that if he did not make his hunting trip in early September, it would have to be put off until well after the birth of his child. Going ahead with something his heart desired, despite other obligations, was an indicative trait Theodore displayed at other times. He sincerely loved and missed Alice, as his letters display, but the chance to live out a fantasy was too tempting for him to ignore. Could this trait be labeled childish? Of course—but then, people who knew the man well said he was the biggest child they ever knew. Theodore never lost the wonderment a child has for life and the various things that crossed his path. It was a trait that endeared him to many—and alienated others.

Bidding Gregor and Lincoln Lang farewell, Theodore and Joe headed north with his prized buffalo trophy. Watching Theodore ride away, Gregor turned to his son and said, "There goes the most remarkable man I ever met. Unless I am badly mistaken, the world is due to hear from him one of these days."[22]

THE HOUSE WITH A CURSE

The light has gone out of my life.

THEODORE REMAINED AT MALTESE CROSS RANCH, AWAITING A TELEgram from Sylvane and Merrifield. During this time, he wrote Alice another letter, informing her that he was becoming a cattle rancher:

All day long I spend, rifle in hand, tramping over the rugged hills, or, much more often, galloping or loping for hour after hour among the winding valleys or through the river bottoms. Of course I am dirty—in fact, I have not taken off my clothes for two weeks, not even at night, except for one bath in the river—but I sleep, eat and work as I never could do in ten years' time in the city.

During these ten days I have also been making up my mind to go into something more important than hunting. I have taken a great fancy to the three men, Merrifield and two brothers named Ferris, at whose ranch I have been staying several days, and one of them has been with me all the time. I have also carefully examined the country, with reference to its capacity for stock raising; and the more I have looked into the matter—weighing and balancing everything, pro and con, as carefully as I knew how—the more convinced I became that there was a chance to make a great deal of money, very safely, in the cattle business. Accordingly I have decided to go into it; very cautiously at first, and, if I come out well the first year, much more heavily as time comes on. Of course it may turn out to be a failure; but even if it does I have made my arrangements so that I do not believe I will lose the money I put in; while if it comes out a success, as I am inclined to think that on the whole it will, it will go a long way towards solving the problem that has puzzled us both a good deal at times—how am I to make more money as our needs increase, and yet try to keep in a position from which I may be able at some future time to again go into public life . . . Even Uncle Jimmie will approve of the step I have taken; but I have long made up my mind that any successful step I take must be taken on my own responsibility. I have been on the ground, I have carefully looked over the chances; I know I run a certain risk, but I do not consider it a very large one, and I believe that the chances are very good for making more of a success than I could in any other way.[1]

Sylvane and Merrifield sent a telegram stating they had been released from their contract. Theodore Roosevelt was now a cattle rancher. The agreement called for Theodore to place four hundred head of cattle on the ranch, not to exceed twelve thousand dollars in value. Both Ferris and Merrifield would act as ranch managers for seven years, and at the end of that period, they would return to Theodore the value of his original investment, plus half the increase. Sylvane and Merrifield could make intermediate settlements on either account of principal or income, provided the sales would not reduce the herd below its original value without Theodore's approval. Any purchase of additional cattle would be managed under the same terms during the seven-year period.[2]

Arriving in St. Paul on September 27, Theodore signed the contract with Sylvane and Merrifield and instructed them to buy an additional three hundred head of cattle. He also asked them to build a better cabin with the basic comforts to make the harsh winters more tolerable.

For the cabin, the two men looked to the Little Missouri River. A large amount of unused pine logs, which had been cut and floated downriver for the Northern Pacific Railroad, were still residing on the riverbanks. The new cabin consisted of three rooms, with wooden floors and whitewashed walls. The steep-pitched roof, which had an attic that served as sleeping quarters for ranch hands, had factory-cut cedar shingles, unlike the common sod or dirt roofs found in many cabins of the area. The three rooms comprised a kitchen, living room, and bedroom. For access to the quarters in the attic, there was a ladder built into the kitchen wall, as well as one outside, next to a square barn-like door. The living room consisted of a small dining table, chairs, a book cupboard, rocking chair, and pot-belly stove to heat the room. The kitchen, like the land itself, was sparse, consisting of a stove and work table, and shelves made from a wooden box. Theodore's small bedroom contained a bed, washstand, small table, chair, a shelf for several books, and a modest bureau. The wooden bed frame either had slats or ropes to hold the tick cloth mattress (filled with either hay or horsehair). A canvas trunk, emblazoned with his initials, sat in the corner of the room. Theodore added two unique items for his frontier living: sheets for his bed (most cowboys simply used their wool blankets on the mattress) and a collapsible rubber bathtub.[3]

When Theodore returned to New York, people noticed a change in him. He wasn't the reedy, sickly young man that had left the city several weeks before. He had a stronger confidence about himself. He had gone to see the elephant.[4] Theodore Roosevelt was now a bona fide frontier hunter, and he had the buffalo head to prove it. He was no longer a dude from the East but a true Western cattleman with a ranch and stock. He would not be one of those absentee owners who wouldn't work with the cowhands. No, Theodore would *live* his dream. In typical fashion, he would embrace it with both hands and heart.

Theodore returned to Albany to begin his third term as a member of the New York legislature, and campaigned vigorously for the position of speaker of the Assembly. Although initially it appeared that he would be elected on the first ballot, many supporters quickly switched their allegiance, and he lost, 30 to 42. Despite the setback, Theodore was made chair of three committees: banking, militia, and cities.[5] The Christmas season of 1883 gave way to the frigid winter days of January 1884 and the upcoming arrival of the Roosevelt's first child.

Alice, entering her final months of pregnancy, was greatly longing for her husband's company. He typically traveled home on the weekends. "How I did hate to leave my bright, sunny little love yesterday afternoon!" he wrote Alice on February 6. "I love you and long for you all the time, and oh so tenderly; doubly tenderly now, my sweet little wife. I just long for Friday evening when I shall be with you again."[6] Missing Theodore was only part of Alice's unhappiness. She suffered miserably from cramps, although the family doctor was not terribly concerned, claiming the malady was a common side effect of her pregnancy.[7]

With assurances from the doctor that the baby would not arrive until at least February 14, Theodore rushed to Albany on Tuesday, February 12, to check on a bill he was sponsoring. With the doctor in attendance, as well as Bamie overseeing the household, Theodore felt confident that Alice and his mother, who was battling a severe cold, were in good hands.

As he left his home, New York City was shrouded under heavy, foggy skies. There was a biting chill to the air, and the sun never broke through during the day. Evening was even darker due to the heavy fog, making visibility extremely difficult. The dense haze muffled the noise of the city to a whisper, except for the croaky call of the foghorns. Train service was limited to the bare essentials, while veteran dockworkers noted that this was the worst fog they'd seen in nearly twenty years. Exterior walls, gates, and iron handrails were covered in a slippery film.

It seemed as if it was the beginning of the end.

Contrasting the bleakness of New York City, Albany's weather was bright and clear, seeming to symbolize that Theodore's bill would have little, if any, obstruction when it came to a vote. Advancing through the halls with his usual no-nonsense, purposeful stride, he set to work with plans to return home within a day. Wednesday morning greeted him with a telegram informing him he was the father of a baby girl, born late the previous night. Theodore was heartily congratulated by members of both parties on this momentous event. He requested, and was granted, a leave of absence after the passage of his bill that day.

Within hours a second telegram arrived. Alice's condition had taken a dramatic turn for the worse, and he was urged to return home at once. Catching the next available train to Manhattan proved to be a grueling ride. Because of the dense fog, the train plodded its way along the 145-mile route at a maddeningly slow pace. Theodore could do nothing but sit and stare out the windows. For a man who was used to taking action, this laggard train ride must have been sheer hell for him.

The train pulled into Grand Central Station around 10:30 p.m. Theodore hired a hack, and the carriage slowly made its way down the wet foggy streets of Manhattan. When Theodore at last rushed up the steps of the house on West Fifty-Seventh, he was greeted at the door by his younger brother, Elliott, who solemnly told him, "There is a curse on this house. Mother is dying, and Alice is dying too."

Theodore went to his wife's bedside on the third floor. Alice, suffering from kidney failure, hardly recognized him. At midnight, church bells tolled. It was February 14—Valentine's Day—the same day, in 1880, on which he and Alice had announced their engagement. Around two o'clock in the morning, the doctor informed Theodore that he should come to his mother's room. Mittie, suffering from typhoid fever, passed away an hour later as Theodore and his other siblings stayed at her bedside. She was forty-eight years old.

Summoning whatever strength he had, Theodore returned to Alice, who had slipped into a coma. As dawn broke, the city was shrouded in a blanket of inky, thick fog, requiring the gas streetlights to remain on. A burst of rain in the middle of the morning cleared the air, allowing the sun to shine for a fleeting five minutes before giving way once more to dark, gray skies. Alice Roosevelt, twenty-two, died in Theodore's arms at two o'clock in the afternoon.

In his diary for that day, he marked an X, and underneath wrote, "The light has gone out of my life."

The two caskets stood next to each other during the service at the Fifth Avenue Presbyterian Church on Saturday, February 16. Throughout the service, Theodore sat in the pew, expressionless. His former tutor, Arthur Cutler, wrote to Bill Sewall that Theodore was in a "dazed, stunned state ... He does not know what he does or says."[8]

The following day, Alice Lee (named after her mother) was baptized. Family and friends recall Theodore's bewilderment at the passing of his mother and wife within hours of each other. He showed little or no interest in his newborn daughter, pacing endlessly in his room. His siblings were worried that he was on the verge of going mad over his grief.

"We spent three years of happiness greater and more unalloyed than I have ever known fall to the lot of others ... For joy or sorrow, my life has now been lived out," he wrote in his diary a day after Alice's funeral.[9]

Now surfaces one of the most perplexing traits of Theodore as a person. Obviously distraught over Alice's death, he would begin to take steps to withdraw her from his life. Aside from writing a parting remembrance for family and friends, it would be the last time he would publicly mention Alice. Within a year of her passing, her name was never mentioned by Theodore or by anyone close to him. Most of the letters between them were destroyed, with only a small handful surviving, including the five Theodore wrote during his buffalo-hunting trip. Pages of Theodore's scrapbook from his days at Harvard are missing, leading one to surmise that those pages dealt with his romantic pursuit of Alice. He completely excludes Alice from his 1913 autobiography. It was as if she had never existed in his life.

In later years, he disliked the name Teddy, claiming it was the name of a child, not a man. Although that may be partly true, the real reason appears to be that Alice had called him Teddy, or Teddykins. He forever refused to have those names mentioned again. After his exploits at San Juan Hill in 1898, the public and the press often referred to him as Teddy Roosevelt. He could only ignore it.

Alice Lee, Theodore's first child, was given to Bamie to raise for the time being. Theodore would refer to her as "Baby Lee," ignoring her first name, another memory of Alice. In later years, although father and daughter were close, there is no documented evidence that he ever spoke to Alice Lee about her mother. It was reported that when Alice would ask her father about her mother, Theodore suggested she ask her aunt Bamie. Like his father's refusal to join the Union Army in the Civil War, Theodore would blot from his memory anything that pained him. For him, looking back was reserved for only the happy memories in his life. Anything involving great pain quickly became a closed door that was never opened or spoken of again. Alice Roosevelt was expunged from his memory, from his scrapbooks and future diaries. Even the home he was building would be renamed, forever distancing the memory of the woman it was initially built for. If Theodore Roosevelt ever thought of, spoke of, or remembered Alice Roosevelt after her death, he took it with him to the grave.

"There is nothing left for me except to try to so live as not to dishonor the memory of those I loved who have gone before me," he said.[10]

The home on West Fifty-Seventh Street was sold within a week of its listing. Theodore sold the brownstone he and Alice had purchased, never again setting foot in the home. He left it to Bamie to handle the sale and disbursement of its contents. In a letter to Bill Sewall, Theodore noted, "I have never believed it did any good to flinch or yield for any blow. Nor does it lighten the pain to cease from working."[11]

After the funeral and Alice's christening, Theodore threw himself back into his work, returning to the New York Assembly on February 18. This was his way of dealing with loss. In a February 21 letter to Carl Schurz, he thanked the man for his "words of kind sympathy," stating he was back at work. "Indeed I think I should go mad if I were not employed."[12]

Theodore set a grinding and endless schedule, from holding investigative hearings to introducing numerous bills on the Assembly floor. Theodore even rewrote his committee's investigative report on political corruption in New York City just hours before it was to be delivered to the Assembly. Rarely sleeping, he would nap on the train going back and forth from Albany to Manhattan. "He feels the awful loneliness more and more, and I fear he sleeps little, for he walks a great deal in the night, and his eyes have that strained red look," his sister Corrine wrote to Elliott.[13]

The Republican presidential convention began on June 1 in Chicago. The party was heavily fractured, with many rallying to nominate James G. Blaine, while others pushed for current president, Chester A. Arthur. Having assumed the presidency after James A. Garfield's assassination in 1881, Arthur decided to run for a full term, although many in the party felt he was too weak (both politically and physically) to survive the upcoming election. Blaine, who had served in the House and Senate since 1863, was the favored choice, despite persistent rumors of financial impropriety. His 1876 bid for the presidency had crashed when rumors circulated that he had received a hefty payment (nearly $64,000) from the Union Pacific Railroad in exchange for bonds he owned of a smaller railroad, the Little Rock and Fort Smith, which were virtually worthless. While charges of accepting a bribe were never proven, Blaine could not shake its shadow. He lost a second bid for nomination in 1880, but was now the leading contender for nomination.

Theodore arrived with the intention of helping to nominate Vermont senator George F. Edmunds, an honest, conscientious, and banal candidate. A contentious battle for the nomination saw votes for Edmunds dwindle on each ballot while Blaine's numbers increased. Both Edmunds and President Arthur, who would die from kidney failure in 1886, lost the nomination to James G. Blaine. With another party machine hack in the running, several Republicans toyed with jumping ship to support the Democratic candidate, Grover Cleveland. Even though he was disgusted with the antics of the Republican Party machine, Theodore told a reporter he would not bolt from the party or the convention, adding that he had "no personal objection" to Blaine.[14]

Politics now lacked the spark it once held for Theodore. The actions that got Blaine nominated only reinforced his distaste of corrupt party hacks pushing their candidate of choice. Obviously, his recent personal tragedy exacerbated his feelings. The grief he suffered was still there, no matter how hard he worked, how little he slept, or how many bills he introduced. Traveling to Manhattan every weekend to visit his baby daughter was a constant reminder of his tragic loss.

In a letter to the *Utica Morning Herald*, Theodore stated that his work in the Assembly had been "very harassing," leaving him tired and restless. He planned to leave public life and return to the Dakotas, spending two or three years hunting and writing.[15]

It was time for a change.

"Black care rarely sits behind a rider whose pace is fast enough; at any rate, not when he first feels the horse move under him," Theodore wrote in 1888 of cowboys riding during a roundup.[16] Like the heroes that appealed to his romantic nature, Theodore would saddle up and ride out into the vastness of the Badlands to lose himself. He would bury his grief in the unbounded rolling hills, the coulees, the dry creek beds, and the bottomland along the Little Missouri River. Cottonwood trees, with the leaves whispering in the wind, would comfort him. The West, as it had done for many others over the recent decades, would allow Theodore to work, ride, and grieve without asking questions. It would also test him as a man. The Western land would force him to face his fears, his grief, and his moral beliefs like nothing he would experience in the East. The West was the proving ground. Many had tried, few had succeeded. He would have to show, as the cowboys would say, that he wasn't "all hat and no cattle."[17] Shooting a buffalo was one thing, but riding the range for hours, or days, branding cattle, and standing up to men who thought the law did not apply to them was another situation entirely.

Unlike others who grieved with emotions, Theodore did just the opposite. He went out in search of a physical challenge to combat his grief. After his father's death, he had hunted endlessly in the Maine woods with Bill Sewall. Hunting was an escape for him, testing his skills against those of wild animals. Who was better? Who would make the kill? He also rode his horses hard, as if to outrun the grief that was constantly dogging his trail. In suffering a loss, he tempted fate; he pushed himself to the edge as if daring death to take him. By conquering his physical obstacle, Theodore gained the strength to vanquish his grief, burying it so deeply that it could not return. Now he would further test himself by living in the West, by living a free but hard life, pushing himself against the elements, the wild animals, and, most importantly, himself. Theodore would now match himself against the likes of Davy Crockett and Daniel Boone, as well as those around him—the Ferris brothers, Merrifield, Sewall, and Dow. He would also, with his romantic nature, become the cowboy found in the dime novels of the time. In some respects, heading west allowed him to indulge in a fantasy, to escape the harsh realities life had recently dealt him.

He was once asked if he had been afraid when he went out west. "There were all kinds of things I was afraid of at first, ranging from grizzly bears to 'mean' horses and gun-fighters; but by acting as if I was not afraid I gradually ceased to be afraid," he replied.[18]

Like those who had gone west before him, seeking to escape a broken heart, the horrors of the Civil War, a failed business, or just answering the itch for adventure, Theodore Roosevelt boarded a train for the Badlands.

The ensuing three years would solidify the beliefs and character of the man whose likeness eventually was carved into the side of a South Dakota mountain.

HEADIN' WEST

Nowhere, not even at sea, does a man feel more lonely than when riding over the far-reaching, seemingly never-ending plains.

"LITTLE MISSOURI AND MEDORA ARE BOTH DESTINED TO HAVE A LARGE and legitimate boom this year. The writer personally knows of three young and energetic business men who will start here, and many others are waiting till spring opens."[1] This optimistic comment was found on page four of the premiere edition of Medora's only newspaper, the *Bad Lands Cow Boy*.

Indeed, Medora was growing, while the hamlet of Little Missouri vainly attempted to maintain its several businesses. It had already seen the train depot moved to Medora, and by the end of 1884, Little Missouri was nothing but a faded memory.[2] At the time of Theodore's arrival in September 1883, Little Missouri boasted four buildings, while a few tents had sprung up in Medora. By the end of the spring of 1884, Medora claimed eighty-four buildings, which included a grocery store, newspaper office, blacksmith shop, photograph gallery, and barbershop. Little Tom's Saloon offered "everything from Cow-boy bitters to Dude Soda." The Marquis built the Hotel De Mores, charging $2.00 daily, or $6.00 for the week, noting that it had "First Class Accommodations for All." Barber H. Lyle advertised "fine work guaranteed," while contractor J. A. Freeze offered carpentry services "done with neatness and dispatch."[3]

Almost all Western towns, despite their size, had a newspaper. Depending on the population—and the news—newspapers were published daily or weekly. The man behind the press could be as itinerant as the gamblers and saloon owners, moving from one boomtown to another, while others put down roots if the town showed promise. These newsmen, while maintaining the lofty principle of being a voice for the truth, nevertheless had to earn a living. Not only did they report on the happenings within the town, but many also served as typesetter, clerk, and printer, not to mention selling subscriptions and ads. Some newspapers became the mouthpiece, or at least a strong supporter, for certain town factions or a political party. Many newspapers tried to maintain a balance in their reporting, but it was rare when an editor did not allow their personal opinions to spill onto the pages.

Arthur T. Packard was no different from any other newspaper publisher in the West. At twenty-two, Packard, a University of Michigan graduate, had already served as an editor and writer for the *Bismarck Tribune* and the *Mandan Pioneer* before arriving in Medora. The Marquis helped fund the paper, supplying Packard with a building—his former blacksmith shop, which stood under a crooked cottonwood tree. It was a long, twenty-by-thirty-foot, single-story building constructed from perpendicular boards, with two-inch strips covering the joints in a vain attempt to keep out the Dakota winters. A small area inside was cordoned off for living space, while the rest of the building was given over to cranking out a weekly edition.[4] Packard, a Republican "clear through to the backbone," was not beholden to the Marquis, or anyone else. He made that abundantly clear in the first editorial of the *Bad Lands Cow Boy*.

> *We do not come as an agent or tool of any man or any set of men. There is a wide field for us to cover, and we intend to cover it. We do come, however, to make some almighty dollars. There is nothing like honesty, and now that we have come out thus plainly our motives cannot be impeached. But to fulfill our mission we must publish a good paper.*[5]

Editorials in the *Bad Lands Cow Boy* were reprinted in other periodicals, including the *St. Paul Pioneer Press*, *New York Sun*, and *New York Herald*, which called the paper "a neat little journal, with lots to read in it, and the American press has every reason to be proud of its new baby . . . It says in its introductory notice to its first number that it intends to be the leading cattle paper of the Northwest, and adds that it is not published for fun, but for $2 a year."[6]

The *Bismarck Tribune*, while noting the newspaper was "bright and newsy," took exception to the "ill-sounding, horrible name chosen for it. The editor cannot be so stupidly blind as to be unaware of the fact that throughout the East the name 'cowboy' is looked upon as a synopsis for lawlessness and cussedness in its most active form, and the 'bad lands' have ever been regarded as barren in the extreme . . . in eastern eyes it means all that is bad, lawless and desperate."[7] Packard quickly responded, stating, "We adopted the name in the first place to attract attention, which it certainly does . . . First, that cow boys in the west are, as a rule, one of the most peaceful and law-abiding classes of citizens that we have . . . The second reason is that cow boys represent cattle . . . This is the reason why we have completed our name into THE BAD LANDS COW BOY."[8]

Packard was extremely supportive of the Badlands cattle industry, stating that his weekly would "preach King Cattle to all men." He noted that the area had an "abundance of unoccupied land," and that any increase "in the number of cattle and cattle raisers will work to the advantage of all concerned. If the Bad Lands were full of cattle it would not decrease the price, as the demand is far in advance of the supply. Word comes from Kansas that the cattle sections there are overstocked and the cattle men there are looking to the Northwest for relief. To all these we would say, come. There is plenty of room and you will be made welcome."[9] Two weeks later, Packard said the land was an excellent winter range. Despite the fact that a few calves suffered from the winter cold, "We have yet to hear of a solitary head ever having died in the Bad Lands from exposure or lack of grass . . . No matter which way the wind is from, there is always a ravine or coulee near, into which the cattle can be entirely beyond its reach. These cross coulees and ravines feel almost warm on the coldest day, and here you will find the cattle as contented as if in a barn."[10]

Packard, like many other new arrivals, had yet to experience a Badlands dry summer or brutal winter.

Medora, similar to other small towns, had few venues by which to entertain the large male population aside from gambling, drinking, and the sporting ladies. The arrival of the train was a major event for those in town; Dutch Wannegan noted that "seeing the trains come in was all the scenery we had."[11] Cowboys, who probably had imbibed too much of

Bob Robert's "bug juice," would watch anyone who disembarked from the train. If a man was wearing a derby or top hat—called "pot hat" and "plug," respectively, by the cowboys—that person became fair game. One cowboy would knock the offender's hat off with a rock, and then display his proficiency with his pistol on the chapeau. This provided great amusement for the cowboys, while the hatless victim could do little but mourn the passing of his headgear. Theodore once stated that he would wear any hat he pleased in town, and, in fact, no cowboy ever attempted to display their shooting skills against him.

Another favorite act of cowboy horseplay was to wait for an arriving train, then let loose with a burst of gunfire inside a nearby saloon. Passengers on the train, hearing the shots, would see two men carrying a dead body out to the rear of the establishment. Within a minute, another volley of gunfire was discharged and, once again, two men carried out another body. As the train left the station, the passengers were aghast at witnessing the violence of the Wild West. Little did they realize that the "dead bodies" were the same very-much-alive cowboy carried out by his colleagues in a revolving circle.[12]

Medora's growth was due solely to the result of the plans and pocketbook of the Marquis de Morès, who was becoming known for ignoring the rights of others, especially when it came to land ownership. He held the opinion that the only enforceable rights belonged to himself, and in the spring of 1884, he sought to challenge Theodore's land holdings. The Marquis placed 1,500 head of cattle on rich bottomland located across the river from Theodore's ranch, which, under the laws of the range, belonged to his Maltese Cross outfit. Bill Merrifield confronted the Marquis's foreman, who said he had his orders, and refused to move the cattle. Riding to Medora, with another cowboy to serve as their witness, Merrifield and Sylvane found the Marquis in his office. It was nearly midnight.

The Marquis demanded to know what the men wanted at such a late hour, and Merrifield related the situation. He asked the Marquis to write an order notifying his foreman to move the cattle off the land. Asking what they would do if he refused to comply, Merrifield curtly responded that they would move the cattle themselves. Attempting to work out a compromise, the Marquis offered to pay $1,500 to graze his cattle in the area for three weeks. The two men flatly refused the offer, adding that either he write the order or they would move the cattle. Returning to the ranch, Merrifield and Sylvane handed a letter to the foreman who moved the cattle that morning. Merrifield later stated, "We knew there'd be no living with a man like the Marquis if you made statements and then backed down for any price."[13]

Theodore arrived in Medora late in the evening of June 9. He stepped off the train into the crisp, cold night air, greeted by the Ferris brothers and Merrifield. They walked over to Packard's newspaper office, where the editor and a few other men were sitting around a stove, talking. With Theodore's arrival, the conversation quickly turned to the Chicago convention and the nomination of Blaine.

The following day, Theodore, Sylvane, and Merrifield rode to Maltese Cross Ranch. It was the first time Theodore saw the new cabin and learned how his cattle had fared during the winter. Thanks to a relatively mild winter, a light snowfall, and early chinook winds, the cattle had had easy access to grass. Because of the favorable conditions, Theodore had lost only twenty-five head of cattle from a total of 440. The even brighter news was that he had gained 155 calves. Encouraged by this report, he increased his investment with an additional thousand head of cattle. His total investment now came to $40,000, nearly 20 percent of his total resources.[14] Roosevelt instructed Merrifield and Sylvane to purchase Eastern cattle instead of the Texas longhorns. Eastern cattle had shorter horns, which meant more of them could be placed in a stock car, and they were heftier compared to the leaner longhorn breed. One major drawback for this breed was that unlike the longhorns, they did not endure the harsh winter weather as well.

Theodore now turned his attention to obtaining a buckskin suit and to shooting a pronghorn.* Lincoln Lang jumped at the chance to help him fulfill both requests. Theodore felt the buckskin suit was "the most picturesque and distinctively national dress ever worn in America. It was the dress in which Daniel Boone was clad when he first passed through

---

* While the pronghorn resembles the antelope found in Africa and Eurasia, it is not an antelope. Many refer to the animal as a pronghorn buck, pronghorn antelope, or simply antelope. I have chosen to refer to the animal as a "pronghorn."

the trackless forests of the Alleghenies . . . it was the dress worn by grim old Davy Crockett when he fell at the Alamo."[15] The clothing appealed to his romantic nature, allowing him, in a small way, to emulate his heroes and live out the role of frontiersman. This feeling was evident when it came to his other Western attire. The Bowie knife he carried was made by Tiffany's in New York. His 1873 Colt pistol, with a seven-and-a-half-inch barrel, was intricately engraved and sported ivory grips, with his initials on one side and the head of a buffalo on the other. On the sides of his spurs, he displayed his initials and the Maltese Cross brand. Theodore wore his chaps in the traditional shotgun style (also called "stovepipes"), in which the legs are straight and narrow.[16] Chaps were a necessity in the Southwest to protect a cowboy's legs from the prickly brush, but their use was more of a personal choice for cowboys in the Badlands. Some cowboys in Medora felt that Theodore's choice of clothing was hardly authentic. J. L. Fisher, the Marquis's new superintendent of the refrigerator car company, held the opinion that the young fellow was "dressed in the exaggerated style" of the West, which only a rank tenderfoot would dare to wear.[17]

Lincoln knew that the only person who could make a buckskin suit in the area was a Widow Maddox. Some folks called her a terror, one to steer clear of. One of the first women to settle in the area, Widow Maddox was a true pioneer. Her husband, while on a drunk one night, attempted to beat her and soon found himself on the losing end of a poker. Soon after that incident, he quickly left her and the ranch. Lincoln Lang described the woman as "heavy set, muscular, rather short of stature, with strong regular features."[18]

Making their way to the Maddox ranch, the two riders heard a commotion in the brush, followed by a loud squeak from an animal in trouble. A large bull snake had a jackrabbit tightly held in its coils and was slowly crushing it to death. Both Theodore and Lincoln quickly dismounted, "basting the life out" of the snake with their quirts. Theodore picked up the panting rabbit and held it in the crook of his arm, gently checking it. After a few moments in the safety of his arms, the rabbit was turned loose. "There goes a sore but wiser rabbit," Theodore noted.[19]

While others may have found Widow Maddox a terror, she took an immediate liking to Theodore, and, as Lincoln stated, was "quite chatty, which was unusual for her with strangers." Theodore described her, without using her name in his autobiography, as "a very capable and very forceful woman, with sound ideas of justice and abundantly well able to hold her own."[20] The two men had a friendly lunch with their hostess before she measured Theodore for his suit. Of his buckskin shirt, Theodore later said it was "first-class," and he used it for many years before one of his sons borrowed it for a winter in Arizona in the early 1910s.[21]

On their return to the Lang ranch, Theodore spotted some pronghorns in the distance. Luckily, the animals neither spotted nor smelled the men as they left their horses and began to stalk their targets. Topping a hill, Theodore and Lincoln saw that the grazing animals were oblivious to the hunters. Lincoln noted that Theodore coolly raised his rifle to his shoulder and shot one of the pronghorns, dropping it in its tracks. "He might have been an old seasoned hunter for any indication of excitement that I could see, although this was his first antelope," he wrote years later. "As the animal dropped, however, his self-possession promptly took wings, wild enthusiasm held the stage, and he was executing a species of war dance around the top of the hill, with his rifle in one hand while waving his hat with the other."[22]

Shouting "I got him!" over and over, Theodore failed to take a shot at the other pronghorns before they ran off to safety. Overjoyed at his success in bagging one of his desired targets, Theodore promptly gave Lincoln "the surprise of my life" when he handed the young man the shotgun that brought down the pronghorn. "But that was Roosevelt, as we had come to know him even then," Lincoln recounted. "Deeply I appreciated his kindness and said no." The young man also knew that Theodore, in the moment of complete euphoria, may have regretted the gesture once the thrill wore off. "It seemed proper for me to decline," he said.[23]

The two rode fifty miles in that one day. Since the pronghorn is so spare, the only real meat on the body is the hams, which they cut out, as well as the head, which became another trophy mount. A few days later, Theodore wrote to Bamie, detailing his feelings about the area and his cattle business:

Well, I have been having a glorious time here, and am well hardened now (I have just come in from spending thirteen hours in the saddle). For every day I have been here I have had my hands full. First and foremost, the cattle have done well, and I regard the outlook for making the business a success as being very hopeful. This winter I lost about 25 head, from wolves, cold, etc.; the others are in admirable shape, and I have about a hundred and fifty-five calves. I shall put on a thousand more cattle and shall make it my regular business. In the autumn I shall bring out Seawall [sic] and Dow and put them on a ranch with very few cattle to start with, and in the course of a couple of years, give them quite a little herd also.

I have never been in better health than on this trip. I am in the saddle all day long either taking part in the round up of the cattle, or else hunting antelope (I got one the other day; another good head for our famous hall at Leeholm). I am really attached to my two "factors," Ferris and Merrifield; they are very fine men.

The country is growing on me, more and more; it has a curious, fantastic beauty of its own; and as I own six or eight horses I have a fresh one every day and ride on a lope all day long. How sound I sleep at night now! There is not much game, however; the cattlemen have crowded it out and only a few antelope and deer remain . . . I will start out alone to try my hand at finding my way over the prairie by myself.[24]

This trip on his own would be his first test. He would ride off into the Badlands and the prairie to prove that he could handle himself in the wilds like Crockett, Boone, and even Sewall. This was a boy's true adventure, enacting the role of the great frontiersman, and—in what would soon become typical fashion—Theodore's way of life. His childlike enthusiasm in embracing such adventures would make him irresistible to his future public, and provide great press.

"I started in the very earliest morning," he wrote in *Hunting Trips of a Ranchman*, "when the intense brilliancy of the stars had just begun to pale before the first streak of dawn. By the time I left the river bottom and struck off up the valley of a winding creek, which led through the Bad

Lands, the eastern sky was growing rosy; and soon the buttes and cliffs were lit up by the level rays of the cloudless summer sun. The air was fresh and sweet, and odorous with sweet scents of the spring-time that was barely passed; the dew lay heavy, in glittering drops, on the leaves and the blades of grass, whose vivid green, at this season, for a short time brightens the desolate and sterile-looking wastes of the lonely western plains. The rose-bushes were all in bloom, and their pink blossoms clustered in every point and bend of the stream; and the sweet, sad songs of the hermit thrushes rose from the thickets, while the meadow larks perched boldly in sight as they uttered their louder and more cheerful music."[25]

Theodore made his way through the Badlands with its rounded hills tinted with scoria and red volcanic rock that peeked up through the growing grass. Clumps of sagebrush and wild rose populated the area, and at one point he spotted "two magpies, who lit on an old buffalo skull, bleached white by the sun and snow." He passed the remaining buttes that acted as a gateway to the "great, seemingly endless stretches of rolling or nearly level prairie." Seeing this land reaching out as far as the horizon leaves a rider with an overwhelming sense of awe and insignificance. The vast openness of the prairie only accentuates one's isolation from civilization, but it also stimulates the sense of adventure for what may lie over the next rolling hill.

However, the prairie can be dangerous. What seems to be level ground can quickly give way to a sharp dip, or to hidden prairie dog or badger holes. Riding at a lope or gallop, many a horse has caught a hoof in one of these holes, sending both rider and mount tumbling. A horse that trips in such a hole on the prairie could be left with a broken leg, having to be put down, while the rider would be miles from any cow camp, shack, or ranch. In the summer, the prairie can be a furnace, reflecting the rays of a blistering sun, drying up creek beds or a once-shallow water hole. As in the desert, water is a very valuable commodity on the prairie. Water means life, not just for people, but for animals. The prairie also offers little shelter from the sun, rain, and snow. The wind uses it as an expressway, blowing hard with little care of what it does to anything in its way. Like the rest of the American West, the prairie, while offering a beautiful view and dreams of wealth, is an exacting taskmaster. As with the Badlands, animals and man do not conquer the prairie; they live with it and accept the daily lessons it hands out.

Theodore was mounted on his favorite horse, Manitou, whom he referred to as "a wise old fellow, with nerves not to be shaken by anything."[26] In his *Hunting Trips of a Ranchman*, Theodore uses the word "we" to describe the travels of horse and rider in the chapter "A Trip on the Prairie." To him, Manitou was not simply a horse but a partner. He carried a telescope that his father had given him, using it to scan the area for game, writing, "The greatest caution was used in riding up over any divide, to be sure that no game on the opposite side was scared by the sudden appearance of my horse or myself."[27] Spotting some pronghorns, he fired at them without much success. "I had fired half a dozen shots without effect; but while no one ever gets over his feeling of self-indignation at missing an easy shot at close quarters, anyone who hunts antelope . . . soon learns that he has to expect to expend a good deal of powder and lead before bagging his game."[28]

As the sun lifted overhead, Theodore followed a dry creek until he found "a small spot of green" near a faint pool of water. Unsaddling Manitou, he allowed the horse to graze and drink while he himself had a biscuit and some water and rested for a few hours. Then they went across the dry creek bed and soon found themselves floundering in quicksand. Both rider and horse struggled but managed to get out of the mess. The authority and detail with which Theodore reports the dangers of being caught in quicksand in *Hunting Trips of a Ranchman* indicate that such material could come only from risky personal experience.

Topping a crest, Theodore's luck soon changed. He came across six or eight pronghorns about a quarter of a mile away. "A group of bucks, six or eight feeding together, started to run across my path, while I was riding alone on the prairie; I was on a first rate pony, and galloped full speed diagonally to their course; I leaped off as they passed within twenty-five yards, and gave them both barrels, killing a fine buck shot through the shoulders," he detailed in his diary.[29] Theodore found a campsite in a rich bottomland with cottonwood trees and pools of water. He picketed Manitou, who grazed on the grass, and spread out on the ground his horse blanket and slicker for his bed. Heating a cup of water for tea and roasting the pronghorn hams, Theodore settled down for the night. "It is wonderful how cozy a camp, in clear weather, becomes if there is a good fire and enough to eat, and how sound the sleep is afterwards in the cool air, with the brilliant stars glimmering through the branches overhead," he commented.[30] In his first day in the wilderness on his own, Theodore was living the experience he had only briefly grasped in tours with Bill Sewall and Joe Ferris. Now he was on his own, a lone rider in the vast American West.

Awakened in the early morning by the sound of prairie dogs emerging from their burrows, Theodore, rifle in hand, walked out onto the prairie. Scanning the open ground, he saw no sign of game, and only the shrill chirps of the prairie dogs and the song of a skylark filled the air. Saddling Manitou, he rode off. The sun was soon beating down on them, causing Manitou to break into a sweat even though they were simply walking. Finding a "bitter alkaline pool," Theodore stopped to rest. The bank was too steep for Manitou to manage, so Theodore filled the inside of his hat with water and brought it up to his friend. Moving closer to the fringes of the Badlands, he spotted more pronghorns, but his attempt to shoot any was unsuccessful. Continuing on, Theodore once again spotted two pronghorns. "On riding round a little knoll, I saw two antelope a long distance off, looking at me; I dismounted and fired off hand, with careful aim . . . By actual measurement the distance was three hundred yards; the best shot I ever made with the rifle," he wrote in his diary.[31]

With his supply of biscuits running low, and pronghorn meat good only for roughly twenty-four hours, Theodore headed back to Maltese Cross Ranch the following morning. As he wrote in his book, the solo trip into the wilds "always has great attraction" for anyone who loves the sport and nature, and can be "his own good companion." Of course, such an excursion depends a great deal on favorable weather, because winter snows or rain make such travel tiresome and dangerous. On the way back to the ranch, a storm rolled in, drenching both Theodore and Manitou. "But when a man's clothes and bedding and rifle are all wet, no matter how philosophically he may bear it," Theodore wrote in his book, "it may be taken for granted that he does not enjoy it."[32] Returning to the ranch on the evening of June 22, the following day he was off on a different adventure.

Although he was comfortable at the Maltese Cross, Theodore found that the location did not always afford him the privacy he desired. Its location—thirty miles south of Medora, and near a well-traveled route that ran north to south—guaranteed that the ranch never lacked company. For Theodore, privacy and remoteness fitted his current frame of mind. In addition, the Maltese Cross was not conducive to the solitude he needed to write a book. The morning after his four-day sojourn, he saddled up and headed north, searching for a new location to build another cabin.

Passing through Medora, he stopped at the office of the town newspaper for a short visit with Arthur Packard, who informed him that reform-minded members of the Republican Party, who had opposed James G. Blaine's nomination, were upset that Roosevelt and his friend, Henry Cabot Lodge, would not leave the party and would support Blaine. Shrugging off the verbal attacks, Packard noted in the next edition of the *Bad Lands Cow Boy* that Theodore was "perfectly non-committal on politics and the alleged interview with him, published in St. Paul Pioneer Press, speaks more for the reporter's asininity than for his perspicacity."[33]

The newspaper office became Theodore's favorite place to stop when in Medora. A virtual teetotaler, Theodore avoided the town's saloons. He preferred to sit in a rocking chair by Packard's stove, drinking coffee or tea and discussing politics or the events of the day. Theodore genuinely liked Packard and his sense of right versus wrong. Packard was also responsible for saving Theodore from potential danger in town. When he'd ride into Medora, Theodore always wore his gun and holster, as did most of the men in the area. Packard, understanding the problems that wearing a gun in town can cause, recommended Theodore leave his sidearm at the newspaper office while in town. When Theodore questioned Packard's request, the newspaperman had William Roberts, a man handy with pistols, demonstrate. Throwing two tomato cans into the air, Roberts quickly blasted them with his pistols while they were airborne. When they landed, Roberts continued to fire away at the cans, moving them along the ground. Claiming it a wonderful exhibition, Theodore also realized Packard's point, and he never wore his pistol in Medora again.[34]

"The cowboys are a much misrepresented set of people," Theodore stated in an interview with the *New York Tribune*. "It is a popular impression when one goes among them he must be prepared to shoot. But this is a false idea. I have taken part with them in the rounding up, have eaten, slept, hunted and herded cattle with them, and have never had any difficulty. If you choose to enter rum shops with them, or go on drinking sprees with them, it is easy to get into a difficulty out there as it would be in New York, or anywhere else. But if a man minds his own business and at the same time shows he is fully prepared to assert his rights—if he is neither a bully or a coward and keeps out of places in which he has no business to be, he will get along well as in Fifth Avenue. I have found them a most brave and hospitable set of men. There is no use in trying to be overbearing with them, for they won't stand the least assumption of superiority, yet there are many places in our cities where I should feel less safe than I would among the wildest cowboys of the west."[35]

Riding out of Medora, Theodore met rancher Howard Eaton and shared with him his desire for a new cabin. Eaton suggested riding north, roughly thirty miles from Medora, to investigate the bottomland along the Little Missouri River. Finding the area Eaton described, Theodore noted a wide grassy stretch that extended a hundred feet from the riverbank, perfect for grazing. Beyond that was a grove of cottonwood trees following the course of the river, which provided shade and more than enough space to build a substantial cabin. The trees also served as a spot for numerous birds to rest and sing their songs, something that was literally music to Theodore's ears. Beyond the grove of trees was a flat area that would house his second cabin, and beyond that stood the wind-worn hills of the Badlands. Near this location, Theodore found a small shack and paid $400 to the owner in return for obtaining proper claim to the land.

The area was isolated. Quiet. Peaceful. Only the birds singing and the wind passing through the leaves of the cottonwood trees muffled the sound of the river making its way north. It was what Theodore wanted—and needed. Not far from his chosen site, he found the skulls of two elks, their antlers interlocked, who had done battle to the death.

He named his new ranch the Elkhorn.

One problem cattle ranchers faced in such remote areas was theft. Cattle rustlers and horse thieves were commonplace in the West, and with vast stretches of open range, stealing a few head—or even a hundred—could easily happen without the owner's immediate knowledge. Thieves generally were cautious about how many head of cattle or horses they stole, in order to avoid detection. One way of aiding their crime was to doctor the brand. A CS brand, for example, could easily be made to look like O8 with a heated cinch ring. Unless the doctoring was poorly executed, it wouldn't be noticed until the cow was butchered; then the inside of the hide would show that two brands had been burned in. When a cattle rustler or horse thief had the misfortune of being caught, justice was swift and unmerciful. Offenders were either shot or hanged, usually without a burial. Law enforcement was often spread thin over wide distances, and traveling to a town for a trial was a great inconvenience for cattlemen. Dispensing justice immediately also served as a warning to other potential thieves.

Rustlers operated in groups of small numbers, generally no more than ten. These men may have worked for an outfit for a while, then quit with the idea of taking a small number of cattle, perhaps twenty, re-branding them, and selling them in another town or military post. Most rustlers frequented saloons, hash-houses, and anywhere else where they could gather information about a herd. Western Dakota Territory, the northwest of Wyoming, and the eastern border of Montana were prime locations for rustlers. The large areas of open range, and few cowboys to protect the herds, made the cattle a tempting target. By June 1884, Granville Stuart, president of the Montana Stockgrowers Association, had had enough of cattle rustling. Rather than seeking the assistance of the law, he formed a private group known as the Stranglers to handle a recent increase in thefts. This group, made up of cattle owners and the loyal cowboys who worked for them, would eliminate the problem on their own. On June 24, Stuart held a meeting to explain his idea to the cattle owners. One of those present was the Marquis, who requested to join the Stranglers. Stuart refused, citing the Frenchman's well-known presence as a distraction.

No one really knows when Theodore and the Marquis actually met for the first time. There is nothing in Theodore's diaries or in the

Marquis's records mentioning an initial meeting. However, both Theodore and the Marquis traveled on June 26 to Miles City in Montana Territory to meet with Stuart. They pleaded their case on why they should be allowed to join, and while Stuart listened patiently, he declined their request. He noted that the two men's distinguished positions within society would draw unwanted attention to their actions, which they hoped to keep secret from the rustlers.[36] "The vigilantes, or stranglers, as they were locally known, did their work thoroughly; but, as always happens with the bodies of the kind, toward the end they grew reckless in their actions, paid off private grudges, and hung men on slight provocation," Theodore commented in his autobiography.[37] Hermann Hagedorn claimed that Arthur Packard had been told that two known rustlers would be eliminated on a following Thursday. On the designated day, which was also the day Packard's weekly paper came out, the editor included an article about their demise. Later in the day, dropping off copies of his newspaper at the Medora train station, he saw the two rustlers. It was a most uncomfortable moment, but, because the two men could not read, they were unaware of the premature announcement of their passing. They boarded the train and were hanged later that night.[38]

As the Stranglers went about their deadly work with a calm efficiency, Theodore returned to New York. One of the first things he did upon his arrival was send a letter to Bill Sewall and Wilmot Dow asking them to join him in the Badlands.

DAKOTA RANCHER

I understand you have threatened to kill me on sight. I have come over to see when you want to begin the killing, and to let you know that, if you have anything to say against me, now is the time for you to say it.

"I HOPE MY WESTERN VENTURE TURNS OUT WELL," THEODORE WROTE to Bill Sewall a month after Alice's death. "If it does, and I feel sure you will do well for yourself by coming out with me, I shall take you and Will Dow out next August. Of course, it depends upon how the cattle have gotten through the winter. . . . [I]f the loss has been very heavy I will have to wait a year longer before going into a more extended scale."[1] Before leaving for the Badlands, Theodore had discussed with Bill Sewall and Wilmot Dow the possibility of their coming out to Medora and working at Theodore's ranch, where he guaranteed the two men a share of anything he made in the cattle business. If he suffered a loss, Bill and Wilmot would still be paid wages and Theodore would absorb the deficit. Sewall said it was a very one-sided offer, but if Theodore "could stand it, I thought we could."

Returning from Medora the first week in July, Theodore stayed at Bamie's home, where he had a reunion with Baby Lee. He sent Sewall and Dow a letter, along with a $3,000 check to pay off mortgages, bills, and anything else that could keep them from heading west. Theodore promised their wives could come out if everything went well after the first year. "If you are afraid of hard work and privation, do not come West. If you expect to make a fortune in a year or two, do not come West. If you will give up under temporary discouragements, do not come West. If, on the other hand, you are willing to work hard, especially the first year;

if you realize that for a couple of years you cannot expect to make much more than you are now making; and if you also know that at the end of that time you will be in receipt of about a thousand dollars for the third year, with an unlimited rise ahead of you and a future as bright as yourself choose to make it—then come . . . So fix up your affairs at once, and be ready to start before the end of this month."[2]

Theodore went to New Jersey to visit his younger sister, Corrine, for several days without bringing Baby Lee. Oddly, in none of his letters home does he ask any questions about his daughter. Returning from New Jersey, Theodore took Baby Lee to Boston to visit her maternal grandparents, where he stayed for only a few days. Leaving Baby Lee with her grandparents, Theodore went to visit Henry Cabot Lodge at his summer home, where they commiserated over the backlash for their standing with the Republican nominee. Theodore told a *Boston Herald* reporter he would not bolt from the Republican Party, and endorsed James G. Blaine as the Republican nominee. "I am going back in a day or two to my Western ranches, as I do not expect to take any part in the campaign this fall," he stated.[3] After Alice's death, Theodore held the opinion that his political life was over, yet on two different occasions he was approached to run for Congress. He declined. Although he liked to keep abreast of political news, for the present time he had had enough. In an August 12, 1884, letter to Bamie, he said he thought it would be "a good many years" before he ever returned to politics.[4] The fire in the belly was not, for the moment, burning within. It is also likely that the uproar for supporting Blaine as nominee from reform-minded Republicans left him disenchanted with the political game.

Sewall, Dow, and Theodore left New York City on July 28, arriving in Medora five days later. A week prior to their arrival, Sylvane and Merrifield had brought in a thousand head of cattle from Minnesota. Theodore cut a hundred head from the group and moved them to the Elkhorn site. Sewall and Dow, under the watchful eye of a man known as Captain Robbins, drove the herd north. Little is known about Robbins other than that he had earned his title from sailing ships, while his knowledge of cattle had been gained from various ranches in South America. He had been a trapper in the Badlands, then gone to work for Gregor Lang.

Sewall dubbed Robbins "the man of many orders," and they did not get along as they moved the cattle. Sewall's only riding experience had come from riding logs down a flume in Maine. He and his horse were not a good match, causing Captain Robbins to lose his temper and yell at Sewall. Replying in his no-nonsense manner, the Maine logger said he was doing the best he could with a green horse, and he "wasn't going to be found fault with." Taken aback by Sewall's comments, Robbins rode away.[5] A few days later, after he had gotten to know the men from Maine, Robbins told Theodore that he had two good fellows. "That Sewall don't calculate to bear anything. I spoke to him the other day, and he snapped me up so short I did not know what to make of it. But I don't blame him. I did not speak to him as I ought," he said.[6] From that point on, Robbins and Sewall got along.

Sewall did not share Theodore's excitement for the area as cow country. In his plain-speaking way, Sewall said he liked the country, but doubted its ability for cattle ranching. Theodore, a bit surprised by his comment, told Sewall he didn't "know anything" about it, adding that everyone said the land was perfect for cattle raising. Sewall agreed that he didn't know much about cattle, but his old woodsman's common sense was not so quick to endorse the area for running beef.[7] The yearly rainfall average in the Badlands was about fifteen inches, compared to forty-plus inches in the Maine woods. Sewall couldn't understand how cattle could survive on grass with such little rain. He said whoever had named the area the Badlands had "hit it about right," and noted that the Little Missouri River was "the meanest apology for a frog pond I ever saw" in a letter to his brother Sam.

Once they arrived at the ranch site, Sewall and Dow got to work felling cottonwood trees that would become the walls and floors of the new cabin. At one point, Theodore jumped in to help his friends. A local cowboy asked Dow one day how the cutting of trees was proceeding. "Well, Bill cut down fifty-three," he noted, "I cut forty-nine, and the boss, the boss, he beavered down seventeen." Overhearing the comment gave Theodore a good chuckle, as his trees looked like a beaver had done the work.[8] Dow, Sewall, and Robbins also built a small shack to serve as living quarters during the winter.

Having planned a hunting trip to the Bighorn Mountains, Theodore was itching to get started, but he had to wait until Merrifield secured more horses for their remuda. During this period, Theodore rode down to the Lang ranch for two days, then up to visit the Elkhorn site, where he received a letter from the Marquis claiming that the Elkhorn site belonged to him. The Marquis stated that in 1883, he had stocked the area with a thousand sheep, and the range, in the Marquis's eyes, rightfully belonged to him. Theodore, like any cattleman, had little use for sheep, as they ate the grass down to the root, leaving nothing for the cattle. His response was blunt: The only sheep on the range were dead, and the Marquis had no claim. For Theodore, the matter was closed, although he warned Sewall and Dow to be careful.[9]

Waiting for the additional horses, Theodore spent his days in the saddle, sometimes riding upwards of seventy-two miles from first light to sunset. It was during this period that most historians believe the famous "Mingusville affair" happened. Of all the adventures that occurred during his time in the Dakotas, this incident (and the one with the boat thieves) demonstrated the traits that would later make him well-known and greatly admired. In Mingusville, Theodore aptly demonstrated his "Walk softly and carry a big stick" maxim. Some question the veracity of this incident, especially those dour historians who wish to debunk the man and his actions, but it did happen. While Theodore had more than a healthy dose of self-confidence, he was not a bragger. True, he could take dramatic license with a story, like any seasoned storyteller, but, as biographer Edmund Morris has noted, Theodore "was almost infallibly truthful," and his spirited tales "have found themselves documented down to the last detail."[10]

Riding for many miles on the lookout for stray horses, Theodore drifted across the border into Montana Territory. Mingusville, named after its first citizens, Minnie and Gus, was a tiny burg consisting of a shack that served as a railroad station, a section house, and a one-and-a-half-story building called Nolan's Hotel.[11] The bottom floor of the hotel was a combination bar and dining room, while the upstairs offered a few rooms for rent. It was just barely a step above the Pyramid Park Hotel.

The sun had dropped below the horizon, and the temperature, even in summer, was sufficiently cold to make camping outside unpleasant. Stabling his horse, Theodore was walking to the hotel when he heard two gunshots. Hesitating a moment, he debated whether or not to enter the establishment, when a gust of wind kicked up, reminding him that Nolan's Hotel was preferable to sleeping under the stars. Walking inside, he found several men, including the bartender, "wearing the kind of smile worn by men making believe to like what they don't like." Standing in the center of the room was a "shabby individual," wearing a broad hat and holding cocked pistols in each hand as he strutted up and down the saloon floor, a streak of blue words cascading from his mouth. The clock on the wall had two or three holes in its face, a demonstration of the man's prowess with a sidearm. Theodore described him as not a "bad man" of the true man-killer type, "but he was an objectionable creature, a would-be bad man, a bully who for the moment was having things all his own way." Spotting Theodore and his glasses, the bully called him "Four Eyes," quickly adding that "Four Eyes is going to treat!" Theodore laughed with the others, hoping to pass it off as a jest, but it "merely made him more offensive." Theodore took a chair at a table near the stove, hoping to avoid any further contact, but the drunken man, pistols in both hands, followed him. Leaning over the table, he expressed his views "in very foul language." Standing with his heels close together, however, made him unsteady.[12]

Talking about being involved in a fight, Theodore once said, "Don't hit at all if you can help it; don't hit a man if you can possibly avoid it; but if you do hit him, put him to sleep."

Repeating his demand that "Four Eyes" treat everyone, Theodore replied, looking past the braggart, "Well, if I've got to, I've got to." Rising quickly, he struck with a hard right on one side of the man's jaw, followed by an equally quick left as he straightened out, and then hitting with his right once again. The man's guns went off as he fell to the floor, striking his head on the corner of the bar, knocking him unconscious. Theodore was prepared to "drop on his ribs with my knees" if the man moved, but no further action was needed. Theodore took the bully's guns away, and the torpid, would-be bad man was dragged out and locked in a shed. The following morning, when he gained his senses, he hopped on a freight train and disappeared into obscurity.[13]

Some Roosevelt historians debate when this incident occurred. Nothing in any of Theodore's diaries gives a date for the incident. Hermann Hagedorn claimed it happened in June 1884, while biographer Edmund Morris favors the summer of 1884. Author Carleton Putnam placed it in April 1885, and Clay S. Jenkinson offers a wide scope, placing it between June 1884 and June 1885. Unless more factual evidence surfaces, based on the facts at hand, this author believes it took place sometime in June 1884.

Once the story became known among the cowboys and residents of the Badlands, respect for Theodore grew. He had proven himself in a moment when backing down would have made him appear weak, afraid, or, as the cowboys would say, "down in your boots."[14] He was no longer looked on as a joke, or an Eastern dude wanting to play at being a cowboy or cattleman. When the time came, he simply did what had to be done. He had demonstrated that he had what cowboys referred to as "sand."[15] In their eyes, he was one of them.

Around this time, Theodore created a printed memorial for Alice. It was a combination of newspaper clippings and eulogies, privately published and distributed among family and close friends. His own tribute was titled "In Memory of My Darling Wife."

She was beautiful in face and form, and lovelier still in spirit; as a flower she grew, and as a fair young flower she died. Her life had always been in the sunshine; there had never come to her a single great sorrow; and none ever knew her who did not love and revere her for her bright, sunny temper and her saintly unselfishness. Fair, pure, and joyous as a maiden; loving, tender, and happy as a wife; when she had just become a mother, when her life seemed to be but just begun, and when the years seemed so bright before her—then, by a strange and terrible fate, death came to her.

And when my heart's dearest died, the light went from my life forever.[16]

Although running a cattle ranch and spending days in the saddle kept him busy, writing this tribute only underscored Theodore's depression. In much of his writings during this period, especially those describing his trips into the wilds of the Badlands, he repeatedly used the words *lonely* and *melancholy*. Perhaps, in some way, he saw the land as both a reflection of his feelings and, for the moment, an emotional anchor. One day Theodore shared his feelings with Sewall, stating he felt it didn't make a difference what became of him, as he felt he had nothing to live for. Sewall replied that he did have a future ahead of him, and, more importantly, he had a daughter to live for. Theodore brushed aside Sewall's comment, stating that he felt the child would be better off without him.

"You won't always feel as you do now," Sewall told his friend, "and you won't always be willing to stay here and drive cattle, because when you get to feeling differently you will want to get back among your friends and associates where you can do more and be more benefit to the world than you can here driving cattle. If you cannot think of anything else to do you can go home and start a reform. You could make a good reformer. You always want to make things better than worse."[17]

❧

"In two or three days I start across country for the Bighorn Mountains, and then you will probably not hear from me for a couple of months," Theodore wrote to Bamie on August 12. "I take a wagon, and six ponies, riding one of the latter. I now look like a regular cowboy dandy with all my equipment finished in the most expensive style."[18]

As the sun was just breaking over the far horizon, Theodore stepped into his saddle to ride out for the Bighorn Mountains in the Wyoming Territory. Bill Merrifield and Norman Lebo accompanied him on the trip. Merrifield, whom Theodore described as a "good-looking fellow who shoots and rides beautifully; a reckless, self-confident man," was a bit *too* full of himself, making him unpopular with many in Medora. With this expedition, Merrifield appeared to be too quick to take credit as the leader of the party, claiming he taught Theodore "to do what he was told." (It is highly doubtful anyone ever told Theodore to do what he was told.) Despite Merrifield's faults, however, Theodore remained loyal to his friend. Norman Lebo was one of those unique characters found frequently in Western history. Hailing from Ohio, he was a Union veteran of the Civil War, showing up in the Badlands in 1883. At the age of fifty, he worked as a trapper, hunter, and blacksmith at the Custer Trail Ranch.[19] A thickset man with a beard, Lebo was an innate wanderer. It was said he once left his family to hunt for a week, only to return three years later. He was allowed to accompany this hunting trip only after Theodore and Lebo's wife reached an agreement: She would receive three years' sustenance should her husband get the itchy foot to meander again.[20] Theodore described Lebo as a "chatty, tough old plainsman, full of expedients and ready with both wit and hands."

Lebo drove the two-horse wagon, while Theodore and Merrifield rode out ahead. They were well fortified with supplies, including a tent for sleeping if they met with inclement weather. Theodore brought along enough weapons and ammunition to withstand a major Indian attack, including a Colt revolver, a ten-gauge shotgun, a Winchester repeating rifle, a .40 caliber Sharps rifle, and a .50 caliber Webley shotgun. He also had 150 rounds for his pistol, 300 cartridges for the ten-gauge, 1,000 rounds for the Winchester, 150 rounds for the Sharps, and 100 cartridges for the Webley shotgun. He wore his buckskin suit, with alligator boots, and also brought along heavy moccasins, sealskin chaps, a raccoon coat, a slicker, two flannel shirts, three light and three heavy suits of underwear, heavy socks, bandanas, and " a little brandy and cholera mixture."[21]

Leaving Maltese Cross Ranch, they rode south, following the Little Missouri River. That afternoon, the men spotted black storm clouds in the northwest; within minutes, the skies opened, letting loose a massive cloudburst with strong winds and hail the size of pigeon eggs. Lebo and the wagon were caught in the open, while Theodore and Merrifield galloped to the edge of a washout and huddled with their horses against the windward bank until the storm passed. Theodore noted that even though it was August, "the air became very cold."

The rain continued throughout the day and evening in a varied routine of drizzle followed by a burst of strong showers, only to return to a drizzle. Roosevelt and Merrifield spent the night at the Lang cabin, leaving Lebo with the horses and wagon.[22] Neither Merrifield or Lebo had ever been to the Bighorn Mountains, and they had only the scantest idea of their actual location. Luckily, on their second day, they encountered a group of cowboys herding cattle to Mingusville, and the head drover set them on the correct course. Theodore and Merrifield estimated that the town of Buffalo in Wyoming Territory was just less than three hundred miles distant. That night, as the rain continued, they slept in the wagon among the supply boxes. Coffee the following morning, August 20, was made from rainwater caught by their rubber blankets. The rain had moved on, but the saturated ground allowed the wagon to make only twelve miles.

Over the next two days, however, with better weather, they covered forty-five miles, and by mid-afternoon on August 24, they had reached the Powder River in Montana Territory.[23] That evening, Theodore wrote a letter to Henry Cabot Lodge, noting, "You must pardon the paper and general appearance of this letter, as I am writing out in camp, a hundred miles or so from any house; and indeed whether this letter is, or is not, ever delivered depends partly on Providence, and partly on the good will of an equally inscrutable personage, either a cowboy or a horse thief, whom we have just met, and who has volunteered to post it . . . I heartily enjoy this life, with its perfect freedom, for I am very fond of hunting, and there are few sensations I prefer to that of galloping over these rolling, limitless prairies, rifle in hand, or winding my way among the barren, fantastic and grimly picturesque deserts of the so-called Bad Lands."[24]

Theodore noted in his diary on August 23: "Crossed the Little Beaver [Creek]. Travelled [*sic*] over great rolling plains bedded with short, brown grass; saw several herds of cattle, which have taken the place of the buffalo, whose carcasses can be seen everywhere." By August 30, they had entered Wyoming Territory and had crossed the Powder River nine times in one day. By nightfall, they made camp at the mouth of Clear Creek. "Country very pretty," Theodore wrote.[25] They reached the town of Buffalo on September 1 ("quite a frontier town"), before heading to a sawmill on Crazy Woman Creek. From that point they left the wagon behind and all the supplies were transferred to pack animals for easier traveling in the mountains.

"Slow progress," Theodore noted on September 5, "as pack animals and loose ponies proved hard to drive. Camped on Widow Creek. Already pretty cold." The following day they only made six miles over a "pretty rough trail." Later that day, Theodore and Merrifield spotted fresh elk tracks, which eventually led to their finding a small herd; Theodore shot a cow and a bull calf. With the horses showing signs of fatigue, they didn't break camp. As the horses grazed, Merrifield, Lebo, and Theodore staked out the elk hides and meat to dry. The following morning, they were greeted with a coating of snow on the ground. As the day wore on, it rained and sleeted. The three men stayed in their tent with "a roaring log fire in front of it."[26]

Supposedly, Theodore and Merrifield went to visit a camp of Cheyenne Indians after they crossed into Wyoming Territory. Merrifield made the decision to ride into the camp to see if there were any possible risks. Even though they had been subdued, eight years earlier, the Cheyenne had fought in the famous Battle at Little Bighorn against Custer and the Seventh Cavalry. Visiting the camp, Merrifield challenged the Indians to a shooting match, which both he and Theodore handily won. "You go among Indians and they find out you are superior to them in anything, especially shooting, they at once have a great deal of respect for you," Merrifield reportedly stated.

While it is a good story, there is one a problem with it: Theodore's 1884 diary *never* details an encounter with Cheyenne Indians. The only notation in his diary during this trip regarding Indians reads, "[P]assed a camp of Cheyennes."[27] If such an event had taken place, it would have made a tremendous impression on Theodore, worthy of some mention in his diary or, certainly, in one of his many books. (In his book *Ranch Life and the Hunting-Trail* [1888], Theodore does detail a separate encounter with some Indians he had on the prairie.) Even though his diary notes everything they did on the trip, including the number of game that was shot, there is no mention of visiting a Cheyenne camp, let alone a shooting competition. According to Hermann Hagedorn's notes, Bill Merrifield is the *only* source for the story, and was told *after* Theodore's death. Hagedorn, as well as another author, quoted Merrifield's story, which gives it a form of credibility. However, no other biography ever mentions the event.

Could the story be true? Certainly. However, such a rendezvous would have greatly appealed to Theodore's ideal of living a frontier fantasy. The nagging question to the story's veracity is why doesn't he include it in any of his books? Given that such an encounter is missing from his diary, or one of his books, only strengthens the argument that it never happened. Unless new evidence surfaces to prove otherwise, this author firmly believes Merrifield's story is complete fiction.

By September 11, they had moved their camp closer to a branch of the Tensleep Creek. From there, Merrifield and Theodore went fishing and caught fifty trout.[28] It was a long ride and hike for them to find the specific lake they wanted. "Glad to get back to camp and a first class trout supper," Theodore noted in his diary. The following day, they moved their camp again, six miles downriver, closer toward the foothills, "in a narrow valley with steep, wooded sides."[29] That afternoon, Theodore killed a bull elk at seventy-five yards. They left the elk's body to lure another prey—a grizzly bear.

The following morning, they found that a grizzly had indeed fed on the elk carcass. They waited in the bushes until darkness, yet no bear returned. On September 13, they went back to examine the carcass and found fresh bear tracks. The two men began tracking "Old Ephraim," the term used by mountain men to describe a grizzly. Crawling over fallen logs, Merrifield quickly went down on one knee. Theodore knew that this meant the grizzly was close. Walking slowly past his partner, Theodore was no more than ten steps away when the male bear rose up on his haunches before dropping down to all four paws. It was then that Theodore pulled the trigger. His shot hit the bear between "his small, glittering evil eyes."[30] The next morning, they skinned the bear for its hide and took the head as a trophy. Before the expedition was over, Theodore and Merrifield had shot another male grizzly, as well as a female grizzly and her nearly adult cub.

According to his diary, it seems that Theodore was hunting any game in sight each day. Many expressed surprise at his "bloodlust" during this hunt, given that he is often referred to as "The Conservation President." How could Theodore preserve millions of acres of land and the animals that live in it, yet be such a prodigious hunter? He called the buffalo and the elk "lordly," yet he hunted both. How does one have such a reverence for these animals, yet have their heads mounted on a wall of his home or office? These questions may remain forever unanswered. Theodore's closest answer was that he had an antipathy for those who simply hunted for the hides and not for the sport or the food. He regarded "game-butchers" (as he called them) the lowest form of hunter. "No one who is not himself a sportsman and lover of nature can realize the intense indignation with which a true hunter sees these butchers at their brutal work of slaughtering the game, in season and out, for the sake of a few dollars they are too lazy to earn in any other and more honest way."[31] In spite of his heavy trigger finger, Theodore's hunting in the Dakotas eventually galvanized him to form the Boone and Crockett Club, an association that pushed for laws protecting game and natural resources. It would mark his first step in conservation.

The trio broke camp on September 17, making their way down the mountain with heavily laden pack ponies. Returning to the sawmill, they retrieved their wagon and loaded the hides, horns, and remaining supplies. Stopping overnight at Fort McKinney, Theodore dashed off a letter to Bamie, which, aside from his comments about the hunting trip, is one of the first letters in which he mentions any feelings for Baby Lee. "I shall be very glad to see you all again. I hope Mousiekins will be very cunning; I shall dearly love her."[32]

The ride home began to wear down some of the horses, which forced the party to rest for two days. "Our bear skins are rapidly spoiling and need to be fleshed and dried. Horses are not in good condition," Theodore noted in his diary on September 22.[33] Three days later they moved their camp to a bend on the Powder River. Then the rain returned, haunting their trail day and night. A combination of rain and heavy winds on October 1 forced them to stay in camp. ("Furious hurricane blowing, with driving rain squall.") The next morning, the horses had strayed, and it took until noon to locate them, plus another two hours to get one of them out of a mud hole. Determining that the wagon would take another three days to reach Maltese Cross Ranch, Theodore and Merrifield rode on ahead, leaving camp at nine in the evening. The two rode the fifty miles to the ranch nonstop, arriving at six in the morning.

While Theodore was in the Bighorn Mountains, Sewall and Dow were busy felling trees for Elkhorn Ranch. Dow lent a hand during the fall roundup and heard from two cowboys that the Marquis was still simmering over Theodore's letter claiming that the Frenchman had no claim to the Elkhorn site. From that point on, both men kept their pistols and rifles close at hand. One day, Sewall heard gunfire, and a half-dozen riders came into view, including Eldridge "Jerry" Paddock, the Marquis's close friend. Sewall greeted them, offering them some freshly cooked beans and coffee. Caught off guard, the men filed in and ate as Sewall refilled their plates and coffee cups. Once they had consumed their share, they went outside. Surveying the area, Paddock commented they had done a nice job, then saddled up and rode away. Shortly after this visit, Sewall and Dow were told that Paddock was making threats that the ranch belonged to him. He boasted that if "Four Eyes" wanted it so badly, he could pay for it any way he wished, including in blood.

The day after he arrived at the Maltese Cross from his hunting trip, Theodore rode out to visit Sewall and Dow. They quickly related the threats Paddock had been making, including shooting him.

Theodore turned his horse around and rode to Paddock's house near the railroad crossing. Answering the knock on his door, Paddock was surprised to find the man he had threatened facing him.

"I understand you have threatened to kill me on sight," Theodore said. "I have come over to see when you want to begin the killing, and to let you know that, if you have anything to say against me, now is the time for you to say it."

A completely flummoxed Paddock could only stammer that he had been misquoted.[34] Ironically, after this incident, Theodore and Paddock became friends.

Theodore Roosevelt once stated he never would have been president if it weren't for the time he spent in the West. AUTHOR'S COLLECTION

Bill Sewall (left) and Wilmot Dow (center) with Theodore (right) near Island Falls, Maine, in 1879. Theodore met the two men the previous year when he first traveled to Maine to hunt. The three men formed a fast friendship, with Sewall and Dow following Theodore to Dakota Territory. THEODORE ROOSEVELT COLLECTION, HOUGHTON LIBRARY, HARVARD UNIVERSITY

Medora, Dakota Territory, in 1884. The building with the large smokestack (upper center of photo) was part of the abattoir built by the Marquis de Morès. The Little Missouri River is just beyond. Today, only the smokestack remains of the abattoir in Medora. STATE HISTORICAL SOCIETY OF NORTH DAKOTA

The Marquis de Morès in 1884. He cut a dashing figure in Medora, and spent a fortune in numerous failed business projects in Dakota Territory. After a brief stop in Medora, in 1887, he never returned. STATE HISTORICAL SOCIETY OF NORTH DAKOTA

In early 1885, Theodore posed for a series of photographs in a Manhattan gallery, portraying himself as a frontier hunter. One photograph from this series appeared on the front page of his *Hunting Trips of a Ranchman* (1885). Note the photographer's floor rug under the fake grass and the painted backdrop. AUTHOR'S COLLECTION

Theodore and his beloved mount, Manitou, in Dakota Territory, 1885. His initials, TR, are carved into the cantle of the saddle, which now resides at the Buffalo Bill Center of the West, in Cody, Wyoming. LIBRARY OF CONGRESS

The Elkhorn Ranch along the Little Missouri River, with two of Theodore's cattle standing on a sandbar. The cabin, built by Sewall and Dow, stands to the right, while the stables and other buildings can be seen to the left. This photograph was taken by Theodore, who had one of the first personal cameras sold to the public. He used the cabin's root cellar as a darkroom. Today, only the stone foundation of the cabin remains.

Sylvane Ferris (right) and two other cowboys pose for Theodore's camera during one of the Little Missouri River Stockmen's Association roundups.

Editorial cartoon that appeared in the *New York World* during the 1886 mayoral election. This is the first known newspaper cartoon portraying Theodore in a cowboy motif. AUTHOR'S COLLECTION

Theodore astride Little Texas in Montauk, Long Island, after returning with his beloved Rough Riders from their fighting in Cuba. THEODORE ROOSEVELT COLLECTION, HOUGHTON LIBRARY, HARVARD UNIVERSITY

As the vice presidential candidate, Theodore traversed the country campaigning for the Republican ticket. On September 16, 1900, during a stop in Medora, he managed to steal some time away for a ride through part of the Badlands.

Theodore's refusal to shoot a black bear tied to a tree became big news. Clifford Berryman's *Washington Post* editorial cartoon made Theodore even more popular with the public, and gave birth to the ever-popular teddy bear. AUTHOR'S COLLECTION

A STRENUOUS LIFE

I do not believe there ever was any life more attractive to a vigorous young fellow than life on a cattle ranch in those days. It was a fine, healthy life, too; it taught a man selfreliance, hardihood, and the value of instant decision . . . I enjoyed the life to the full.

ALTHOUGH THEODORE CLAIMED TO HAVE PUT HIS POLITICAL LIFE ASIDE, saying he had no interest in campaigning on behalf of James G. Blaine, that was just what he was going to do when he left for New York City on October 7. Politics, as much as he may have tried to convince himself otherwise, was a major force in his life. It was answering a call to duty. To do battle and fight for the right thing was one of his innate traits. He fought not only for what he believed was right, but also for those who had no voice or leader, be it the cattlemen, the coal workers, or the average American. The fight, like the chase of the hunt, fed his desire. Sometimes he was blind to the cause he believed in, as in his 1912 presidential campaign. In such instances—and they were few—he took counsel from no one. He relied on his instincts, rightly or wrongly, and proceeded. It was a characteristic that left people either adoring or loathing him.

One thing was certain: Theodore left little doubt where he stood on any subject.

Arriving at Bamie's home, Theodore spent, albeit minimal, time with Baby Lee. He hardly had unpacked his suitcase before jumping into the election campaign with both feet, giving three speeches on behalf of the party's ticket. His support for James G. Blaine gave the reform-minded Republicans enough material to label him a traitor to the cause. While Blaine was not an ideal choice—it's likely Theodore must have had to swallow hard when speaking for the nominee—he also knew that Blaine had to be elected to keep the presidency from falling into the hands of the Democrats.

The campaign became terribly partisan, with each party throwing mud at the other party's candidate. Grover Cleveland, the Democratic nominee, was revealed to have fathered a child out of wedlock eight years earlier. Cleveland, a bachelor, never denied fathering the child, and had provided support through the years. The Republicans, and the newspapers that favored the party, leapt to paint Cleveland an adulterer. At campaign stops, hecklers would cry out to Cleveland, "Ma! Ma! Where's my Pa? Gone to the White House, Ha Ha Ha!"[1]

As Election Day neared, James G. Blaine held a very strong lead, but then two serious blunders sunk his chances—again. During a meeting before a thousand ministers at the Fifth Avenue Hotel on October 29, a Reverend Dr. Burchard stated that the Democrats were "the party whose antecedents have been rum, Romanism and rebellion." On the surface, the comment could be dismissed as typical of a firebrand preacher. However, it blew up in Blaine's face when he said nothing to distance himself from the slander. By ignoring it, Blaine seemed to endorse a statement that insulted anti-prohibitionists, Catholics, and Southerners—important groups Blaine needed to get elected. The candidate told friends he had heard the words but was so focused on his speech that the impact escaped him.[2] It did not escape the Cleveland campaign or the Democratic press.

The catastrophe wasn't finished, however. That evening, Blaine accepted an invitation to a dinner party at Delmonico's Restaurant on Fifth Avenue with a guest list of very important business leaders, including the notorious "robber baron" Jay Gould. (The Democratic press dubbed it "The Millionaires' Dinner.") Known for its fine dining and creative dishes such as Lobster Newburg, Eggs Benedict, and Baked Alaska, Delmonico's customers included actress Jenny Lind, Mark Twain, "Diamond Jim" Brady, and Lillian Russell—hardly a place the average American could afford. While Blaine consumed an extravagant meal, his critics charged, thousands of children in the city went hungry.

The damage was done. Blaine lost to Cleveland, and for the first time since 1860, a Democrat sat in the presidential chair.

Henry Cabot Lodge lost his chance for a seat in the House of Representatives, likely due to his supporting Blaine. Theodore wrote to Lodge: "I cannot say how glad I have been to hear from all sides of the gallant front you showed in defeat . . . Of course it may be we have had our day; it is far more likely that this is true in my case than in yours . . . Blaine's nomination meant to me pretty sure political death if I supported him; this I realized entirely, and went in with my eyes open. I have won again and again; finally chance placed me where I was sure to lose whatever I did; and I will balance the last against the first . . . we fought a good winning fight when our friends the Independents were backing us; and we have both of us, when circumstances turned them against us, fought the losing fight grimly out to the end. What we have been cannot be taken from us; what we are is due to the folly of others and to no fault of our own."[3]

Winter was settling in on the Badlands when Theodore returned on November 16. Once again, he sought solace in the West after a loss. The Western outdoors became a salve for him, a way to escape and renew himself.

Despite the cold weather, the following morning, Theodore, Sylvane, Merrifield, and Dutch Wannegan drove a herd of cattle to Medora to be shipped to Eastern markets. (There is no evidence that Theodore availed himself of the Marquis's slaughterhouse and refrigerated cars when it came time to ship his cattle.) With his business completed, Theodore bade the others a farewell and rode on to the Elkhorn site.

It was early afternoon when he started the thirty-three-mile ride. He was barely at the halfway point when the sun began to set, and the temperature dropped considerably. He made several crossings along the Little Missouri River, which he called "difficult and disagreeable." The river had frozen over a few days earlier, but the ice wasn't solid, with snow hiding any thin patches. In one crossing, the ice broke under rider and horse, dropping them into the cold water. The horse furiously grappled its way to the opposite bank, with Theodore following. They continued on as the sky grew darker and the stars began to glisten. Theodore was hoping to make it to the small shack he had found near Elkhorn Ranch. As darkness fell, though, he worried that he might not be able to find it with the clouds moving in to cover the shining stars. The horse's steps were muffled by the snow, and the only noise was the far-off wailing of a wolf. Theodore came across a large section of cottonwood trees but could not readily locate the shack. Backtracking, he found the shanty and stabled his horse. Inside it was vacant, with no food stores. After getting a fire going, Theodore made good use of the only thing he had with him—a packet of tea. "The hot tea did not prove such a bad substitute for a cold and tired man," he commented.[4]

As morning arrived, Theodore saddled his horse and rode onto Elkhorn Ranch. The following day, November 19, Theodore chose the exact site for his ranch house, as Sewall and Dow laid the large stones that would serve as the foundation.[5] The three men rode back to Maltese Cross Ranch in anticipation of the arrival of a herd of ponies that Sylvane and Wannegan were bringing in from Spearfish.[6] The snow continued to fall, as did the temperatures. It was 20 below zero on November 22, followed by several days of rain. Theodore rode into Medora on November 29 and had lunch with the Marquis. While he mentions this luncheon in his diary, there is no further information as to what the two men may have discussed.

One of the subjects they may have addressed was the formation of a local cattlemen's association, much like the one Granville Stuart had formed in Montana. Such an association had been on Theodore's mind for a while because of two matters to be confronted: thefts, and cattle overpopulation in the area. Even though the Stranglers were still going about their business, thefts continued, albeit scaled back. Overgrazing was becoming a growing concern to many established ranches in the area due to an influx of new cattle herds, and many called for rules to protect them. The *Bad Lands Cow Boy* announced that a meeting for the new cattlemen's association would be held on December 19 in the hall above Bob Robert's saloon.

"Iron cold" was a term that described the bitterly harsh days of winter in such places as the Dakotas, where the daytime temperature could sink below zero. Theodore readily embraced the winter cold, hunting with the same vigor he displayed in the summer. He made the thirty-three-mile trek on horseback from the Elkhorn site to Maltese Cross Ranch in conditions that hovered around zero degrees. Interestingly, in his diary, he makes few comments about the conditions other than to note the temperature. There are never any complaints, or wishing for a warmer climate.

Because of the harsh weather, the arrival of the horses from Spearfish was delayed. Using this to his advantage, Theodore spent a few days hunting with Merrifield for Bighorn sheep. On December 6, Sylvane "arrived with 52 ponies, spent day breaking," he noted in his diary.[7]

Breaking means taming a wild horse to be a saddle horse. The old style for breaking a horse was to run a horse into a corral, throw a rope over the animal's head, and pull it tightly around its neck. The other end of the rope was wrapped around a wooden post (called a *snubbing post*) that was sunk into the ground in the middle of the corral. The protesting horse was then pulled up to the post and blindfolded with either a bandana or a coat. A *hackamore* (a looped halter) was placed over the horse's head. Sometimes a bridle with a metal bit was used, usually at the discretion of the cowboy who was breaking the horse. One or two men would hold the horse by the rope as the rider attached a saddle and quickly mounted the animal. "Let 'er rip!" was the cue for the men to remove the blindfold and let go of the rope on the post.

The horse and the rider would then battle it out.

A horse, especially an untamed one, will buck to get the thing off its back. Horses can jump several feet into the air, arching their backs, pulling their heads down, and kicking furiously with their back legs. The rider breaking the horse is generally called a bronc buster, but can also go by the name flesh rider, hazer, bronc scratcher, and bronc snapper. He holds the reins (usually made from rope), valiantly trying to stay in the saddle. The bronc buster's intention is to let the horse tire itself out, and once the animal "settles down," the rider will attempt to lift the animal's lowered head, helping it to get used to the commands of the reins. As this happens, he will get the horse to walk around the corral, making turns by use of the reins, and generally get the horse accustomed to the rider on its back and to taking commands. Some horses adapt to being tamed more quickly than others do, but there is always an "owl head"—an unridable horse—that will just not get along, no matter what.

During such a breaking period, the rider is thrashed in all directions, with jarring jolts that jam his back and spine into the saddle. If he's lucky, he will "stay with 'em" and not be thrown to the ground. Some cowboys have said that being thrown from a horse hurts more than the grating ride. Indeed, landing on dirt hurts and can be dangerous, depending on how one lands. Riders have broken their backs or been killed by breaking their necks. No matter what part of the body hits the earth, it will be painful. Cowboys say that any time you don't break something (other than the wild horse!), it is a good landing.

Theodore did not abide by this rough method of breaking a horse. He felt that it damaged the animal and made it unsuitable for use. He favored a horse that already displayed something of a benign attitude. He would "gentle" a horse by daily contact, slowly working the animal to accept a saddle and rider. Most cowboys had a time limitation in breaking a herd of horses, which did not allow them to indulge in Theodore's methods. "I have a perfect dread of bucking," Theodore once stated, "and if I can help it I never get on a confirmed bucker."[8] Bill Sewall was still a greenhorn when it came to riding horses, and some of the more-experienced cowboys taunted Bill when he refused to ride any of the wild horses. "I suppose you fellows can ride broncos," he warned them, "but you cannot ride me, and if you get on, your feet will drag." In a case of true irony, Sewall, requiring a mount, thought he had picked out a gentle horse, but it turned out to be one of the more-disagreeable ones in the remuda. When Sewall himself sat the animal, the horse behaved like a gentleman. However, when Wilmot Dow, who had become a very good rider, mounted the same horse, it let loose its bad character. After that episode, no cowboys bothered Sewall again about riding a horse.[9]

Early each morning, the cowboys would have breakfast at five before going out to get the horses and start the breaking process. On the last day of handling the horses, one of the men commented that he had spotted two bears in a nearby washout. Quickly giving up gentling any horses, Theodore and Merrifield followed the cowboy in hopes of bagging the animals. Already planning a trip in hopes of shooting Bighorn sheep, Theodore had found an excuse to start right away. George Myers would follow them in a buckboard with the needed supplies and meet them later in the day.

Myers had become a regular hand at Maltese Cross Ranch, handling all sorts of chores, including cooking. When Theodore returned from his solitary four-day trip in June 1884, he requested that George make some of his tasty biscuits for dinner. To please the boss, George added an extra dash of baking powder so they would be light as a feather. He placed the biscuits into the oven, and when the time came to remove them, he discovered they were a vivid emerald green. It appears that Sylvane or Merrifield had mistakenly dumped a can of baking soda into the baking powder can. On this expedition, George would once again create a culinary disaster when he mistakenly cooked beans in a pan that had the remains of rosin in it. (Rosin is a derivative from pine trees or other plants, used primarily as bases for adhesives and soap.) Reportedly, after taking a spoonful of the unsavory beans, Theodore told George that he could "eat his green biscuits and most of your infernal concoctions, but I am hanged if I can eat your rosined beans."[10]

The sun was still below the horizon when Theodore and Merrifield started out, wearing heavy fur coats and caps. After going up a long valley, they topped the highlands in time to greet the rising sun, but found no trace of any bears. They quickly spotted two dark objects ahead of them coming out of the washout onto the plains; unfortunately, they were not bears but dark-colored horses. Theodore said the cowboy's "chap-fallen face" foretold the "merciless chaff" he would endure for his mistake. He had the cowboy escort the two wayward horses back to the Maltese Cross, as he and Merrifield pressed on.

Theodore observed that hunting Bighorn sheep was "the hardest and most difficult" of any big game, as it was "equally trying to both wind and muscle." As hard as it was, he also found it to be "the noblest form of sport with the rifle."[11] Reaching broken country, they tied up their horses and went on foot. Having shucked their chaps and fur coats, the hiking into the hills kept the two men warm as they sought out the wary animal. Male Bighorn sheep are recognized for their large, curved horns (female horns are smaller and less curved). The animal is extremely agile and can easily maneuver along some of the sheerest cliffs on a mountain, requiring the hunter to be equally agile in his tracking. In winter, it becomes doubly dangerous; Theodore and Merrifield, without their heavy coats, had to climb slippery, ice-covered rocks and buttes. The two made their way to the top of some rocks but found only hints of tracks. The cold began to chill them and numb their hands.

Returning to their horses, they headed to a hut where Myers had a fire blazing. "Throughout the night the temperature sank lower and lower, and it was impossible to keep the crazy old hut anywhere near freezing-point," Theodore wrote.[12] The following day left them empty-handed, cold, and trying to make the best of it in the chilly hut at night. The third morning, Theodore and Merrifield saddled the horses and headed toward a group of buttes where they had spotted some tracks. In the distance was "a towering mass of grayish white clouds" that Theodore described as a "weather-breeder." The area, surrounded by high, sharp peaks and ridges, "broke off abruptly into narrow gorges and deep ravines." It was not the type of country one wanted to be caught in when the storm hit. They needed to find their Bighorn quickly.

Climbing up a peak, they inched out on "knife-like ridges" covered with ice. Descending into a narrow chasm, they inched their way along, with the sides rising up at "an acute angle." Signs indicated their quarry had gone up to the top. Theodore scrambled up the side, "digging my hands and feet into the loose snow," grasping any rock or projection he could. Reaching the height, the men saw a couple of Bighorns ninety yards away, the one with the larger pair of horns standing broadside to Theodore. Dropping to one knee, he fired. The Bighorn staggered before crossing over the ridge. Merrifield and Theodore did their best to catch up with their potential prize, sliding down the ravine, lungs burning from the cold air. "He had most obligingly run around to a part of the hill where we could bring up one of the horses without much difficulty," Theodore later commented of the hunt.[13]

With the storm approaching, the two men returned to the hut with their prize, loaded up the buckboard, and made a hasty departure for the Maltese Cross. As they had in their previous hunt, Merrifield and Theodore nudged their spurs into their mounts' flanks, leaving Myers and the buckboard behind. "Merrifield and I rode on ahead, not sparing the horses, but before we got home the storm had burst, and a furious blizzard blew in our teeth as we galloped along the last mile of the river-bottom, before coming to the home ranch-house," he recalled.[14]

The first meeting of the Little Missouri River Stockmen's Association was called to order at 11:30 a.m. on December 19. In attendance were representatives from eleven ranches, as well as the Marquis's Northern Pacific Refrigerator Car Company. Theodore was elected chairman, and Henry Royce, vice-chairman. It was agreed that the positions of chairman and vice-chairman would be for one year, with elections to follow the fall roundup. The group also agreed to hold their next meeting by April 1, 1885, and the chairman was given the power to draft a set of bylaws that would reflect those of the Eastern Montana Stockmen's Association.

With those issues taken care of, the members appointed the Marquis as a "committee of one" to work with the Eastern Montana Stockmen's Association to obtain measures "favorable to the interests of the cattlemen" from the Dakota Territory legislature. They also agreed that if any cattle were hit by a train and the railroad refused to pay full value for the animal, the chairman was to be immediately notified so the association could bring it before the courts, at the association's expense, as "a test case." The association also agreed that no member would gather any cattle or brand calves between the first of December and the "date of the general spring round-up" without informing other ranches in the neighborhood with "reasonable time." Another resolution was passed that each member would not have more than ten bulls to every head of stock on their range.[15]

Theodore left Medora the next day, arriving at his sister's New York home in time to celebrate Christmas. It would obviously be a somber holiday, being the first without his mother or his wife. As the snow fell over Manhattan, Theodore made himself comfortable in front of a cozy fire in the living room fireplace and began to draft the bylaws for the cattlemen's group.

Once he was done with that, he began work on a book. In this effort, Theodore began by providing a brief history of the horse and cattle in North America, describing how the cattle had come to the Northern Plains. His love of history and the thrill of the hunt, as well as his awakening appreciation of the land, were evident in his writing. The book wasn't just something he chose to write; it was something he clearly *had* to write. He had great passion for the subject, explaining the habits of the animals he hunted, how they moved, ate, and ran. Although portions of his writing are a bit stiff and episodic, it was the first, major step in authoring what would become his trilogy of experiences out west.

The book was titled *Hunting Trips of a Ranchman*.

ROUNDUP

Nobody ever gets enough sleep on a round-up.

THROUGHOUT JANUARY 1885, THEODORE WORKED ON HIS BOOK, recounting his experiences hunting grouse, deer, mountain sheep, buffalo, elk, and a grizzly. The manuscript was handed over to his publisher, G. P. Putnam's Sons, in early March. At the same time, he arranged a session at a Manhattan photography gallery where he posed, minus his spectacles, against a painted backdrop simulating a wooded area. In the series of photographs, Theodore wears a buckskin suit, his Tiffany Bowie knife tucked behind a canvas ammo belt, over-the-ankle moccasins, fur hat, and bandana around his neck. In one image, Theodore firmly clutches his Winchester rifle, ready to fire at an unknown target, while in another he stands with the rifle held across his chest in a "port arms" stance. In both, his facial features are taut, as if expecting trouble. In another portrait, he sits with the rifle across his lap while looking at the camera lens. The fourth pose, a profile shot, has him standing like an old hunter, the butt of the rifle resting on the ground, and his hands wrapped around the barrel.

It is hard to take the photographs seriously, as both his posing and the painted backdrop are very theatrical. By comparison, three photographs taken in the Badlands, in 1884, are far more realistic. Although he appears to be squinting (probably due to the sun), Theodore looks more authentic, even with his buckskin clothing. His pistol is worn on his hip in the cross-draw fashion, and he sports fringed gauntlets and a wide-brimmed cowboy hat. In all three photographs, he wears his glasses and looks directly at the camera. There is no dramatic pose, no staged look of a hunter or cowboy. You see a young man living his dream, with an absolute resolve to do whatever job needs to be done. In two of the images, he stands next to his saddled horse, Manitou (one can see Theodore's initials etched into the cantle of the saddle),[1] while in the third photo, he sits astride his mount. Although his clothing is more elaborate than that of other cowboys of the time, in these photographs, Theodore truly appears to be a man of the West.

Winter's iron grip on the Badlands left much of Medora and the surrounding area in a state of suspended action. The Marquis's abattoir shut down, and the butchers went back east. A Badlands winter forces everyone—even the horses and cattle—to hunker down, doing their best to stay as warm as possible. Arctic winds blow down through northern Canada and onto the Dakota plains with a ferocious, numbing chill. Most ranches became ghost towns during this season because there was little work for cowboys in this type of weather. Outfits who could afford to do so kept their men on salary, usually having cowboys "riding the line." As line riders, two men would go out to a certain area from the main ranch and settle into a one-room cabin for the winter. Their job was to ride out in the early morning and keep the cattle on their own range (and another's outfit on theirs). They also kept an eye open for any cattle that got caught in a bog or strayed too far out, potentially leaving them to be caught in a blizzard or attacked by wolves. It was a hard, thankless job in conditions that could only be described as miserable. Food, which had to last up to four months, was packed in. The cabin was equipped with two rough beds and either a fireplace or wood-burning stove for heat and cooking. More often than not, the cabin had gaps between the logs or planks, letting the cold wind come in to torture the inhabitants. Unless an ample stockpile had been assembled before the snows, one of the cowboys had to go out daily to chop wood. Bathing was nonexistent, and almost every cowboy grew a beard to help keep his face warm.

For line riders, spring could not come soon enough.

Cowboys who stayed at the main ranch might be allowed the luxury of riding into town, if they were hardy enough to endure the cold ride. Those who did often bunked at a hotel and indulged in drinking, gambling, and being entertained by a sporting lady before returning to the ranch a few days later. Most ranches maintained a small contingent of cowboys during the winter, letting the rest go for the season. Some of the men would drift to other parts of the country, while the heartier souls became "grub line riders." They were panhandlers, riding from ranch to ranch, seeking meals and shelter. Eventually, they would wear out their welcome and head over to another outfit. Some men actually managed to survive the winter doing this—but not many.

Shortly after handing in his manuscript, Theodore suffered another serious intestinal attack, which forced him to delay his return to Medora for nearly four weeks. Arriving in the cow town on April 19, he stepped off the train wearing city clothes, including a derby. No cowboys attempted to shoot his hat off his head.

Winter had given way to the spring thaw, which meant the Little Missouri River quickly swelled. If one wanted to cross the river in Medora, the logical—and safest—way was to go across the train trestle. There was another route, but it was riskier. One could attempt to cross on the top of a dam that had been built by the Marquis. However, with the river overflowing, it was capricious at best for a man to cross the top of the dam, let alone a horse and rider. Theodore was warned not to take the precarious route, but he waved off concerns. "If Manitou gets his feet on that dam, he'll keep them there and we can make it finely," he stated with confidence.

True to his nature, Manitou got on the dam and was slowly making his way when he slipped. Both Manitou and Theodore were thrown into the swiftly moving river, and workers near the dam lost sight of the two as they went under, only to quickly pop up. Both horse and rider pawed at the water, with Theodore pushing ice floes away from them. Manitou gained his footing on the river bottom and struggled up the bank, as did Theodore, who did not even lose his glasses. Once on dry land, Theodore rode over to the general store owned by Joe Ferris, where he purchased a pair of socks. Ferris, watching his friend change into the dry socks, admonished him for his behavior. "I suppose it might be considered reckless, but it was a lot of fun," Theodore admitted.[2] To prove to himself that he could do it, several days later, Theodore crossed the dam with Manitou when no one was around, making it safely.

"My home ranch-house stands on the river brink. From the low, long veranda, shaded by leafy cotton-woods, one looks across sand bars and shallows to a strip of meadowland, behind which rises a line of sheer cliffs and grassy plateaus," he wrote in *Hunting Trips of a Ranchman*. "This veranda is a pleasant place in the summer evenings when a cool breeze stirs along the river and blows in the faces of the tired men, who loll back in their rocking-chairs (what true American does not enjoy a rocking-chair?), book in hand—though they do not often read the books, but rock gently to and fro, gazing sleepily out at the weird-looking buttes opposite, until their sharp outlines grow indistinct and purple in the after-glow of the sunset."[3]

Theodore was writing about the Elkhorn, which he considered his "home ranch." (The Maltese Cross now served as his business ranch.) At the end of April, he settled into his new home. It was ideally suited for him at the time. His nearest neighbors were ten to twelve miles away. The cottonwood trees and the river offered him solace, and the silence of the area allowed him to write or read without any disruption.

The cabin, made from cottonwood trees, measured thirty feet wide by sixty feet long and sat on six stone slabs. A central hallway divided the rooms, four on each side. Theodore had two adjoining rooms in the southeast corner. The end room was his bedroom, complete with his rubber bathtub, and a door opened into a combination library and office. The kitchen and dining area were on the northwest side of the building, while a large sitting room next to the fireplace occupied the northeast portion. A large porch faced the cottonwoods and the river, while a smaller piazza was on the southern end of the cabin, next to his bedroom. A root cellar under the cabin served as a darkroom for Theodore's new portable camera. The ranch also boasted a well, a blacksmith shed, a barn with two stables (both were sixteen by twenty feet) connected by a twelve-foot roof, a cattle shed, a chicken house, and a horse corral with a snubbing post. Theodore kept two or three dairy cows at the ranch, unlike many other outfits in the area, which provided him with milk and butter.

In the spring and summer evenings, he sat on the porch and read until the sun disappeared, or simply listened to the birds sing in the cottonwoods. When the weather got colder, evenings were spent by the fireplace, where he sat in his favorite rocking chair and read to others from one of his many books, or gave a lecture on some aspect of history. Depending on the subject, Theodore was known to become so animated in his story-telling that he and his rocking chair would literally move across the floor. While the fireplace provided warmth, each room had abundant buffalo and bear hides to keep the occupants warm at night.

As much as he loved his new residence, Theodore did not spend much time in it. The spring roundup of 1885 was about to begin.

The fifteen hundred head of cattle Theodore had purchased shortly after his return from New York, arrived in Medora on May 6. Theodore sent five hundred head to Maltese Cross Ranch, while the rest were driven to the Elkhorn. It took six days to get the cattle to the Elkhorn, mainly because of the swollen river and an unexpected snowstorm, which forced Theodore to move the cattle inland, away from their water source.

Cattle, as cute as they may look with their brown eyes, can be cantankerous animals. One moment they are as gentle as lapdogs, then the next, they suddenly get a notion and become anything but gentle. Even cattle without horns can be dangerous. When their sense of fear is triggered, they will stop at nothing to get away, knocking down sturdy fences, tipping over a fully loaded chuck wagon, and plowing up the ground to the extent that it takes months to rejuvenate. One of the greatest fears for a cowboy was a stampede—especially at night. It was a grim sight to find a colleague after he had been run over by several hundred head of cattle.

A stampede generally happened when the herd was uneasy or thirsty. Any type of noise could set them off—a couple of tin pans clanging together, a clap of thunder, even a cowboy sneezing. That was why riding "night herd" was so important. Two riders, working a two-hour shift, would circle the herd in opposite directions, singing a tune softly to calm the cattle. If the herd broke out, these two riders were in the thick of it. They would yell "Stampede!" and, with luck, be on either side of the running herd. The yell of that dreaded word quickly awakened other riders, who grabbed their horses and joined in. To stop a stampede, riders on both sides of the running herd would position themselves next to the lead runners and start to turn the cattle into themselves, as if forming a circle.

This would cause the animals to stop, but it was no guarantee they would settle down, because anything could set them off again.

Theodore's first stampede happened as he was moving the cattle to the Elkhorn. He and another rider took the first shift of riding night herd. They had gotten the herd bedded down for the night, when the stock got it in their mind to move. Theodore knew their only hope was to keep the herd together and not let them scatter.

I kept on one side, and the cowboy on the other, and never in my life did I ride so hard. In the darkness I could but dimly see the shadowy outlines of the herd, as with whip and spurs I ran the pony along its edge, turning back the beasts at one point barely in time to wheel and keep them in at another. The ground was cut up by numerous little gullies, and each of us got several falls, horses and riders, turning complete somersaults. We were dripping with sweat, and our ponies quivering and trembling like quaking aspens, when, after more than an hour of the most violent exertion, we finally got the herd quieted again.[4]

Despite the stampede, Theodore brought in all one thousand head of cattle to the ranch. With this completed, he dashed off a letter to his friend Henry Cabot Lodge on the eve of the spring roundup.

I have just come in from taking a thousand head of cattle up on the trail. The weather has been very bad and I had my hands full, working night and day, and being able to take off my clothes but once during the week I was out.

The river has been very high recently and I have had on two or three occasions to swim my horse across it. A new experience to me. Otherwise I have done little that is exciting in the way of horsemanship; as you know I am no horseman, and cannot ride an unbroken horse with any comfort. The other day I lunched with the Marquis de Morès, a French cavalry officer; he had hunted all through France, but told me he never saw in Europe such stiff jumping as we have on the Meadowbrook hunt.[5]

The Little Missouri Stockmen's Association spring roundup started at the mouth of Box Elder Creek and the Little Missouri River. (According to Lincoln Lang, it was about fifty miles south of their ranch.[6]) The spring roundup would brand all new cattle, including newborns, and take a tally of the stock that survived the winter. (The fall roundup would gather the steers, which were sent to market.) The spring roundup, which would take one to two months, was looked upon by cowboys and cattle owners as a social gathering despite the workload.

Roundups were divided into sections by the cattlemen's association ahead of time. The ranches in each section would meet at a designated location to begin their roundup, and over the next several weeks, they would gradually move from one end of their chosen section to the other. The section that included Theodore's ranches encompassed over 150 miles, from Beaver Creek, east of the Little Missouri River, to Little Beaver Creek, in the west.[7] Each cattle outfit brought along its own chuck wagon, while smaller cattle ranches would join another ranch and share expenses. Each outfit brought four to six cowboys, along with a string of eight to ten horses for each rider. Two men, known as horse wranglers, were assigned to handle the string of horses and create a rope corral to keep their horses from joining another outfit's remuda. Arriving at the meeting place, the outfit would make camp, cowboys dropping their sleeping gear and claiming their preferred spot, while the cook started making the first meal. Ranchers outside the divided section would send four men as representatives to take any cattle from their ranches that may have strayed.

Once all outfits had gathered at the meeting area, they would report to the "captain" of the roundup, a ranch foreman chosen for the job. He would assign various tasks, whether it was riding out to drive in the cattle, roping cattle and calves, or smoothing off the rough edges of some horses. Morning began early, at three a.m. A cup of coffee, biscuit, beans, and a couple slices of bacon was breakfast. The cowboys would select a horse from the remuda for the morning's work, and if a cowboy was smart, he'd place the metal bit of his bridle under his arm for a few minutes to warm it. A horse was more willing at that hour to accept a bit if it wasn't cold. Once the rider stepped into the saddle, he might find his mount to be a bit frisky, or just plain uncooperative. "Topping him off" was a cowboy term for letting the horse buck until he calmed down. Eventually, the horse would settle down, and the two companions would be off on their daily mission.

During this roundup, Theodore found himself with a horse that simply did not want him on his back. "He [the horse] would balk and then throw himself over backward: once, when I was not quick enough, he caught me and broke something in the point of my shoulder, so that it was some weeks before I could raise the arm freely."[8] With no doctor nearby, Theodore had to let the break heal itself and live with the pain.

As the cowboys moved out to gather loose cattle from the various coulees and washes, the chuck wagons and the remudas would move to the next spot, setting up by midday. "It is rather picturesque to see the four-horse teams filing down at a trot through a pass among the buttes— the saddle-bands being driven along at a smart pace to one side or behind, the teamsters cracking their whips, and the horse-wranglers calling and shouting as they ride rapidly from side to side behind the horses, urging on the stragglers by dexterous touches with the knotted ends of their long lariats that are left trailing from the saddle," Theodore reminisced.[9]

Most cowboys have certain ways of driving cattle or horses. Some simply use a whistle, while others will make a clucking sound, and others shout out a *hee-yah* or a *git-git-git*. It becomes rather repetitive and second nature for the rider. But the men riding with Theodore one day were more than surprised when he yelled, in his high voice, "Hasten forward quickly, there!" It was all his men could do not to laugh at their boss. When the men became bored with their usual calls, one would break the monotony with a yell of "Hasten forward quickly!" They had a good laugh at Theodore's expense, but he saw the humor in it, taking it as a sign of acceptance by his men.

Normally, the boss of the outfit always had first pick of a horse for the morning's work. Theodore accepted no favors, choosing to draw straws with the men when it came to selecting a mount. The cowboys of his outfit, and the others, were impressed that this dude from the East pulled his own weight, saddled his own horse, and did whatever was asked of him. Because of his poor eyesight, Theodore did not participate in roping or cutting out the cattle, but he was very involved in the branding. He did have his quirks during the roundup: He shaved every day, used a toothbrush, and brought along his rubber bathtub.

Lacking the practical experience of working a roundup, Theodore's willingness to try anything earned him the respect of the cowboys and owners. John Goodall, foreman of the Marquis's ranch, stated that "he was game to the core," while Lincoln Lang noted that Theodore "was right on the job, holding his own with the best of them."[10]

"These long, swift rides in the glorious spring mornings are not soon to be forgotten. The sweet, fresh air, with a touch of sharpness thus early in the day, and the rapid motion of the fiery little horse, combine to make a man's blood thrill and leap with sheer buoyant light-heartedness and eager, exultant pleasure in the boldness and freedom of the life he is leading," he recalled of the morning's work.[11]

By noontime, each man rode in to exchange his horse for a fresh one, grabbing a quick lunch of beans, bacon, biscuit, and a cup of coffee. At this point, it was time to cut the cattle from the herd. Bunching the cattle together, cowboys and their mounts would form a ring around them. A few men from each ranch looked over the group for their respective brands and cut them out from the herd. This is very difficult work because the herd does not simply stand still, but moves around in its tight circle. Cowboys who do this work need a horse they can rely on, known as a "cutting horse." A cowboy would rope a perspective target around the horns or neck. (Roping around the horns was the preferred choice, because a lariat around the neck of a cow, especially one that does not want to comply, could end up strangling the animal.) With the rope around the horns, the cowboy quickly wrapped the other end of the lariat around his saddle horn (called "dallying"). "A good horse takes as much interest in the work as does his rider," Theodore wrote, "and the instant the noose settles over the victim wheels and braces himself to meet the shock, standing with his legs firmly planted, the steer or cow being thrown with a jerk."[12] (A rider or horse that is not prepared for the hard jerk of the rope can easily be yanked to the ground.) In cases in which a brand could not be easily spotted, two cowboys would rope a bovine, with one throwing his rope over the horns, while the other roped the back legs, allowing them to inspect the brand. (Today, this exercise is a very popular contest in American rodeos, known as team roping.)

The chosen cow, steer, or calf would be dragged to the fire for branding. A fire was built, with the outfit's branding irons placed deep into the flames. Two cowboys would hold the animal down, one grabbing its front legs and placing his knee on its neck. The other cowboy grabbed the top hind leg and stretched it out, while bracing his other foot against the other hind leg. In this type of position, the animal can do nothing but wail in its unhappiness. The yell of "Hot iron!" serves as a warning that a branding iron is on the way. The cry of the animal being marked would fill the air, along with the pungent smell of burning hair and flesh.[13] (If the calf happened to be a bull calf, it would also be castrated at this time.) The animal was released and quickly joined the others who had suffered the same indignities. Cattle without markings were called "mavericks," and were divided up evenly among the outfits. Those that did not need to be branded were cut loose, returning to the area the cowboys had already ridden through.

Outfits would continue this process of gathering cattle, branding, and letting them return to the range as they made their way through their section. "The cowboys look forward eagerly to the round-up, where the work is hard, it is true, but exciting and varied, and treated a good deal as frolic," Theodore later noted. "There is no eight-hour law in cowboy land: during round-up time we often count ourselves lucky if we get off with much less than sixteen hours; but the work is done in the saddle, and the men are spurred on all the time by the desire to outdo one another in feats of daring and skillful horsemanship."[14] When there was free time during a roundup, cowboys held horse races, foot races, or wrestling matches, as well as the occasional card game. They also played practical jokes on each other.

Even though the cowboys respected "Mr. Roosevelt," as they called him, they couldn't resist playing a prank on him. Knowing his penchant for hunting, even while on a roundup, they concocted a story that a few of the cowboys had spotted a herd of a dozen pronghorns about five to six miles back from their current camp. Theodore took the bait and quickly left to find them. Once he was gone, the cowboys prepared themselves for his return from what they expected would be a wild goose chase. Several hours later, Theodore rode into camp with two pronghorns behind his saddle. He shot them a quarter-mile from where the cowboys had claimed to have spotted them.[15]

◆

As May gave way to June, the roundup moved its way to Garner Creek, two miles south of Maltese Cross Ranch.* June 2 proved to be muggy, with dark clouds forming in the west as the sun began to make its final departure for the day. A storm was in the offing. The outfits had gathered a large herd of cattle and settled the animals in a meadow near Chimney Butte. Sensing the approaching storm, the cattle grew uneasy. As the evening progressed, the rain began, eventually becoming a downpour. Then came the thunder and lightning.

The lightning struck right by the herd, and away all the beasts went, heads and horns and tails in the air. For a minute or two I could make out nothing except the dark forms of the beasts running on every side of me, and I should have been very sorry if my horse had stumbled . . . Then the herd split, part going to one side, while the other part seemingly kept straight ahead, and I galloped as hard as ever beside them. I was trying to reach the point—the leading animals—in order to turn them, when suddenly there was a tremendous splashing in front. I could dimly make out that the cattle immediately ahead and to one side of me were disappearing, and the next moment the horse and I went off a cut bank into the Little Missouri.

I bent away back in the saddle, and though the horse almost went down he just recovered himself, and, plunging and struggling through water and quicksand, we made the other side. Here I discovered that there was another cowboy with the same part of the herd that I was with; but almost immediately we separated. I galloped hard through a bottom covered with big cottonwood trees, and stopped the part of the herd that I was with, but very soon they broke on me again, and repeated this twice.

---

* An endpaper map of the Little Missouri River–Badlands area in Hermann Hagedorn's book, *Roosevelt in the Badlands* (1922), lists it as Gardiner Creek.

Finally toward morning the few I had left came to a halt . . . I got off my horse and leaned against a tree, but before long the infernal cattle started on again, and I had to ride after them. Dawn came soon after this, and I was able to make out where I was and head the cattle back, collecting other little bunches as I went. After a while I came on a cowboy on foot carrying his saddle on his head. He was my companion of the previous night. His horse had gone full speed into a tree and killed itself, the man, however, not being hurt. I could not help him, as I had all I could do to handle the cattle.[16]

Returning to camp with the cattle he found, Theodore ate a hasty breakfast while another cowboy saddled him a new mount. Gulping down coffee, he quickly mounted his fresh horse and rode out to find more of the scattered beasts. Ten hours later, he returned to switch mounts and went back out until nightfall. "By this time I had been nearly forty hours in the saddle, changing horses five times, and my clothes had thoroughly dried on me, and I fell asleep as soon as I touched the bedding . . . Nobody ever gets enough sleep on a round-up," he commented.[17]

The following morning, at four a.m., Theodore was up to start that day's work.

By the second week in June, the roundup was completed. On June 20, Theodore signed a deal with Sewall and Dow, giving them eleven hundred head of cattle (worth $25,000 in 1885 dollars). The two men would hold on to the cattle for three years, returning Theodore's original investment, and Theodore would keep two-thirds of any increase, with Sewall and Dow splitting the other third.[18]

The following day, Theodore boarded a train for New York, eager to see the publication of his new book. Reporters who met Theodore as he came east noticed a change. He was no longer the reedy young man with wan skin. "Rugged, bronzed, and in the prime of health . . . There was very little of the whilom [former] dude in his rough and easy costume," a reporter for the *St. Paul Pioneer Press* noted.[19]

DEEDS, NOT WORDS

I have a perfect horror of words that are not backed up by deeds.

HUNTING TRIPS OF A RANCHMAN, RELEASED IN JULY 1885, BOASTED A FIVE-hundred-copy print run with an astounding price of fifteen dollars. The *New York Times* stated that Theodore's book would "take a leading position in the literature of the American sportsman."[1]

George Bird Grinnell, editor of *Forest and Stream* magazine, commented, "Mr. Roosevelt is not well known as a sportsman, and his experience of the Western country is quite limited, but this very fact in one way *lends* an added charm to this book . . . We are sorry to see that a number of hunting myths are given as fact, but it was after all scarcely to be expected that with the author's limited experience he could sift the wheat from the chaff and distinguish the true from the false."[2]

To say Theodore was hurt by the less-than-flattering review is an understatement. He was very familiar with Grinnell and his magazine, which had previously praised his legislative work in halting the damming of streams that spilled into the Hudson River. In typical fashion, Theodore went to Grinnell's office to speak to him. Instead of a shouting match, the two men spent many hours talking about his book, as well as conservation.

Grinnell, a native of Brooklyn, New York, had been born in 1849 to a wealthy family. As a boy, he became friends with John James Audubon's widow, who introduced him to the world of birds. He obtained a bachelor's degree and PhD in osteology from Yale University. While assisting at the Peabody Museum in 1874, he was selected as the naturalist to accompany the Black Hills Expedition, led by Lt. Col. George A. Custer. The army officer enjoyed Grinnell's company and invited him on his ill-fated

June 1876 campaign, but the young man declined, citing his workload at the museum. He was part of the exploration team that visited Yellowstone Park and the surrounding area in 1875, cataloging 40 mammals and 139 species of birds. The most important aspect of his Yellowstone report was documenting the poaching of buffalo, deer, and elk for their hides. This led Grinnell to become a champion for conservation, founding the first Audubon Society and organizing the New York Zoological Society. *Forest and Stream* magazine, for which he served as editor from 1876 to 1911, provided him an outlet to inform the country about conservation issues.

The book review, which had hurt Theodore's feelings, sparked a long friendship between the two men, who shared a deep interest in conservation, especially saving wildlife. "He was always fond of natural history, having begun, as so many boys have done, with birds; but as he saw more and more of outdoor life his interest in the subject broadened, and later it became a passion with him," Grinnell commented.[3]

The release of his book coincided with Theodore's move into his new home at Oyster Bay. Designed by the Manhattan architectural firm of Lamb and Rich, the construction cost was estimated to be $16,975. (Theodore purchased the 155 acres for $30,000.) A massive three-story Queen Anne–style home, it boasted twenty-two rooms, including thirteen bedrooms, and three bathrooms. It was large enough to hold his growing collection of hunting trophies and books, although, in 1905, Theodore added the North Room. In the autumn of 1885, Theodore changed the name of the home from Leeholm to Sagamore Hill. The new name (*Sagamore* translates to "chief" or "head of tribe") was chosen because the area had been frequented by the Algonquin tribe. It was also another way for Theodore to erase the memory of Alice from his life. He spent many days hiking, swimming, and playing with Baby Lee on the large lawn. Friends and family members came for extended visits, including Eleanor, the youngest daughter of his brother Elliott. It was an idyllic time for Theodore, even if many thought the home was terribly large for just a widower and his baby daughter.

As much as he loved his new home, Theodore returned to Medora on August 25. Once in town, he placed an announcement on behalf of the Little Missouri Stockmen's Association in the *Bad Lands Cow Boy* for a

September 5 meeting. This meeting would require members to choose the time and location for the fall roundup, as well as hold elections for officers. (Despite Theodore's suggestion that the chairman's position be appointed to someone who lived year-round in the Badlands, he was reelected.)

While at the newspaper office, Theodore learned that the Marquis de Morès, who had been indicted by a grand jury in Mandan for the killing of Riley Luffsey, was being held in the town's jail until his trial.[4] Theodore and the Marquis maintained a cordial association, dining together on several occasions, including a dinner at Bamie's home in New York. Only once had the two men had a disagreement, when, in the spring of 1885, the Marquis had agreed to purchase nearly one hundred cattle from Theodore at the price of six cents a pound. Upon delivery of the herd, the Marquis stated he was reducing the purchase price by half a cent due to a price drop in the Chicago beef market. Insisting a deal was a deal, Theodore took back his cattle, refusing to ever do business with the Marquis again.[5]

Frank B. Allen, the Marquis's lawyer, successfully petitioned to have the trial moved to Bismarck, as a lynch mob was making threats around the Mandan jail.[6] Sitting in his jail cell gave the Marquis plenty of time to contemplate who was behind this latest judicial action. He suspected Joe Ferris was paying witnesses to testify against him, including Dutch Wannegan, one of two survivors of the 1883 ambush. In reality, Ferris, who owned a general store, acted as an informal banker for many residents of Medora, holding their money until they requested the funds. Those who went to Bismarck to testify had simply used their funds, held by Ferris, for train fare. The Marquis also began to question Theodore's motives because he was a close friend of Joe Ferris, and had recently hired Wannegan as a ranch hand.

This could explain, no matter how dubious the reasoning, why the Marquis sent a letter to Theodore from his cell on September 3, 1885.

My Dear Roosevelt,

My principle is to take the bull by the horns. Joe Ferris is very active against me and has been instrumental in getting me indicted by furnishing money to witnesses and hunting them up. The papers also publish very stupid accounts of our quarreling—I sent you the paper to

N.Y. Is this done by your orders? I thought you my friend. If you are my enemy I want to know it. I am always on hand as you know, and between gentlemen it is easy to settle matters of that sort directly.

Yours very truly,
Morès

I hear the people want to organize the county. I am opposed to it for one year more at least.[7]

Theodore, in dramatic fashion, assumed the Marquis was challenging him to a duel. As the challenged party, he could choose the weapons. Since he wasn't as handy with a pistol, Theodore decided he would pick a rifle if it came to a duel. Three days later, Theodore sent his reply.

Most emphatically I am not your enemy; if I were, you would know it, for I would be an open one, and would not have asked you to my house nor gone to yours. As your final words, however, seem to imply a threat, it is due to myself to say that the statement is not made through any fear of possible consequences to me; I, too, as you know, am always on hand, and ever ready to hold myself accountable in any way for anything I have said or done.

Yours very truly,
Theodore Roosevelt[8]

Many years after the fact, Bill Sewall and Frank Roberts claimed that Theodore stated the Marquis sent him a second note (which no longer exists), saying they could settle their differences without trouble.[9] It was highly unlikely that the Marquis was seeking a duel; it sounded more like wounded feelings, as he believed that Theodore was a friend. Reading the note the first time, Theodore likely jumped to the impression he was being challenged, and overexaggerated the intent of the letter. Also, Theodore paid the Marquis a visit on September 16 while he sat in the Bismarck jail, awaiting trial[10]—hardly the action of a man expecting a duel.

The trial began on September 12, and thirteen days later, the jury returned a not-guilty verdict within a few minutes. However, a more serious matter awaited the Marquis: His business ventures were failing. The Medora and Black Hills Stage and Forwarding Company, announced with the typical flourish one would expect from the Marquis, was a prime example. Deadwood, the gold town best known for being where Wild Bill Hickok had cashed in his chips in August 1876 after Jack McCall shot him in the Number 10 Saloon, was still thriving as a mining town. However, it lacked any direct transportation from the north. The Marquis quickly seized on the idea of running a stage from Medora to Deadwood, promptly hiring A. T. Packard to supervise the stage line, in addition to his editorial duties with Medora's newspaper. The Marquis was banking heavily on obtaining a government contract to deliver mail to Deadwood, which would provide his venture with welcome and needed capital. A single ticket for the thirty-five-and-a-half-hour ride, which began operation in October 1884, was $21.50. The stage would make a thrice-weekly run, leaving Medora at eight-thirty in the morning on Monday, Wednesday, and Friday, arriving in Deadwood at six in the evening on Tuesday, Thursday, and Saturday. Among the many headaches for the infant stage line were half-broken horses that had no desire to be hooked up to harnesses, providing passengers with a wild ride many were not expecting. Failing to obtain the government contract to carry mail doomed the stage line. Commenting on the stage's last run on May 19, 1885, the *Dickinson Press* noted "the Medora Stage and Forwarding Company is a total wreck."[11]

In addition to the stage line's failure, the Marquis's cattle-dressing operation was severely in need of more cattle to process through his slaughterhouse. By June 1885, the Marquis's abattoir was processing only 40 to 80 cattle a day, when he needed at least 400 to 500 a day to make a profit. He tried bringing in sheep and pigs during November and December of 1884, with little success.[12] Aside from the high costs of running his business, the Eastern beef trust was his biggest opponent. They did everything to damage his chances of success, including not having ice for the refrigerated cars at certain stops along the way to New York. Another problem was with the public, who preferred the taste of corn-fed beef to the Marquis's grass-fed herds. Despite the setbacks, the Marquis maintained a brave front.[13]

The Elkhorn Ranch had some of its roughness smoothed over that summer with the arrival of Bill Sewall's wife, Mary, and daughter, Kittie, along with Wilmot Dow's new bride, Lizzie.[14] The cabin windows sported curtains, and meals were supplemented with bread, cakes, and wild-berry jam. It took the two women a while to adjust to ranch life, because they had no neighbors nearby as they'd had in their Maine village. The vegetable garden plants withered and died in the heat of that summer, while the water contained so much alkaline, it made Kittie sick. The only way to make it potable was to buy lemons from a grocer in Medora and mix their juice into the water.[15] Mary Sewall saw the beauty in the area, but Bill remained skeptical about raising cattle in this territory.

Grass fires broke out that summer near the Elkhorn, which many ranchers suspected were started by a small group of Indians. Prairie-grass fires, like any blaze, are dangerous, and these had plenty of fuel to feed upon. Most grass fires in the Badlands area were caused by lightning strikes, embers from a passing train, a piece of burning coal from a nearby vein, or by cattle thieves covering their tracks.[16] Theodore said the quickest way to fight such a blaze was to kill a steer, splitting "it in two length-wise, and then have two riders drag each half-steer, the rope of one running from his saddle-horn to the front leg, and that of the other to the hind leg . . . the two would then ride forward, dragging the steer bloody side downward along the line of flame."[17] Other men on foot would follow with wet blankets to beat out any remaining flames. Although Theodore said it was exciting work, he also noted that it was very exhausting.

◆

Even though the tribes of the Northern Plains had been defeated and removed to various reservations, ranchers in the Badlands area still had to deal occasionally with some young men who left the reservation in hopes of stealing cattle or horses to prove their manhood. Most white settlers failed to understand that for a male Indian, fighting was a way of life. It was their way of proving themselves, advancing into manhood. Another way that these men distinguished themselves was in their display of valor and bravery by riding alone to an enemy, either alive or dead, and touching him with their hand or a stick. The warrior would then cry out that he had vanquished his opponent; his fellow tribe members were witnesses. Among many tribes this was known as "counting coup." Those who performed such acts were given the right to wear an eagle feather in their hair, a prized honor. Warriors well known for their acts of counting coup were highly regarded within their tribe.

Raiding a different tribe, or ranch, and taking as many horses or cattle as possible was another identification of a brave fighter, not to mention that this made him a strong provider for his family and tribe. As the farmers and ranchers settled in the Western lands, their stock became prime targets for Indians desiring to increase their standing within their tribe. (During the fur trade era, it was not uncommon for Indians and mountain men to engage in a running game of stealing mounts, stealing them back, and then getting them stolen once again.)

Young males on the various reservations felt the need to prove themselves to their elders, whether by counting coup, stealing livestock, or simply hunting to provide for family members. Life on a reservation was not what a young male was accustomed to, and simply sneaking off without the reservation agent knowing about it was a successful step. Ranchers in the Little Missouri River area, however, had minimal, if any, dealings with the Indians. Their experience was generally confined to losing some stock, although most thefts were the acts of cattle rustlers. Some Indians came by various ranches looking for food; as Lincoln Lang noted, "they were *always hungry*."[18]

Theodore said he got along particularly well with the Indians that visited his ranch, commenting that he treated them as fairly as any white man. However, he once came across a band of young braves out to prove themselves. Describing such young braves as "truculent, insolent, and reckless," he said any man that met such a party ran the "risk of losing his horse, his rifle, and all else he has."[19] Theodore's encounter happened in September when he was on the range, north and east from the Elkhorn, with the Killdeer Mountains in the distance. He said it was close to the noon hour when he topped a small rise and moved out onto a plateau. There, he stated, he spotted four or five Indians abruptly coming up over the edge in front of him.

"The second they saw me they whipped their guns out of their slings, started their horses into a dead run, and came on at full tilt, whooping and brandishing their weapons," Theodore recalled. Quickly dismounting and using his horse, Manitou, as a shield, he realized the level plain where he stood was the best of all terrain on which to make a stand, instead of broken country, because "a white man is at a great disadvantage if pitted against such adepts in the art of hiding as Indians." Unlike other horses that would run off from a running Indian charge, complete with whoops, Manitou stood his ground, "steady as a rock." Waiting until the band was about a hundred yards off, Theodore threw up his rifle and took aim on the leader. His actions caused the group to scatter, forcing them to double back, "bending over alongside their horses."[20] Gathering a distance away from him, the Indians briefly talked among themselves before one came riding up. He dropped his rifle and waved his blanket over his head.

When he came within fifty yards I stopped him, and he pulled out a piece of paper—all Indians, when absent from their reservations, are supposed to carry passes—and called out, "How! Me good Indian!" I answered, "How," and assured him most sincerely I was very glad he was a good Indian, but I would not let him come closer; and when his companions began to draw near, I covered him with the rifle and made him move off, which he did with a sudden lapse into the most canonical Anglo-Saxon profanity.[21]

Theodore led Manitou out onto the prairie, while the band of Indians lingered, watching him. He headed in one direction, the Indians, in another. "It had passed all too quickly for me to have time to get frightened," he wrote, but during the rest of his ride, he was uneasy, and "pushed tough, speedy old Manitou along at a rapid rate." He never saw the Indians again and admitted that they may not have intended any mischief, but he was not about to give them an opportunity. Later that night, he met two riders who told him the Indians he had encountered were young Sioux "bucks," and had stolen two of their horses earlier in the day.[22]

Like other men of his time, Theodore's opinions about Indians were very direct and likely leave today's readers uncomfortable. He distributed the blame equally for depredations, with neither side free of criticism. "I could recite a dozen instances of white outrages which, if told alone, would seem to justify all the outcry raised on behalf of the Indian; and I could also tell of as many Indian atrocities which make one almost feel that not a single one of the race should be left alive," he once stated.[23] Theodore felt that the main trouble derived from each side holding "the race, and not the individual, responsible for the deeds of the latter." He noted that whites or Indians that did not commit any outrages were also quick not to prevent his fellow men from stealing or attacking a rival race. To Theodore's way of thinking, it was not the entire race that was the problem but the individual, or groups of individuals, that were the root of the problem. Yet he was also keen to point out others who either simply stood by and did nothing or eventually took part in the action.

In his *Ranch Life and the Hunting Trail*, Theodore cited two instances that backed up his opinion. The first story was of a German-born ranch hand who had once worked for him. In Minnesota, this man's family grew up around many Sioux, two of whom became very close friends to his family. When the 1862 Sioux uprising took place over unfair annuity payments by the Indian agents, many settlers were killed or taken prisoner. The two friendly Sioux tried their best to rescue this man's family, and pleaded that their lives be spared. The chief killed the boy's mother, and the two friendly Indians killed the other family members, except for the boy.

In Theodore's second narrative, a cowboy related how a small group of Indians had spent a winter near the ranch that employed him. The chief of this group owned two fine horses that the cowboy admired. He took such a liking to them that he drove the two horses off, hiding them in a location where the Indians would not find them. The chief was upset at the loss of his two fine animals and searched for them in vain. A few weeks later, one of the cowboy's horses strayed and could not be found. With the spring thaw, the Indians moved on. The chief returned to the ranch a few days later with the cowboy's stray mount. Feeling guilty, the cowboy led the chief to where he had hidden the leader's two horses.[24]

However, when it came to the claim that white settlers had taken the Indians' land, Theodore was unapologetic. Calling it "sentimental nonsense," he was quick to note that "gross wrong" was committed by the government and individuals over and over. "The government makes promises impossible to perform, and then fails to do even what it might toward their fulfilment," he commented.[25] Theodore also noted that when one combines "brutal and reckless" frontiersmen with "treacherous, revengeful, and fiendishly cruel" Indians, a "long series of outrages" from both sides will follow. When it came to the claims that the Native Americans' land had been taken by whites, Theodore flatly stated that, at least as far as the Western Indians were concerned, "the simple truth is that the latter never had any real ownership in it at all. Where the game was plenty, there they hunted; they followed it when it moved away to new hunting-grounds, unless they were prevented by stronger rivals; and to most of the land on which we found them they had no stronger claim than that of having a few years previously butchered the original occupants."[26]

Theodore noted that the first white hunters who populated the Little Missouri region had as good a title to the area as "that of most Indian tribes to the lands they claim," but no one "dreamed of saying that these hunters owned the country." He felt that the Indians, like the white settlers, should be given 160 acres as their claim. Should they decline the offer, "then let him share the fate of the thousands of white hunters and trappers who have lived on the game that the settlement of the country has exterminated, and let him, like these whites, who will not work, perish from the face of the earth which he cumbers."

Agreeing that such a doctrine was merciless, Theodore felt it was "just and rational . . . it does not do to be merciful to a few, at the cost of justice to the many. The cattle-men at least keep herds and build houses on the land; yet I would not for a moment debar settlers from the right of entry to cattle country, though their coming in means in the end the destruction of us and our industry."[27]

CHANCE MEETING

Her face stirred up in me homesickness and longings for the past which will come again never, alack never.

THEY HAD BEEN FRIENDS SINCE CHILDHOOD. THEIR PARENTS WERE friends, and the young girl, who was born Edith Kermit Carow in Norwich, Connecticut, on August 6, 1861, often thought of the Roosevelt household as her second home.

She had been born a few weeks after Theodore's younger sister, Corinne, who became her childhood friend.[1] The daughter of Charles and Gertrude Carow, Edith, like Theodore, enjoyed a life of privilege. Her father ran the family shipping company, one of the richest in America. A well-educated child, she was known to favor a quiet corner of the house to read a book rather than join a party. It was obvious, even in those early years, that a special relationship was growing between Edith and Theodore. She had stood next to Theodore and his brother, Elliott, in the window at their grandfather's home, watching President Lincoln's funeral procession. (Both Theodore and Edith shared a deep admiration for the slain president for the rest of their lives.) They loved books, often reading to each other. Edith would let "Teedie" play house with her, but she excluded his brother when they came to play at the Carow home.[2] Yet they were complete opposites in personality. Theodore was passionate and impetuous, while Edith was perceptive and circumspect. It was said that Edith was the calm center of Theodore's cyclone.

As a twelve-year-old boy, Theodore had wept openly over leaving his friend behind when the Roosevelt family traveled to Europe. He wrote

Edith letters detailing his adventures, and when her written reply met him in a foreign city, he was overcome with homesickness. In Paris, he noted in his diary, "Mama showed me the portrait of Eidieth [*sic*] Carow and her face stired [*sic*] up in me homesickness and longings for the past which will come again never, alack never."[3] Edith was a constant visitor at the Roosevelt summer home, Tranquility, which the family rented on Long Island, not far from where Theodore would later build his own home. When he was old enough, Theodore would take her out in his small rowboat. They both attended the same social events, and his name appeared more than any other boy's on her dance card.[4]

Despite Edith's idyllic times with Theodore and the rest of his family, the Carow family was anything but unspoiled. Her father fell into the cargo hold of one of the company's ships and struck his head. It appears that after this accident, his instability advanced, especially with his fondness for alcohol. At the end of the Civil War, the family business began to decline, eventually leaving Charles Carow penniless. Edith's mother, Gertrude, who already suffered from the pangs of a loveless marriage, became a hypochondriac. The family began living with various relatives in Manhattan starting in 1867. Little wonder Edith eagerly sought the stability of the Roosevelt household.

Gertrude Carow's father died in November 1882, leaving her $40,000. His will stipulated that the money was to remain invested, with the interest ($5,000) paid semiannually for the rest of Gertrude's life.[5] While not an exorbitant sum, it allowed the Carows to live somewhat comfortably. However, the money couldn't help Charles Carow, who died on March 17, 1883, at the age of fifty-eight.

In the fall of 1877, Theodore left for Harvard. In his few letters to his family, he neither mentions Edith, nor asks anyone to give her his regards. It wasn't until December of that year that Theodore and Edith had a chance to spend time together. During May 1878, when his family traveled to Boston to visit him, he asked Edith to come with them. When she returned home, in a brief letter to Theodore, she described the visit as "three perfectly happy days."[6]

Family members on both sides expected Theodore and Edith to marry when he finished his studies at Harvard. During August 1878, they spent a great deal of time together at Tranquility. In his diary entry for August 22, he noted that they went up to the summer house, yet after that date Edith is not mentioned in his diary for several weeks. Many believe Theodore had asked Edith to marry him on August 22, but she refused. No one can state with certainty what happened that night, including family members. Both Theodore and Edith never discussed the matter, although he indicated in a letter to his sister, Bamie, that they both had tempers. Edith once ambiguously noted, "Theodore had not been nice."[7]

After August 22, Theodore's personality took on a darker tone. He rode his horse, Lightfoot, so hard, he later worried he had hurt the animal. When a neighbor's dog ran after them, nipping at Lightfoot's hoofs, he turned around and shot the dog. Anger burned in him.

Two months later, Theodore met Alice Lee at a party.

Edith, despite the break from Theodore, did not walk away from the Roosevelt family. She remained close to Bamie and Corinne, even attending Theodore's wedding, where she spent the night "dancing the soles off her shoes."[8] She was also a bridesmaid at Corinne's 1882 wedding, and hosted a party for her former love when he won his Assembly seat.[9] From the time of their breakup, it appears that Edith never showed any true romantic interest in another man until early October 1885.

One has to wonder whether Theodore's romantic feelings for Alice, at least when they first met, were simply those of a broken heart on the rebound. It's obvious that he did love Alice, and that her death greatly affected him. Why, in 1885, did he ask Bamie and Corrine to warn him when Edith might visit? Why would he want to avoid her at all costs? The likely answer is that Theodore still held deep feelings for Edith. Evading her was his way to avoid confronting his emotions. Just as he had done in burying Alice's memory so deeply, if he shunned any contact with Edith, she did not exist.

Leaving Medora in the middle of September 1885, Theodore returned to New York City for the Republican convention, where he would help to draft the party platform. He received little notice at the convention, and it does not appear that he did much to attract attention. A few weeks later, in early October, walking into Bamie's house one day, he was met by a lovely woman of twenty-four coming down the stairs.

It was Edith Carow.

There is no record of what they said to each other. Their romance was one of the best-kept secrets, with not even Bamie or Corinne having any knowledge of it. In his diaries for 1885 and 1886, Theodore does not mention Edith by name, but a simple "E" appears on various pages. In some instances, he mentions attending a dinner party or the theater, with the solitary "E" noted alongside the event.[10] It was not considered good form in "polite society" for a recent widower to jump into another romance too quickly. A widower, no matter what age, had to show restraint and, at all times, remain a gentleman. To outsiders, it appeared that they had simply renewed their old childhood friendship.

On November 17, Theodore asked Edith to marry him, and she accepted. They agreed to hold off on publicly announcing their engagement for a year. Instead of returning to his ranches, he remained in New York to be as close to Edith as possible. He attended numerous dinners and balls during the society season in Manhattan, usually with Edith discreetly nearby. The day before his twenty-seventh birthday, he invited Edith to attend the Long Island Meadowbrook Fox Hunt, which began at Sagamore Hill. Although a fox hunt was considered by Eastern blue bloods to be far more dignified than the grizzly bear or buffalo hunts of the West, it was just as intense. In typical fashion, Theodore led the hunt, galloping for over three miles ahead of the other riders. Five miles into the ride, his horse showed signs of being lame and, at the next jump, tripped over a wall, hitting a group of stones. Thrown from the saddle, Theodore's face hit something hard, possibly some rocks, and he felt a snap in his left arm. Once his horse had regained its footing, Theodore was back in the saddle chasing the other riders, this time using just one hand. His left arm dangling at his side, his face bloodied, he rode on and arrived in time to see the hounds corner the fox. When, in this condition, he approached Baby Lee at the stables, the child ran away in complete horror. Writing to his friend Lodge, an avid fox hunter, Theodore commented that he did not mind the broken arm. "I am always ready to pay the piper when I've had a good dance; and every now and then I like to drink the wine of life with brandy in it," he added.[11]

◆

February 14, 1886.

It had been two years since that tragic day in Theodore's life. On that day in 1884, he had drawn a bold X in his diary, with the comment "The light has gone out of my life." His 1886 diary contains no entry for February 14, but two days, later an arrow and a heart are drawn next to each other. (That date, February 16, he attended a dinner at Whitelaw Reid's home.)[12]

During this time, Theodore was a young man torn by two emotions. The first was his elation at being in love and his expectation of sharing his life with someone who knew him very well. The second emotion was the deep guilt he felt in not honoring Alice's memory. The Victorian era had many formalities that, from a current-day perspective, seem antiquated, oppressive, and nonsensical. In that period, of which Theodore was very much a part, it was generally accepted that a widower would remain faithful to his deceased spouse for the rest of his life, and not remarry. There were no exceptions, even for a young widower. One was duty-bound to honor such a tradition.

The guilt he felt weighed on him—at times heavily. Because both Theodore and Edith were very careful not to write anything that would divulge their engagement, let alone their personal feelings, the historian is left to surmise the feelings each harbored. This tendency on the part of the historian can easily become a very slippery slope. One is left to wonder whether the guilt Theodore felt led to verbal clashes with Edith; both of them were, after all, strong personalities. Did Theodore ever have second thoughts about marrying Edith? This may have been possible when he was deep in the throes of guilt pangs; still, whatever the two of them may have felt, they worked through it.

Despite his bouts of guilt, Theodore attended numerous social events with Edith. (In January and February 1886, he attended more than two dozen parties.) On January 11, 1886, his diary simply notes, "E.K.C. dinner," while the entry for February 12, 1886, mentions "Theater with E.K.C."[13]

In February, through the help of his friend Henry Cabot Lodge, he agreed to write a biography of statesman Thomas Hart Benton for the American Statesman series.[14] (Lodge was writing a book on George

Washington for the same series.) In a February 7 letter to Lodge, Theodore exhibits uncertainty over the project. "I feel a little appalled over the Benton; I have not the least idea whether I shall make a flat failure of it or not. However, I will do my best and trust to luck for the result."[15]

His lack of any strong feelings over the Benton book could have been due to the fact he was starting to research another book that was of greater interest to him. The book he envisioned would detail the westward expansion of the country in the nineteenth century. Theodore reached out for help, sending a letter to the leading authority on that period, Lyman Copeland Draper:

> *I am now engaged on a work in reference to the extension of our boundaries to the southward from the day when Boone crossed the Alleghenies, to the days of the Alamo and San Jacinto.*
>
> *I know of no one whose researches into, and collection of material for, our early western history, have been so extensive as your own; so I venture to ask you if you can give me any information how I can get at what I want. I wish particularly to get a hold of any original or unpublished mss; such as the diaries or letters of the first settlers, who crossed the mountains, and their records of early Indian wars, the attempt at founding the State of Franklin, etc.*[16]

Theodore probably looked upon the Benton book as more of a work-for-hire assignment, while his effort on the early West was truly a passion project.

Aside from attending parties and researching material for his two upcoming books, Theodore also found time to deliver some speeches, including one at Princeton and another at Morton Hall.[17] On October 17, 1885, he had been the featured speaker at the Young Republican Club of Brooklyn. Although some party leaders and reformers might have still harbored ill feelings toward Theodore and Lodge (who also appeared at the meeting), the rank and file had greeted them with "great enthusiasm."[18] Theodore spoke of civil service reform, which he noted would soon lead to a very discernible division between the Republicans (who favored it) and the Democrats (who were against it). But that, as he noted, was just one difference between the two parties. "Throughout the North the bulk of the honesty and intelligence of the community is to be found in the Republican ranks. If the Republicans take a false step it is usually because the politicians have tricked them into it; while if the Democrats make a good move it is almost always merely because the astute party leaders have been able for a short time to dragoon their dense-witted followers into the appearance of deference to decent public sentiment," he said.[19]

His speeches were not limited to politics. Theodore spoke about the West and his life as a cattle rancher, noting that the worst thing a frontiersman had to deal with was skunks. "Yet, says Mr. Roosevelt, this is not so bad as politics in New York," the *Bismarck Daily Tribune* observed after one of his New York speeches.[20]

The winter was beginning to lose its luster for Theodore, even though Edith was always around. He missed his ranch, and was concerned about how Sewall and Dow were getting along. Theodore planned to leave for Medora on March 15, while Edith, her sister, and her mother would move to England in April, in an effort to extend what remained of the family inheritance.

Theodore, while making plans for his departure, spent his last ten days in Manhattan almost exclusively with "E."

A MATTER OF JUSTICE

The capture itself was as tame as possible.

THEODORE'S TRAIN PULLED INTO THE MEDORA STATION ON MARCH 18. This trip, encompassing a total of fifteen weeks, would mark the longest amount of time he stayed in the Badlands. That night he bunked in his room at Joe Ferris's general store, where he met Joe's bride. The new Mrs. Ferris was a bit apprehensive about meeting Theodore, especially when he arrived in his city clothes. "I was scairt to death," she reportedly said. When she tried to treat him like a big-city gentleman, Theodore smiled broadly and told her to treat him like one of the boys. Sitting down to dinner with the couple, he exclaimed to Joe, "A white tablecloth in the Bad Lands! Joe, did you ever expect to see it?"[1]

Weather in the Badlands had been capricious in recent weeks. The cold froze the Little Missouri River; a few days later it would be as warm as late spring before freezing temperatures returned. The teetering difference in the temperature caused the river to create huge ice floes that would break apart, then once again freeze, jamming the river and its banks. The jagged piles of ice along the riverbank only added to the eerie appearance of the Badlands.

The following morning, Theodore left Medora, with Sewall and Dow, for the Elkhorn, reaching the ranch "long after sunset, the full moon flooding the landscape with light." Describing to Bamie an ice gorge that had formed on the river in front of the cabin, he noted that "The swelling mass of broken fragments [have] been pushed almost up to our doorstep. The current then broke through the middle, leaving on each side of the stream, for some miles, a bank of huge ice floes, tumbled over each other in the wildest confusion." He stated that no horse had a chance of getting across the river, but he had bought a boat in St. Paul (for thirty dollars) that could take him and his men across the river easily. With the river running high because of the spring thaw, they could take the boat across the river to check on their horses and cattle, although he noted it was "most laborious. We work like Arctic explorers."[2]

At night, lying in bed under buffalo hides, he could hear the "dull roar and crunching" of the ice floes outside his cabin.[3] Fortunately, the line of cottonwood trees standing in front of the cabin served as a barrier that kept the ice floes from reaching the cabin's front door. Defying the weather, Theodore, Sewall, and Dow went hunting, bagging four deer. They left them tied up in a thicket of dwarf cedar trees overnight, as the cold weather would help keep the game fresh. Returning the following morning, they discovered that some mountain lions had feasted on the carcasses, leaving behind fresh tracks. The men followed until they lost the tracks in a morass of rocky hills. Returning to the Elkhorn, Sewall moved their small boat further onto the bank, tying it securely to a tree to avoid being dragged off into the river's current.

In the early-morning hours of March 24, the boat went missing.

The boat was not carried off by the river, but by Mike "Redhead" Finnegan, a recent arrival with a very bad attitude. Described as a surly man with a brick-red complexion and long, red hair and beard, he was also a notorious consumer of any saloon's "Kansas sheep dip." During one visit at Bigmouth Bob's Bug Juice Dispensary, he absorbed too much and passed out. John Goodall, the foreman at the Marquis's ranch, found the plastered bad man on the floor and decided to have some fun. Placing him on a billiard table, Goodall acquired a pair of scissors and proceeded to shear the long locks of Finnegan's hair on one side, as well as cutting off a side of his beard and mustache.[4]

When he awoke from his drunken stupor, Finnegan was not amused with his new look. Taking refuge in a patch of bushes, he proceeded to shoot up the town, starting with the offices of the *Bad Lands Cow Boy*. He was stopped when A. T. Packard charged him with his horse and knocked him unconscious. Locked up in a boxcar, he was set free by an unknown friend and disappeared. Finnegan returned to Medora in December 1885, and resumed his shooting spree until he was arrested. He spent three weeks in a Mandan jail and was fined five dollars.

Residents were unhappy not only with Finnegan's recent shooting demonstrations, but also with his rustling horses. The Stranglers let it be known in March 1886 that Finnegan, who was now traveling with a "half-breed" named Burnsted and Chris Pfaffenbach, an old German whose mind was cankered from whiskey, would have a rope "accident" if he stayed in the area. The night of March 23 was punctuated with a fierce, howling wind, which gave the trio perfect cover for their departure. Launching a small scow, they made good an escape via the Little Missouri River. After a while on the river, their scow began leaking; it was obvious the craft was doomed. That is when they spotted Theodore's boat on the bank tied to a tree. Quickly taking advantage of opportunity before them, the trio took their newly acquired skiff and continued on down the river.

As the sun broke on the morning of March 24, Theodore was ready to renew tracking the mountain lions. The previous day he had spoken to W. J. Tompkins, an experienced hunter in the area, who would accompany him on the hunt. As breakfast was being readied, Sewall went out to check on the boat. Finding only the cut rope and a red woolen mitten on the ground nearby, Sewall went back to the cabin to inform his boss about the theft. Finnegan and the other two were surmised to be the likely culprits. Theodore immediately wanted to go after the thieves, but Sewall reminded him that no horse could make it along the river in such weather. Instead, he suggested that he and Dow build another boat, which would be ready to go within a few days. With the river jammed with heavy ice floes, the chances of the outlaw trio making good their escape would be heavily curtailed. As Sewall and Dow worked on a new scow, Theodore sent another ranch hand to Medora to obtain necessary supplies, as well as to telegraph authorities in Mandan to watch for Finnegan and his accomplices.

Theodore's blood was up. The theft violated so many of the things he held dear: They had stolen personal property, exhibited a complete lack of personal honor, and, most importantly, they had shown a flagrant disregard for law and order. More than anything else, it was a matter of justice for him. In his *Ranch Life and the Hunting Trail*, Theodore devoted an entire chapter ("Sheriff's Work on a Ranch") to the pursuit and capture of the boat thieves. Not only is it an entertaining read, but the passage also provides insight into Theodore's mind-set, as well as providing the words of a man taking on the role of a determined leader.

In any wild country where the power of the law is little felt or heeded, and where everyone has to rely upon himself for protection, men soon begin to feel that it is in the highest degree unwise to submit to any wrong without making an immediate and resolute effort to avenge it upon the wrong-doers, at no matter what the cost of risk or trouble. To submit tamely and meekly to theft, or to any other injury, is to invite almost certain repetition of the offense, and this in a place where self-reliant hardihood and the ability to hold one's own under all circumstances rank as the first of virtues.[5]

Not only did the theft of his property inflame his moral code, but Theodore was, in effect, a deputy sheriff of Billings County due to his position as chairman of the Little Missouri Stockmen's Association. This gave him, in his opinion, the legal ability to pursue the miscreants with the backing of the law, not just as a matter of personal honor. Although he did not admit it, he would soon be off on another boyish adventure, living out the fantasy of a Western lawman.

The worst thing for Theodore at this point was waiting. He never could sit idly by, waiting for something to happen or begin. He had to start it, seize the moment, run with it. As he would do on many future occasions, Theodore wanted to take immediate action. In this case, he had no choice. Constructing a new boat, as well as the hostile weather, added to the delay. With time on his hands, Theodore began work on the Thomas Hart Benton book, and by the time all were ready to start, he had completed the first chapter. "At any rate," he wrote Lodge on March 27, "I have made a start. Writing is horribly hard work to me; and I make slow progress . . . my style is very rough and I do not like a certain lack of sequitur that I do not seem to get rid of. At present we are all snowed up by a blizzard; as soon as it lightens up I shall start down the river with two of my men in a boat we have built while indoors, after some horse thieves who took our boat the other night to get out of the country with; but they have such a start we have very little chance of catching them."[6]

Sewall completed the boat on March 27, but it was "too cold to start" after the trio. While the three pillagers were contending with the unforgiving elements, Theodore, Sewall, and Dow were comfortably ensconced at the Elkhorn. In his diary entry for March 28 Theodore stated it was "bitterly cold," and the following day they experienced a "furious blizzard." The weather cleared on March 30, and the three men began their pursuit. Carrying two weeks' worth of provisions (including flour, beans, coffee, bacon, blankets, and fur coats), they also were each armed with a Winchester repeating rifle, pistols, and a double-barreled shotgun. For reading, Theodore brought along his new copy of Tolstoy's *Anna Karenina*.

As the homemade scow slipped into the icy river, the wives of Dow and Sewall, both pregnant, watched them disappear around the bend. Theodore expressed little concern about a matchup against the trio, as long as they were able to have a fair fight. What he, Sewall, and Dow worried about was being spotted and ambushed from the riverbank.

All through the early part of the day we drifted swiftly down between the heaped-up piles of ice, the cakes and slabs now dirty and unattractive looking. Towards evening, however, there came long reaches where the banks on either side were bare, though even here there would every now and then be necks where the jam had been crowded into too narrow a spot and risen over the side as it had done up-stream, grinding the bark from the big cottonwoods and snapping the smaller ones short off. In such places the ice-walls were sometimes eight or ten feet high, continually undermined by the restless current.[7]

That night they camped at "a point of wood-covered land jutting out into the stream," just below the Eaton VI Ranch. Theodore shot three sharp-tailed grouse, which served as the men's supper. As they rolled into their blankets, the cold grew even more bitter. Morning greeted them with bitingly frigid temperatures, and despite spotting many tracks of white-tailed deer, they found none. Casting off after their prey, the chilly air left them with little to say. It was nearly noon when the sun was high enough to provide a minimal hint of warmth, which was quickly dashed by an icy north wind. Lunch was taken on a sandbar, where they cooked bacon and coffee. Back on the river again, the cold never let up.

As they slept under their blankets and buffalo hides, the temperature dropped below zero. The morning of April 1 wasn't much better, as the river had thickened with ice. Theodore, Dow, and Sewall went in search of game. Four deer jumped out of a thicket, and they managed to shoot two of the four. ("A man doing hard open-air work in cold weather is always hungry for meat.") After breakfast, they once again pushed off into the river.

Despite not making as swift a departure from the Little Missouri area as they had hoped, Finnegan and his two followers felt confident that the jammed river and brutal temperatures gave them the advantage. No one, especially a dude from the East, would venture out in this weather after them. Like many criminals, Finnegan was not the brightest of men, and certainly underestimated Theodore's tenacity.

As the late morning gave way to afternoon, the trio from the Elkhorn made as little noise as they could in case they stumbled upon the thieves. Rounding a bend in the river, they spotted their missing boat moored on the riverbank. A few yards from the boat, in a cluster of bushes, they noticed smoke from a campfire.

"We had come on the camp of the thieves," Theodore observed.[8]

◆

They had just passed the point where Cherry Creek merges with the Little Missouri River. Sewall quietly guided their boat onto a portion of the riverbank that was free of ice. Theodore and Dow quickly shucked their jackets, and as the scow touched land, they were off the boat, rifles in hand. Sewall tied the boat to a tree and joined his friends. Of the three men, Finnegan would be the one to approach with the greatest caution. He was a gunman on the run. Such a man could either submit like a beaten puppy or fight like an angry grizzly. They reasoned, however, that Burnsted, who was half Indian, was another one to consider carefully. He was muscular, and his having thrown in with the likes of Finnegan made him a potential danger. Only the old German, Pfaffenbach, would be the one of least concern, since his mind was so rotted from alcohol.

They carefully made their way to where the smoke was rising. The fugitives' camp was on a bank of the river, about fifteen feet wide; behind it was another bank that rose six feet, supported by thick brush. Theodore would approach from the center, with Dow on the right and Sewall on the left. Theodore had his Winchester, while the other two had shotguns filled with buckshot. "We were all three going to shoot if they offered to raise a gun," Sewall later said. "It is rather savage work, but it don't do to fool with such fellows. If there was killing to be done we meant to do it ourselves."[9]

Pfaffenbach was the only one in the camp, sitting by the fire. Theodore, Dow, and Sewall waited a few minutes to make sure the other two were not hiding, or farther back in the bushes. Certain the old German was alone, they quickly swept down on him and disarmed the befuddled man. Pfaffenbach related that Burnsted and Finnegan had gone off to hunt, leaving him at camp. Assuring the German no harm would come to him as long as he did what he was told, the men resumed waiting in the bushes for the other two.

Burnsted was first to appear. As he came into camp, Theodore, rifle cocked, jumped up, ordered him to put his gun down, and raise his hands. The man readily did as ordered and was tied up.

Now they waited for Finnegan.

A half-hour passed before the leader walked in. Theodore jumped up and ordered him to drop his weapon.

Finnegan hesitated for a second, his eyes fairly wolfish; then, as I walked up within a few paces, covering the center of his chest so as to avoid overshooting, and repeating the command, he saw that he had no show, and, with an oath, let his rifle drop and held his hands up.[10]

One thing Theodore left out of his narrative was that, when Finnegan hesitated for a moment, Dow popped up and yelled out, "Damn you! Drop that gun!"[11] (Hearing such a command from a man holding a shotgun would be quite persuasive, even to a criminal such as Finnegan.) Of course, it was not in Theodore's nature to share the spotlight with this story. It is an undisputed fact that Theodore was the one who ordered

Burnsted and Finnegan to stand down, with Dow and Sewall serving as backup. However, when creating a written narrative, which Theodore was doing, it is always more dramatic when the sole protagonist (in this case, Theodore) captures the deadliest of the fugitives. Sewall himself observed that Finnegan appeared to be more angry than scared, probably because he had been caught by a dude from the East. Theodore informed the fugitive trio they would be treated fairly, but should they try anything, they would be shot.

The three men were searched and their weapons removed. Theodore had to decide how to keep his prisoners from escaping. Tying their feet and hands would not work, as the extreme cold would cause them to freeze. The only way to be certain that their quarry didn't escape was to maintain a twenty-four-hour guard. While Sewall and Dow chopped down some old cottonwoods for the fire, Theodore kept first watch, shotgun firmly in his hands. After dinner, the prisoners were ordered to take off their boots before they bedded down. Theodore stayed up to watch the men for half the night, noting that the only danger of such a task was "the extreme monotony" of sitting in the dark.

The following morning, with the three prisoners in tow, they made their way on the river to Mandan. Their provisions had been allotted for three men, but now with the captives in hand, their food supply began to rapidly decrease. Game in the area was scarce. If they ran low on supplies, they might be forced to let the fugitives go, something that Theodore was loathe to do.

Knowing Finnegan would likely be the one to try an escape, Theodore had him sit next to him in the boat Sewall had built. Sewall and Dow followed in the stolen boat, with Burnsted and the German and the plunder they had amassed, including saddles. For a time they made good progress; the river moved along swiftly, despite some ice chunks between the boats. As the miles wore on, however, ice jams caused them to slow down until the ice broke apart.

It was slow going.

One ice jam brought the boats to a complete halt. Leaving Sewall and Dow to guard the prisoners, Theodore climbed a hill, where he had a clear view of the river, which was blocked solidly. Pulling the boats to shore, they pitched camp for the night. Theodore, Sewall, and Dow held a brief conference on the situation. It was agreed that the men would stay on their current course, with hopes that the harsh weather would let up before their supplies gave out.

"The next eight days were as irksome and monotonous as any I ever spent: there is very little amusement in combining functions of a sheriff with those of an arctic explorer," Theodore noted.[12] The weather did not let up. Each night, as the temperature dropped, water in a pail froze solid, and ice built up on the banks. The next morning, the ice floes would break up, letting the flotilla make a bit of headway before jamming up and forcing them to stop and wait. This was repeated day after day, and with no game in sight, the supplies continued to dwindle.

Passing the Killdeer Mountains, Theodore kept a wary eye for any Indians on the banks. Some cowboys had earlier reported seeing a band of Indians, likely from the nearby Sioux reservation, along this stretch of land. Their presence could explain why game was virtually nonexistent in the area.

The landscape added to the tedium of the trip. Theodore noted that the unceasing rows of barren hills offered no feeling of advancement. Rounding the bend of the river offered a repetitive view. Combined with the winter's bleakness, it was as if they were caught on a bone-chilling, never-ending merry-go-round.

Although progress was slow, tension among the prisoners eased as they realized they were not likely to be strung up on a rope. In one moment of bravado, Finnegan stated that if he had "any show at all," Theodore would have had a fight on his hands. But, the criminal conceded he knew that if he tried to make a break, he'd be shot. Theodore nodded, chuckling. With nothing to do but sit and be watched, the prisoners would occasionally read material they had in their stash—dime novels, as well as "drearily silly society novels." Theodore found the "surroundings were quite gray enough to harmonize well" with his reading his copy of the Tolstoy novel.[13] Completing the book, Theodore borrowed one of Finnegan's dime novels.

As they slowly made their way on the river, supplies ran lower and lower. They were forced to mix flour with muddy river water for unleavened biscuits. After covering nearly thirty miles on the river, on April 8, they spotted a cow camp for the C-Diamond Ranch. Landing the boats, they found a lone cowboy in the camp. It was decided that Theodore would arrange to get a wagon and take the prisoners to Dickinson, as the town was relatively closer than trying to reach Mandan via the river. The cowboy lent Theodore his pony, which proved a bit of a rough ride as soon as he stepped into the saddle. Sewall was heard to exclaim, as Theodore and the horse danced around, "The boss ain't no bronco-buster!"[14] Once the horse settled down, Theodore rode it to the main ranch (fifteen miles from the cow camp), where he made an agreement with the ranch owner to drive the wagon to Dickinson. The following morning Theodore, Sewall, and Dow marched the prisoners, along with their plunder, the fifteen miles to the ranch.

Sewall and Dow returned to the river and eventually landed the boats in Mandan. From there, they boarded a train for Medora, transporting Theodore's boat. Arriving in Medora, they launched the boat in the river to return to Elkhorn Ranch. Meanwhile, Theodore started off for Dickinson. Not knowing the ranch owner well, and not waiting to turn his back on his prisoners by sitting on the bench seat, Theodore made the decision to follow the wagon on foot to Dickinson.

It was a forty-five-mile trip.

Trudging through ankle-deep mud, with the wagon moving along— at best—at a walk, it took two days and a night to reach Dickinson. As darkness fell the first night, the group took shelter in a small lean-to that belonged to a granger. Inside, with a fire to help warm them, Theodore sat with his back to the door, shotgun in hand, keeping an all-night vigil over the prisoners. The following day, Sunday, April 11, the wagon carrying the three prisoners rolled into Dickinson, Theodore walking behind them. "I was most heartily glad when we at last jolted into the long, straggling main street of Dickinson, and I was able to give my unwilling companions into the hands of the sheriff," Theodore stated.[15]

For his efforts as a deputy sheriff, making three arrests and traveling over three hundred odd miles to deliver his prisoners, Theodore received fifty dollars. With his prisoners locked up, Theodore sought medical aid for his feet. Trudging through muddy, cold clay for several days nearly left him with a case of frostbite.

A doctor in the Western lands was as valuable as a good horse or an ample supply of water. When the town had only one doctor, he could be responsible for the care of patients within a range of fifty miles. Smaller towns, such as Medora, had no physician. In such cases, a barber *might* offer some aid for minor problems, including extracting teeth, or even a bullet. In Theodore's situation, he was lucky. The first man he approached on the street in Dickinson happened to be Victor Stickney, the town's doctor. Stickney noticed "the most bedraggled figure I'd ever seen" limping down the street. The man, the physician observed, wore glasses (which "in itself was immoral out in that country"), and his buckskin shirt and pants were covered with sticky gumbo mud.

> *He was all teeth and eyes . . . He was scratched, bruised, and hungry, but gritty and determined as a bulldog . . . As I approached him he stopped me with a gesture, asking me whether I could direct him to a doctor's office. I was struck by the way he bit off his words and showed his teeth. I told him I was the only practicing physician, not only in Dickinson, but in the whole surrounding country.*
>
> *"By George," he said emphatically, "then you're exactly the man I want to see. I've just come 40 miles on foot from the Killdeer Mountains, bringing down some horse thieves at the point of a Winchester, and my feet are blistered so badly that I can hardly walk. I want you to fix me up."*
>
> *I took him to my office, and while I was bathing and bandaging his feet, which were in pretty bad shape, he told me the story of his capture of the three thieves.*[16]

Despite his patient's lack of sleep for thirty-six hours straight, the doctor noted that Theodore "did not seem worn out or unduly tired," and was "pleased as punch" about the adventures he had experienced. "He was just like a boy," Stickney said. The doctor later told his wife over lunch that he had just met "the most peculiar, and at the same time, the most wonderful, man I had ever come to know."[17]

Staying overnight in Dickinson, Theodore appeared the following morning in court for the preliminary hearing before a justice of the peace,

Western Starr, who happened to have been a classmate of Theodore's when they attended New York's Columbia Law School. The justice set a trial date in early August in Mandan. As the afternoon sun began to set, Theodore caught the train for Medora. By the time his train pulled into the station, his capture of the boat thieves had become well-known around the Badlands. While everyone admired his pluck, many shook their heads in amazement that Theodore had wasted his time taking the men to jail, instead of hanging them on the spot.

They did not understand Theodore Roosevelt.

For Theodore, going after the culprits wasn't about revenge; it was about justice. Theodore had no interest in meting out "Western justice" as others did. He had no desire to kill Finnegan, Burnsted, or Pfaffenbach, unless they attempted to escape. Theodore wanted what he believed in—justice. Although he had been willing to join the vigilantes (the Stranglers), given his strict moral code, there is serious doubt over whether he would have allowed anyone to kill a suspected rustler outright. Even if one were caught altering a ranch's brand or stealing stock, Theodore would have insisted that the accused be arrested and have his day in court. He once stated, "The greatest benefit to the people, I am convinced, is the enforcement of the laws, without fear or favor."[18]

Enforcing the law using the fear of vigilantes, as he might have done in this case, was against his beliefs. He could not—would not—allow it then, or in his later years. Going after these thieves was a demonstration, on a small scale, of the type of action he would later take when going after certain trusts, or enforcing laws. With the theft of his boat, Theodore showed he would not be bullied. Anyone who attempted to get away with such action soon learned a hard lesson. His actions also illustrated that people should not mistake him as a "dude from the East." Theodore had proven he could ably handle himself in any circumstances, whether it was on a bucking horse, when capturing thieves, or subduing a drunken cowboy. His pluck in these kind of circumstances manifested itself during his presidency, and beyond.

Theodore traveled to Mandan on August 9, 1885, to testify in his boat theft case. He requested the judge drop the charges against Pfaffenbach, stating that the man "did not have enough sense to do anything good or bad." The German, jumping to his feet, thanked Theodore. Amused by the German's comments, Theodore stated it was the first time he had ever been thanked for calling a man a fool.[19] Finnegan and Burnsted were found guilty, with each receiving a twenty-five-month sentence. Theodore later remarked to Sewall that he didn't "think we [would] have anything more stolen from us."[20]

There's a unique epilogue to this story.

In the fall of 1887, Finnegan wrote to Theodore from his prison cell in Bismarck. He apologized for taking the boat, explaining that his intention was not to steal it, but with the lynching threats, it had been "die dog or eat the hatchet." Finnegan explained that if he'd sought Theodore's help in trying to leave the area, he expected to "look down the mouth of a Winchester . . . When people talk lynch law and threaten a person's life, I think it is about time to leave." Finnegan "supposed" he deserved the punishment, but not the sentence he received. Saying he had been punished enough (he had served seventeen of his twenty-five months), he asked Theodore to speak to the territorial governor about having his remaining sentence commuted. Ending his letter, Finnegan said, "I have read a good many of your sketches on ranch life in the papers since I have been in here, and they interested me deeply." After signing the letter, he added a postscript: "Should you stop over at Bismarck this fall on your western tour, make a call to the prison. I should be glad to meet you."[21]

There is no evidence Theodore replied to Finnegan's letter, visited him, or attempted to get his time commuted. Such an act by Theodore, based on his moral principles and his devotion to enforcing the law, was highly unlikely. He was a strong believer that those who committed the crime should take their medicine. Understanding that Pfaffenbach was incapable of discerning right from wrong due to his mental state, Theodore demonstrated he was capable of rendering mercy when it was truly required.

Despite Finnegan's avowal that he had learned his lesson and would never forget it, he had a short memory. Mike "Redhead" Finnegan's life ultimately ended with a rope around his neck for stealing.[22]

ENTERING THE ARENA

No people were ever yet benefitted by riches if their property corrupted their virtue.

THE NIGHT HE RETURNED TO MEDORA, AFTER TURNING OVER HIS PRIS-oners to the sheriff in Dickinson, Theodore stayed in town, taking his room above the Ferris general store. Writing a letter to his younger sister, Corinne, he briefly mentions the capture of the boat thieves, noting he was "done out" from the lack of sleep and strain, but assured her he was "brown and tough as a pine knot and feel equal to anything." He went on to discuss *Anna Karenina*, which he read "with very great interest . . . I hardly know whether to call it a very bad book or not. . . . Tolstoi [sic] is a great writer. Do you notice how he never comments on the actions of his personages? He relates what they thought or did without any remark whatever as to whether it was good or bad, as Thucydides wrote history."[1]

Concluding his letter, he asked Corinne when Edith would depart for Europe, and for how long. (Theodore already *knew*, but it was part of the charade the couple played to keep their upcoming marriage a secret.) He requested that his sister send Edith some flowers from him on her departure. Three days later he dashed off another letter to Corinne with a sealed card to send with the flowers to Edith. He also requested "three or four cakes of that nice transparent soap . . . I have nothing but castile soap here."[2]

The April 13 meeting of the Little Missouri Stockmen's Association appointed John Goodall, the Marquis's foreman, as captain of the spring roundup. Beginning on May 21, the various outfits would start in Medora and work their way north. In other business matters, Theodore was chosen to serve as the association's delegate at the Montana beef owners meeting that would be held in Miles City. The rough-and-ready town had been born out of a necessity—to sell liquor to soldiers at Fort Keogh. Tiring of his soldiers being drunk, Gen. Nelson Miles barred the fort sutler from selling any alcohol in the spring of 1877. Not one to lose a demanding business, the inventive dispenser of bug juice moved his business two miles east, naming the location Miles City (after the general), while locals called it Milestown. With the influx of cattle ranches and the building of a stop for the Northern Pacific Railroad, the city quickly expanded within the Montana Territory.

Arriving by train on April 18, Theodore, accompanied by Sylvane Ferris, observed that Miles City was a "raw, thriving frontier town." Making their way to the MacQueen House, they were greeted by many cowboys riding "hell bent for leather" down the streets. It was apparent that the saloons, gamblers, and sporting ladies were doing a brisk business. The following morning, promptly at nine-thirty, Fort Keogh's Fifth Infantry band kicked off a parade starting at the MacQueen House. (The band's resounding renditions of military marches were not greatly appreciated by hungover cowboys.) The parade included carriages carrying various officers from the cattlemen's association, followed by a "cavalcade of wild cowboys" and 150 cowmen marching four abreast. Things got interesting when the horses pulling the carriage of the association's president, vice president, and secretary became spooked and ran into the band. "The procession then broke up with a wild charge of cowboys, accompanied with such yells as would strike terror to the heart of the tenderfooted," a Minnesota newspaper commented.[3] Fortunately, the actual meeting was much calmer, where the members focused on two major matters—Texas fever and overgrazing.[4]

Texas fever was a dreaded cattle disease that brought high fevers, enlarged spleens, an engorged liver, and, ultimately, death to many herds. The fever had gained national attention in the 1850s when the first Texas cattle headed north to the Missouri railheads. Although the disease initially sickened only Texas cattle, it soon killed other cattle in the northern ranges. State legislatures quickly passed quarantine laws forbidding the driving or selling of any Texas cattle within their state boundaries.

Doctors Theobald Smith and F. L. Kelborne, both of the US Department of Agriculture, discovered that the disease was caused by a cattle tick. The fever could be controlled by immersing the cattle in an arsenical bath, known as "cattle dipping."[5]

Overgrazing was becoming a serious problem on the northern ranges. The cause was an influx of cattle owners and investors who populated open ranges with more cattle than the land could properly sustain. The Badlands area, as well as eastern Montana, had yet to suffer a severe winter, and many newspapers, including the *Bad Lands Cow Boy*, inaccurately claimed that winters, no matter how harsh, did not adversely affect the herds. Although Theodore and Gregor Lang, among others, asserted that overgrazing was a serious problem, their concerns were ignored by the majority. Lincoln Lang noted that many of the cattlemen, boosted by the previous mild winter, planned to "stock heavily that season."[6]

During the meeting, a heated debate erupted between two cattlemen. As tempers cooled, most attendees thought that the matter was settled, but later in the evening, the disagreement once again flared, and the cowboys for the two outfits showed up, armed and ready. Theodore, fearing a gunfight, quickly jumped into the fray, ordering the two warring men to settle their differences with their fists while he served as referee. The two cattlemen squared off, but the name of the winner of the bout is lost to history.[7]

No sooner had he returned from Miles City than Theodore and Merrifield left for a week's hunting trip. The spring roundup was a month away, and would consume almost two months of his time. Theodore had only completed one chapter of the Thomas Hart Benton book before going after the boat thieves, yet he showed no sense of urgency to complete it. Unlike his *Naval War of 1812*, *Hunting Trips of a Ranchman*, or other volumes he authored on subjects that ignited his passion, it appeared the Benton book was becoming more of a chore than a desire. After his hunting foray, Theodore returned to Elkhorn Ranch and devoted the next three weeks to working on the Benton book, as well as tending to ranch duties. This was the longest amount of time Theodore lived at the ranch, and the three weeks filled him with a joy he never forgot. Spring was in full bloom with wildflowers everywhere, and cottonwood trees provided shade while the wind rustled through their leaves. There was the babbling of the Little Missouri River, and the songs of many birds. All of this provided Theodore with a sense of peace; yet it is very likely he knew deep inside this would soon change for him. Within a year, he and Edith would marry, and she was not the type of woman who would take to frontier living. A visit to the area for a week or two would be enough for Edith, but living in such a place for the rest of her life was impossible. Theodore was at a crossroads. He loved the life of the open range, riding alone, living among those hardy souls that made up the American West. He understood and liked them. He was, at least in some small part, one of them.

However, his interest in ranching appeared to be waning. His period of melancholy was coming to an end. Meeting Edith showed him, despite any guilt pangs he may have suffered, that he could love again. The depression and loneliness he had endured after Alice's death had abated, at least sufficiently for him to realize that his life held more promise for him than just ranching. One must wonder if he was ever completely able to shake off his loss of Alice. He certainly did everything he could to bury, or erase, any thought of her. But inwardly, one has to wonder if it ever truly left him. Theodore was strong enough to suppress anything that bothered him, such as his father's lack of military service. He could force himself to banish these thoughts into oblivion, but certainly there must have been moments when a sliver of memory, of places visited, dinners shared, and, of course, his daughter, reminded him, albeit briefly, of his deceased wife.

Like the weather that would soon change things in the Badlands, Theodore was ready for a change. A great, unseen movement of events would take hold and push him into another direction. Theodore Roosevelt likely did not realize, sitting in his rocking chair on the porch of his cabin that spring, that his destiny, and that of the country, were on the brink of a new direction.

❧

"If I was not afraid of being put down as cold blooded I should say that, though I honestly miss greatly and all the time think longingly of all you dear ones, yet I really enjoy this life," Theodore wrote Corinne on May 12. He went on to say that he spent three or four days "reading and working at various pieces I have now on hand. They may come to nothing whatever; but on the other hand they may succeed; at any rate I am doing some honest work, whatever the result is."Theodore was amused when he occasionally heard that he harbored a "secret and biting regret" relating to his political career. He admitted to Corinne that when he was alone, he hardly gave it "two thoughts," as he was much more "wrapped up in hunting, ranching, and bookmaking as I ever was in politics."[8]

In some of his letters during this period, it is hard to tell whether Theodore's remarks relating to his ranch life were meant to reassure his siblings, or himself. Even though his ranches kept him busy, the pull of politics was never far from his mind. It was always brought up in conversations when he visited Gregor Lang or A. T. Packard's newspaper office. Although he may have been trying to reassure his sisters, and even his friend, Henry Cabot Lodge, of his disinclination to become involved again, it is doubtful that any of them really believed he was finished with the political arena. Politics was too tempting for a man of Theodore's ego and desire. He was a warrior at heart, and politics, unlike a war, was a fight that never ended. The constant battle to see wrongs righted appealed to his sense of justice and fair play. Being a rancher or a natural scientist, as much as those roles interested him, did not provide sufficient action or excitement. The thrill of the fight, much like the thrill of the chase in hunting, fed his soul. He disliked bullies; this sentiment dated back to the two boys who had made his life miserable at Moosehead Lake in Maine. His dislike of anyone who took advantage of others was never far from the surface, and as with his encounter with the drunken cowboy in Mingusville, Theodore demonstrated that he could handle bullies. In confrontations with them in the political field, he was less apt to use his fists, but his mind and wit were just as effective.

Whether or not Theodore cared to admit it, politics was in his blood. It was, for him, the bugler blowing "Charge!" in the field. Politics allowed him to be a hero, to do what he honestly felt was right for the good of the country. Whatever office he occupied, Theodore wasn't worried by the demands of the "party machine." To him, they were the source of the problem. However, being a good politician, he knew there were certain times one had to play along with the party machine in order to obtain backing for a bill, or, at the very least, get into office. After that, all bets were off when it came to Theodore's supporting the party machine desires.

A few days prior to the spring roundup, Theodore was busy writing letters, even chipping away at the Benton biography. In a letter to Bamie, he asked if she could help the Sewall's daughter, Kitty. "The poor little mite of a Sewall girl, just Baby Lee's age, has neither playmates nor play toys. I don't appreciate it as a table companion, especially when fed on, or rather feeding itself on, a mixture of syrup and strawberry jam (giving it the look of a dirty little yellow-haired gnome in war paint); but I wish the poor forlorn little morsel had some play toys . . . send me a box with the following toys, all stout and cheap: a big colored ball, some picture blocks, some letter blocks, a little horse and wagon and a rag doll," he requested. Revealing a bit of his blue-blooded upbringing, Theodore notes that if she came to visit next summer, he dreaded "seeing you at table, for we have no social distinctions, and the cowboys sit down in their shirt sleeves."[9]

One of the last letters he wrote before leaving for the roundup was to Henry Cabot Lodge. "I have got the Benton about half through," he noted. "If I could work at it without interruption for a fortnight I could send Morse the manuscript; but tomorrow I leave for the round up, and henceforth I will have to snatch a day or two whenever I can, until the end of June. I have really become interested in it; but I cannot tell whether what I have done is worth anything or not."[10]

The roundup began on May 22, just south of Medora. Like the previous spring event, it was hard, dusty work, although it appears it was free of any stampedes. Being close to Medora provided Theodore the opportunity to ride into town and sleep in his room at Ferris's general store. On one occasion, Theodore dined with the Marquis at his chateau, where he had cherries ("the only fruit I [have] had since I left New York"). When dinner was over, the Marquis gave him a French copy of *War and Peace*, which Theodore finished in two weeks.

As busy as he was with the roundup, the Benton book was not far from his mind. This was obvious in a letter he sent to Lodge, giving him a progress update and asking for assistance. Noting he had little information relating to Benton after he left the Senate in 1850, Theodore asked his friend if he could hire someone "to look up, in a biographical dictionary, or elsewhere, his life after he left the Senate in 1850? . . . the Bad Lands have much fewer books than Boston has."[11]

The roundup worked down South Hart Creek on June 20, through to Rocky Ridge and Davis and Andrews Creeks, ending at Bullion Creek on June 26.[12] (These creeks are all located south of Maltese Cross Ranch.) When the roundup was completed, Theodore returned to work on the Benton book, which by now seemed to have ignited some of his creative flow. Between June 29 and July 2, he awoke every morning just as the sun was breaking over the hills in the east at the Elkhorn. Theodore drank in the visual and aural beauty as the sun rose, a soft breeze stirring the cottonwood leaves as the birds sang their songs. Inspired by what he saw, Theodore would go to his sitting room and write until noon, when the cabin became too stuffy for any type of constructive writing. From there, he would go off hunting or do some physical ranch chores, including breaking horses. Sewall said some days Theodore would simply stay in his room and write all day long. Merrifield recalled, "He used to walk up and down this room, then sit down awhile, then jump up and grab a gun and go out hunting. Then he would come back in again and start to write . . . and would work sometimes until early in the morning."[13]

After arriving in England, Theodore received letters from Edith. However, after his death, for reasons known only to her, she destroyed the majority of their correspondence. However, a letter dated June 8, 1886, survives. It allows an insight into their relationship at the time, when both tightly held it from anyone's eyes. The letter illustrates a tender love that had manifested since their childhood.

Indeed, my dearest Mr. T. R., I think imagination is one of the greatest blessings of life, and while one can lose oneself in a book one can never be thoroughly unhappy. I don't for a moment defend the morale of the Arabian Nights. Indeed I rarely open them now, and most of the heroes and heroines never seem more than glittering phantoms hung with gold and jewels; but it is the whole atmosphere of the book which is so fascinating and somehow Kubla Khan and Aldrich's little lyric "When the sultan goes Ispahan," give me the same feeling. I have always had a passion for fairy tales . . . I cannot explain very coherently on paper, but some very hot day, I will pull my tattered old copy of Arabian Nights from the bottom of the box where it now reposes

*and show you what I mean . . . London is perfectly lovely now, every-
thing is so bright and gay. Last night we heard your cousin Mr. Scov-
ell, poor Marcia Roosevelt's husband, sing in Carmen. He is middle
aged, ugly, and uninteresting with not enough voice to redeem his bad
acting. His one idea of making love is to seize the prima donna's arm
and shake her, violently. I am so glad that is not your way . . . You may
not believe it, but I never use[d] to think much about my looks . . . now
I do care about being pretty for you . . .*

*You know I love you very much and would do anything in the
world to please you. I wish I could be sure my letters sound as much
like myself as yours do like you . . . You know all about me, darling. I
never could have loved anyone else. I love you with all the passion of a
girl who has never loved before, and please be patient with me when I
cannot put my heart on paper . . . Please send me your photo in hunting
costume. Not that there is any danger of my forgetting you, but I want
to show it to Emily [Edith's younger sister].*

*I am more glad than I can say that you have been enjoying the
western life and do hope the cattle will turn out well, but be good and
patient and do not worry too much; please take your hunting trip, for
I am quite sure it will pay for itself. You must take me out west, or I
shall repent all my life, not having seen the place my dearest is so fond
of . . . I perfectly love your description of life out west, for I almost feel
as if I could see you and know just what you are doing, and I do not
think you sentimental in the least to love nature; please love me too,
and believe I think of you all the time and want so much to see you.[14]*

—

During the roundup, Theodore received an invitation from Dr. Stickney
to be the featured speaker at Dickinson's July Fourth celebration. At first
Theodore was hesitant, but after reconsidering the offer, he accepted. The
Dickinson Press proudly announced the festivities on June 26:

GRAND 4TH OF JULY CELEBRATION!
Parade of Lady Equestrians
G. A. R. Veterans
Oration by
HON. THEO. ROOSEVELT![15]

Theodore rode his horse, Manitou, from the Elkhorn to Medora on July 3, staying with Joe Ferris overnight. The following morning, he and other Medora residents caught the eastbound freight train to Dickinson. At ten o'clock in the morning, the Silver Cornet Band led the parade, followed by two floats. The first one offered an interpretation of Lady Liberty, while the second featured thirty-eight schoolgirls all dressed in white, representing the states in the Union. A phalanx of carriages and horses carrying the many townspeople followed, and viewers were so overtaken, they joined the procession, leaving only a few drunken cowboys to watch.[16]

It was a hot day in Dickinson, with the temperature well over 110 degrees. Yet it did nothing to stop the public's desire to celebrate; many attended a noon luncheon at the town hall. After the meal, justice of the peace Western Starr read the Declaration of Independence, followed by the band playing anthems, while a local choir sang "My Country, 'Tis of Thee." Dr. Stickney stood on a soapbox and introduced the featured speaker. Taking his place on the box, Theodore looked over the crowd and began his speech.[17]

We are now doing in the Northwest exactly as our forefathers did in the East when that famous Declaration of Independence was declared by those great men of America—building up free homes for ourselves and families, but under different circumstances. Here we have a grand country, a territory that will make one of the grandest states in the Union. The hardships of the pioneer life in Dakota are not what they were in 1776 . . .

The Declaration of Independence derived its peculiar importance not on account of what America was, but because of what she was to become. She shared with other nations the present, and she yielded to the past; but it was felt in return that to her, and to her especially, belonged the future. It is the same with us here. We—grangers and cowboys alike—have opened a new land; we are the pioneers, and as we shape the course of the stream near its head, our efforts have infinitely more effect in bending it in any given direction than they would have if they were made farther along. In other words, the first comers in a land can, by their individual efforts, do far more to channel out the course in which its history is to run than can those who come after them . . .

Like all Americans, I like big things; big prairies, big forests and mountains, big wheat fields, railroads—and herds of cattle too; big factories, steamboats and everything else. But we must keep steadily in mind that no people were ever yet benefitted by riches if their property corrupted their virtue. It is of more importance that we should show ourselves honest, brave, truthful and intelligent than that we should own all the railways and grain elevators in the world . . .

All American citizens, whether born here or elsewhere, whether of one creed or another, stand on the same footing. We welcome every honest immigrant, no matter from what country he comes, provided only that he leaves behind him his former nationality and remain neither Celt nor Saxon, neither Frenchman or German, but become an American desirous of fulfilling in good faith the duties of American citizenship . . . We must never exercise our rights either wickedly or thoughtlessly . . . I am myself at heart as much a westerner as an easterner; I am proud indeed to be considered one of yourselves, and I address you in this rather solemn strain today only because of my pride in you, and because your welfare, moral as well as material, is so near my heart.[18]

As Theodore sat down, the audience applauded and vocally lauded him before rushing off to watch the horse races between the cowboys and the Indians. It was noted that his voice was "between a squeak and a shriek."[19]

Theodore had delivered his first major speech, which was carried by several newspapers. His discourse highlighted many subjects that he would return to time and again during his political life: extolling the duties and responsibilities of being a good American citizen; cautioning that corruption would lead to the downfall of the country; and exhorting his fellow citizens to not be consumed with benefiting from riches while corrupting their goodwill and moral excellence.

Theodore Roosevelt had entered the arena.

As fireworks illuminated the evening sky over Dickinson, the train made its way to Medora. Theodore sat with A. T. Packard of the *Bad Lands Cow Boy*, discussing the day's events. Packard, impressed by his speech, listened as Theodore said he felt his future and best work was not in raising cattle, but to be involved "in a public and political way."

"Then you will become president of the United States," Packard replied.

Theodore showed no surprise in his friend's assessment.

"If your prophecy comes true, I will do my part to make a good one," he replied.[20]

DARK CLOUDS

Sooner or later there comes a winter which means ruin to the ranches that have too many cattle on them.

SUMMER TEMPERATURES IN THE BADLANDS GENERALLY RANGE BETWEEN the high 80s to low 90s. It is a dry heat, often mixed with seasonal rains that cool everything for a brief time. The hot weather turns the green grass to brown by mid-July, yet still provides adequate feed for the cattle.

The summer of 1886 was different.

During the first two weeks of July, the temperature reached 114 degrees in the open and 102 in the shade. The Little Missouri River, usually no more than two to three feet deep, was completely dry in sections. Creeks that fed into the river were barren, and the grass that the cattle relied on became parched and brittle. Summer rains were a distant memory.

Ranchers began to worry that if a hard winter were to follow this extreme heat, it could lead to serious trouble. Many began a frantic search for supplies of hay, only to be told there was little, if any, to obtain. Cattlemen as far away as Texas and Kansas saw their land dry up. Driving their herds north in hopes of finding green grass, they were greeted with only disappointment. Theodore and Gregor Lang had voiced concerns about the possible results of overgrazing, and unfortunately, they were now coming to fruition.

Historically, beaver in the area built dams in various creeks which provided a yearly supply of water for the roaming cattle. By the summer of 1886, however, the majority of the beaver in the Badlands had been hunted out, and with their destruction, the dams disappeared. With no dammed water to drink from, the cattle were forced to roam farther to find water. In doing so, herds moved in a long, stretched-out fashion, as they did in cattle drives, trampling the grass and creating their own trails, leaving a thin line of erosion on the ground. As Lincoln Lang noted, "The White Man had undertaken to reverse Nature's plans and already she was coming back at him in no uncertain manner."[1]

The few water holes that did exist quickly became trampled, turning them into mud holes before vanishing into the dry earth. Weeds, not indigenous, and poisonous, began to sprout across the landscape. The sun was diffused by a curtain of haze. As the summer wore on, ranchers began to panic, sending their beef to market early in hopes of making a profit. Instead, their actions flooded the market, and drove the price down.

Summer eventually made way for the fall. The change of seasons was filled with hope for better times.

Despite the extreme summer, Theodore felt that his cattle were doing reasonably well, and he remained upbeat about cattle ranching. Although he had planned to spend the summer at the Elkhorn, three days after returning from Dickinson, he hopped a train for New York City.

Part of his decision to head east had to do with his Benton book. With his manuscript almost completed, Theodore needed to do further research at the Astor Library before sending his final draft to the publisher. Another reason for traveling to New York was political. He was offered the position of president of the board of health by the city's mayor. Writing to Corinne, he related that Henry Cabot Lodge was "strongly against" his accepting the job, feeling that it was beneath Theodore's status. He confided that if he did accept the post, he'd have to give up his life in the West, noting it would "fairly break my heart."[2] Although this emotional comment could be attributed to his consideration of the job offer, it was more likely a reflection that, once he was married to Edith, his time in the Dakotas would either be sharply limited or come to an end. As for the job offer, it amounted to nothing, since the current president of the board of health, who had been indicted for corruption, refused to resign.

Theodore's time in New York was brief—just three weeks. He spent days at the Astor Library, reviewing material for the Benton book, as well as spending time with Baby Lee. As he traveled back to Medora, Theodore focused on a hunting trip in the Rocky Mountains. Returning to the Elkhorn, he found a letter from Edith that confirmed their plan to marry in London in December. Meanwhile, the ranch had two new guests, courtesy of Mrs. Sewall and Mrs. Dow, as both ladies had given birth to boys within a week of each other. "The population of my ranch is increasing in a rather alarming manner," he noted to Bamie.[3] Despite the distractions of Edith's letter and the newborns, Theodore's mind was on his upcoming hunting trip, until news broke of a potential war with Mexico.

US Army captain Emmet Crawford and a group of nearly one hundred Apache scouts, including the Apache Kid and Tom Horn, had entered Mexico in December 1885 in hopes of capturing Geronimo and his band. On January 11, 1886, Crawford's group was attacked by the Mexican military and despite Crawford's waving a white flag from a rock, the Mexican army continued its barrage. (Crawford was killed when a bullet struck him in the head.) After an hour of fighting, the Mexicans waved a white flag, and the shooting ceased. Many in Washington, DC, including the US Army, were livid over the young officer's death, caused by the Mexican military's deliberate attack. Tensions began to rise, with calls for a war against Mexico.

As the rumor of a potential war on the horizon grew, Theodore was eager to join in. He wrote to Lodge asking if he had heard anything more in Washington regarding military action. "Will you telegraph me at once if war becomes inevitable?" he pleaded. "Out here things are so much behind hand that I might not hear the news for a week." He also wrote to Secretary of War William Endicott with the offer of raising a group of mounted riflemen from the West. "I think there is some good harum-scarum rough riders out here," he told Lodge. Hopeful as he was for an opportunity, Theodore soon realized that any chance of being involved in military action grew "continually smaller," yet he would continue to "grasp at every opportunity that turns up."[4]

Military action was one way of achieving something worthwhile. His desire to be part of something productive paints the picture of a young man still uncertain about his future. As he neared his twenty-eighth birthday,

Theodore was already a published author of two books and several magazine articles, as well as having served three terms in the New York legislature. Despite these accomplishments, he felt his future would not likely present any worthy challenges. Perhaps this was a moment of self-pity on his part, something he rarely, if ever, allowed. It could be that, with his upcoming marriage to Edith, and having no stable form of employment, he was feeling useless. A job that had been offered to him—no matter how seriously he may have thought of accepting it—quickly disappeared. Ranching was enjoyable for him, yet whatever challenges it had held seem to have been met. Nor had this venture established a healthy recurring profit for him. A life as an author was, like other professions in the arts, fraught with instability. Politics, although he strongly felt it to be a closed door, was still a possibility. Theodore Roosevelt was at another crossroads, with no conviction as to which direction he should take. Even if he wouldn't readily admit it to himself, the uncertainty scared him.

One day in Medora, he visited a local taxidermist with the head of a mountain goat. Of all the animals he had hunted in the West, the mountain goat had eluded him. Theodore learned that Jack Willis, a hunter in Montana, had shot that goat. Writing to Willis, he asked, "I have heard it is the hardest animal in the Rockies to find and the most difficult to kill. I have also heard that you are a great hunter. If I come to Montana, will you act as my guide, and do you think I can kill a white goat?"[5]

Willis's first impression was that it was a joke, and he intended to ignore it, but Theodore's penmanship was so bad, it irritated him "to have to wrestle with his almost illegible note." His reply was to the point. "If you can't shoot any better than you can write, NO!" A very independent man, Willis had lived in Thompson Falls in the Montana Territory since 1882, where he hunted and sold animal skins in large quantities. He also made money by furnishing the railroad with venison and bear meat for their dining cars. Like many others in true Western towns, he regarded Medora as something of a "joke town." "It was a lively community," he commented, "while it lasted, but it didn't last much longer than a tenderfoot at a roundup."[6] Typically, Theodore paid no attention to the reply from Willis and sent him a telegram two days before he and Merrifield arrived in Thompson Falls. Curious to see what this fellow looked like, Willis waited at the station.

> *Two men climbed down from the Pullman. One of them had on the corduroy knickers and coat of [a] tenderfoot. I knew he was Roosevelt, and he looked too much like a dude to make any hit with me . . . The only thing about him that appealed to me at all was his eyes. They were keen and bright and dancing with animation. From them I knew he was honest and had a mind that worked fast and smoothly and was set on a hair trigger. But in spite of that I didn't like his looks.*[7]

Merrifield, Willis observed, was "properly garbed" in buckskins. Theodore shouted to Willis, "I'm here!' and shook his hand as if he were working a water pump. Anxious to get started, Willis quickly threw cold water on Theodore's plans. He informed him that he didn't work for anyone on a salary, adding, "I go where I like and when I like and do as I damned well please." Theodore managed to convince Willis to come to his hotel room and talk further. In his room, he gave Willis a Sharps rifle as a gift, which the hunter promptly handed back to him. Willis admitted, however, as did others who were at first put off by Theodore's enthusiasm, that the more the man talked to him, the better he liked him. "There was something of the savor of the West in his manner and his frankness, and, so long as I could keep my eyes away from his foolish pants, I cottoned to the things he said and the way he said them," Willis recalled.[8]

Willis struck a deal with Theodore and Merrifield where they could accompany him as guests on a hunt he had already planned in two days. He refused to let Theodore pay for supplies, saying the two men "might get sore and walk off and leave me afoot." Happy with the arrangements, Theodore was raring to go.

Hunting mountain goats is a tough task for even an experienced hunter. The animals, which are sure-footed climbers, are generally found in the higher altitudes, usually along rocky cliffs and mountainous areas that are heavily iced. Their black, sleek horns contrast with their thick white wool coats, which allow them to withstand temperatures of minus-40 degrees and winds of one hundred miles per hour. Because mountain goats primarily stay above the timber line, hunters have to track them on foot, which means scaling the sheer cliffs and the rocky shale that covers them. It is dangerous, hard climbing—especially for a man like Theodore, who had no experience with such locations. Willis, who expected the dude to slow him down, admired Theodore's gameness in keeping up with him, while pausing only occasionally to acclimate himself to the altitude or to wipe the sweat from his glasses.

Their first day out, they located a salt lick, which was something that would attract the mountain goats. Willis positioned them above the salt lick, noting that a goat always runs uphill when attacked. Within thirty minutes, a large male, called a "billy," came to the salt lick.

The animal was less than two hundred yards away. Theodore took aim and fired.

He missed.

As the goat ran off, Theodore fired off another shot, and Willis saw a bit of the animal's wool coat fly off around the foreleg. Certain that Theodore had wounded the animal, they followed the blood trail over the rocks until late in the afternoon. Then the two men hiked the nine miles back to camp.

That night, Theodore complained not of his blistered feet but of his poor marksmanship on such an easy shot. The next morning, leaving Merrifield in camp to nurse his own blistered feet, Theodore and Willis went back and scouted the previous day's trail in hopes of finding the mountain goat. At daylight, Willis spotted a mountain goat on a butte, at least a quarter-mile away. Pointing out the target to Theodore, they both realized that it was the goat he had wounded the previous day. Placing his Winchester against his shoulder, Theodore sighted down on the target. Willis told him he was wasting ammunition, not only because of the distance, but also because a strong wind was blowing.

It was, Willis said, an "impossible shot." Theodore decided he'd give it a try.

His shot hit the goat through the heart, dropping him instantly.

As he had done before, Theodore jumped and hollered. "The yell of delight he let loose could have been heard for two miles in any country," Willis said. Theodore pressed a hundred-dollar bill into Willis's hand, but the hunter refused it. It turned out that the goat was indeed the same one he had wounded the previous day. Theodore had Willis hike back to camp to get his portable camera and asked him to bring Merrifield along, sore feet and all, to record the event. While Theodore was full of joy over his new trophy, poor Merrifield offered a lackluster smile through gritted teeth to conceal his pain.[9]

The following day, Theodore and Willis were once again hiking through the highlands on the trail of another goat. Crossing along a narrow ledge of slate rock, with a high cliff on one side and a very sheer drop on the other, Theodore's smooth, soft-soled shoes slipped on the loose shale, and he fell off the ledge. Willis wasn't close enough to grab him, but saw Theodore fall headfirst, still holding his rifle. "When I saw him fall I wouldn't have given two-bits for his life," Willis wrote, adding that the fall was at least sixty feet, the bottom covered with jagged rocks. Fortunately for Theodore, he struck the top of a pine tree, which cushioned his fall. He continued downward through several branches before coming to rest on a thick bunch of moss, rifle in hand. Assuring Willis that he wasn't hurt, he asked for a moment to locate his glasses before climbing back up the hill to continue his hunt.[10]

During the time he spent with Willis, Theodore continually preached to the man that his hunting skins for profit was not sportsmanship but wholesale murder. Willis, who enjoyed Theodore's company, chose not to argue the issue. Theodore continued his proselytizing, and finally, either his words, his magnetic personality—or both—convinced Willis that killing game for the skins was wrong.

> Up to the time I met him I had been killing game for years, by the thousands and tens of thousands . . . And until Roosevelt began telling me about the error of my ways it had never occurred to me that there was anything at all wrong about it. Others were doing it, though perhaps not so successfully, so why shouldn't I? And game of all kinds was so plentiful that it didn't seem possible there could ever be anything approaching extinction of it . . . It took Roosevelt to set me thinking along new lines, in that as well as in some other directions.[11]

In later years, Theodore took delight in saying how he made Willis "a Christian" in turning from his hunting ways, while Willis would jokingly say that he had made a man out of Theodore. His sermons to Willis did change the hunter's life. He gave up hunting skins for profit, eventually opening one of the largest department stores in northern Montana.

With their hunting expedition completed, Willis waited at the Thompson Falls train station with Theodore and Merrifield. As they boarded the train, Theodore handed Willis a roll of bills with a rubber band around it. Willis had told his new friend that $150 would cover expenses for the hunting trip. Once the train left, Willis discovered the roll contained twelve $100 bills.[12]

Returning to Medora on September 18, Theodore was greeted with a big headache. All the careful planning and subterfuge that he and Edith had undertaken to mask their romance and engagement was now for naught. The *New York Times* reported that Theodore and Edith were engaged, which brought an instant reply from Bamie that the newspaper was incorrect. Who the newspaper's source was for the story remains unknown. Edith eventually told her mother and sister when they were in London, with the promise to keep it confidential. No one in Theodore's family knew of the engagement, let alone suspected a romance between them.

Theodore now had the unpleasant task of admitting to Bamie that it was all true.

> *On returning from the mountains I was savagely irritated by seeing in the papers the statement that I was engaged to Edith Carow . . . But the statement itself is true . . . You are the first person to whom I have breathed one word on the subject . . . On returning to Medora I received letters giving definite shape to my [wedding] plans; I did not write you at once, because a letter is such a miserably poor substitute for talking face to face . . .*
>
> *I utterly disbelieve in and disapprove of second marriages; I have always considered that they argued weakness in a man's character. You could not reproach me one half as bitterly for my inconstancy and unfaithfulness, as I reproach myself . . . But I do very earnestly ask you*

not to visit my sins upon poor little Edith. It is certainly not her fault;
the entire blame rests on my shoulders. Eight years ago she and I had
very intimate relations; one day there came a break, for we both of us
had, and I suppose have, tempers that were far from being of the best.
To no soul now living have either of us ever since spoken a word of
this.[13]

He also assured Bamie that she could keep Baby Lee and that he would pay the expenses. Theodore stated he would write Elliott and Corinne, as well as his aunt Anna and uncle James, but asked her to say nothing to anyone else. Interestingly, unlike his other letters to his sister, which he signed as "Thee," on this one he signed his full name.

There is no doubt that, while writing this letter, Theodore was filled with guilt and shame, leaving him feeling like a coward. As much as he loved Edith, he was overwhelmed with bouts of guilt because he was being unfaithful to his deceased wife's memory. (There is no published record of what Alice's parents thought of his remarrying.) Staying at a friend's home in Mandan, or at the room in Joe Ferris's general store, he was often heard pacing and repeating that he was not steadfast. It was a difficult time for him, now made worse by his having to confess to family members that he had hidden the truth from them.

Theodore was also forced to make serious decisions regarding his cattle business. The predictions and beliefs that Bill Sewall had harbored were, sadly, coming true. While Theodore was in the Rocky Mountains, Wilmot Dow went to Chicago to sell some of the Elkhorn cattle. With other ranchers flooding the beef market, the going price in Chicago was now ten dollars less than it would have cost to raise and transport the cattle. "It looked like we were throwing away Roosevelt's money, and I didn't like it," Sewall said.[14]

The three men met to look at the figures. It was obvious to Theodore that Sewall and Dow were not terribly happy in the Dakotas and longed to return to the Maine woods. He agreed to release them from their contract, asking how long it would take them to pack and leave. Sewall told him ten days.[15] Theodore would leave the Elkhorn a day before his Maine friends departed, turning over management of the Elkhorn to Merrifield and Ferris. The evening before he left, Theodore took a long walk around the ranch property with Sewall. He told his friend that he was thinking of going back into politics, and asked his opinion. Sewall told him he should do it because good men like him were needed in the political arena, adding that he would likely become president. Theodore laughed off the comment, claiming that such an idea was "a long ways ahead."

"He never cared about making money and didn't go to Dakota for the money he expected to make there," Sewall later stated. "He came because he liked the country and he liked the people and he liked the wild, adventurous life. The financial side of the ranch was a side issue with him."[16]

Theodore stopped in Mandan for a few days, visiting with some friends before returning to New York. If he were debating with himself about reentering politics, he did not have to wait long before making a decision. On the afternoon of October 15, Theodore was visited by a number of leading Republicans who asked him to run for mayor of New York. Entering what would become a three-man race, with a slim chance of winning, Theodore accepted as a loyal party member. "It is of course a perfectly hopeless contest, the chance for success being so very small that it may be left out of account," he informed Lodge.[17] He was running against Henry George, who was on an independent Labor Party ticket, while the Democrats sponsored Abram Hewitt, a former congressman. Henry George worried Democrats and Republicans alike because he was a strong believer in the theory that it took many poor men to make one man rich. While the Republicans originally gave serious thought to supporting Hewitt, they finally chose to have their own candidate in the race.

No seats were available in the Cooper Union building the night of October 27, 1886, when New York Republicans gathered to ratify Theodore Roosevelt's nomination for mayor. (It was also his twenty-eighth birthday.) As a student of history, Theodore could not help but be moved that the ratification vote was held in the same building where Abraham Lincoln gave a speech in 1860 that many say led to his presidential nomination. Chairman Thomas C. Acton introduced Theodore as "The Cowboy of Dakota."

While the phrase to describe him would change over the years, eventually becoming "The Cowboy President," the reference to him as a cowboy would forever be part of Theodore's life. The image of a hard-riding, no-nonsense cowboy in politics was born. It was an epithet, based on real-life experiences that Theodore heartily embraced. The cowboy was indeed part of his being. Even though cartoonists and reporters would enhance his Western pedigree, embellishing some incidents as the years went on, the foundation was solid and true. He had lived the life, eaten trail dust, ridden in stampedes, crossed paths with Indians, and dealt with outlaws. No one could ever take that away from Theodore, or dismiss what the life had done for him. In his heart, he considered himself a Westerner.

Despite the appellation, and his active campaigning, when it came to counting the votes, Hewitt won the contest, with Theodore coming in third.[18] Four days after the election, November 6, Theodore and Bamie quietly boarded the liner *Etruria*, early in the morning to avoid any reporters, under the name of Mr. and Mrs. Merrifield. Arriving seven days later in Liverpool, Theodore took a train to London while Bamie visited their mother's relatives in the port town. Prior to the wedding, Theodore spent time traveling around London and the countryside, visiting with Edith and sharing a lunch with George Bernard Shaw. The wedding was held at St. George's Church in Hanover Square on December 2. The day was christened with an impervious fog that blanketed not only London but also the inside of the church. Bamie would not have made out her brother at the altar if it had not been for the bright orange gloves that his best man, Cecil Arthur Spring Rice, had provided him.[19]

The couple honeymooned in Europe until March. It was a long, not to mention expensive, trip for a man who had no real job waiting for him. In a January 3, 1887, letter to Bamie, Theodore expresses his concerns over finances, noting that he and Edith have seriously discussed closing up Sagamore Hill and moving out to his ranch for a year or two. He had instructed Corinne's husband, Douglas, to sell his favorite horse, Sagamore, with great reluctance. (He later rescinded this decision.) "I *must* live well within my income and begin paying off my debt this year, at no matter what cost, even to the shutting up or renting of Sagamore Hill, bitterly as I should hate such an alternative," he wrote.[20]

◆

One old-timer in the Badlands noted that "Nature was fixin' up her folks for hard times."[21]

The fall season offered warnings to those who could read the signs. The hot weather continued. A continuous haze in the October sky was not residual smoke from summer grass fires, as some folks claimed, but an indication of moisture in high suspension. Lincoln Lang noted that there were frequent "sun and moon dogs together with halos and an uncanny stillness prevailing over all."[22] Muskrats along the river were building their houses twice the customary height and the walls double thick. Geese and ducks, which normally headed south in October, left a month earlier. The few remaining beavers in the area were storing up twice the amount of willow brush, their primary food source. Deer, pronghorns, horses, and cattle all had exceptionally long winter coats.

Then came the arctic owls.

Legend held that sightings of arctic owls indicated a harsh winter.

WISHING FOR A CHINOOK

It is hard to fail, but it is worse never to have tried to succeed.

It began on the afternoon of November 13, 1886.

No one paid much attention at first to the soft snowfall because it was not terribly unusual for the area. As the night wore on, however, the temperature dropped, and a fierce wind began to blow. The worst blizzard ever to strike the Badlands had begun. No one expected it. No one was prepared for it.

During the night, the temperature sank to 40 degrees below zero. Ice formed everywhere and on anything—including cattle. Cabins that had any kind of an opening in the walls, however small, were hit with the chilly blast of air. Anyone daring, or foolish, enough to venture outside was hit in the face with ice-dust particles that were said to be sharp as glass. The freezing air would burn a man's lungs and face within seconds. The few who tried to travel in this numbing cold quickly lost any sense of direction, leaving them to wander aimlessly until they froze to death.

The following morning, things did not get any better.

Drifts were averaging six to eight feet deep, with the snow continuing to fall. Visibility was limited to a few yards at best. On opening their cabin door, the inhabitants were greeted by a solid block of snow several inches thick.[1] As evening set in, the snow and the temperature both dropped, bringing equal misery. For the rest of the month, the snow fell, temperatures dropped, and the wind blew powdery, white destruction over the land. Some cattle, unlike buffalo or horses, which had better sense, stood facing the wind. The blowing snow was so fine that it plugged up the nostrils and throats of the animals until they were asphyxiated.[2]

Many of the cattle did their best to find forage. They would scrape the ground with their noses, often leaving their flesh bloodied and raw, only to freeze over. Unfortunately, there wasn't much grass to be found. What little there had been in the summer had been consumed, and with no summer rains to replenish the grass, very little remained to feed what was estimated to be more than two hundred thousand head of beef.

The cruelest of ironies came in early December.

An Indian summer, accompanied by a warm chinook breeze, swept over the land. In one day, the temperature rose to 50 degrees. The snow began to melt down to about six inches before Nature changed its mind. The evening temperatures dropped once again to subzero, quickly turning the mushy snow into a hardened crust of ice. The Little Missouri River glazed into a sheet of thick ice, providing wolves and coyotes a roadway to find prey—and there was plenty.

As December wore on, the snow continued to fall, and the cold hung on like a tenderfoot on a bucking horse. Christmas Day the temperature stood at minus-35 degrees; seven days later, January 1, 1887, it hovered at 41 below zero.[3] January offered no relief for man or beast. The wind blew the powder snow, filling in coulees and cuts. Cattle that had sought shelter in such places were buried alive, and the snow kept rising. Sage hens died in the drifts; rabbits and prairie dogs were smothered in their holes. Many coulees and gulches were filled in with snow that rose to one hundred feet. With the snow layering over itself, cattle nibbled on bark from tree branches that normally would be several feet off the ground. Conditions became so bad that some of the cattle began stripping off tar paper from cabins for some form of nutrition. Some cattle's hooves froze in the ice, leaving the animal stranded, awaiting a miserable death.[4]

The animals tried to find shelter wherever they could. One of the more unfortunate places was in the railroad cuts. In late November, a westbound train smashed into a herd between Belfield and Medora. "The engineer was compelled to keep a continual tooting while passing through these famous grazing lands but the blinding storm made it impossible for him to see the cattle until it was too late to stop. It was a wild and cruel night for the cattle of the Bad Lands," the *Bismarck Daily Tribune* reported.[5]

Cattle weren't the only ones to die. Many men attempting to get supplies or check on a small herd found themselves victims of the blizzard, as did a few children, while more than one woman went "off her head." Henry Jackson wrote to his friend Pierre Wibaux, who was out of town, that a cowhand killed another, while "your wife's hired girl blew her brains out in the kitchen."[6]

Nature still wasn't finished spreading her pain.

On January 28, a blizzard that made the previous ones look like a summer rain let loose with a fury. The cattle, too weak to move on the range, simply fell over and waited for death. Stray animals that had sufficient strength made their way into Medora or outlying ranches. They banged their heads against doors or windows in mad acts to escape the cold. Windows and doors were boarded up to prevent the animals from breaking in, but their cries of agony were a haunting reminder of the death that was sweeping the Badlands.[7]

As February gave way to March, Nature's winter whirlwind released its grip. A chinook wind blew through, bringing warm temperatures. The snow and ice began to melt. The Little Missouri River began to break up its ice crust and was soon overflowing its banks to the cottonwoods and some points beyond. The engorged river took down trees standing in its way, ripping and smashing into anything that dared to stop it. It was as if the fierce river itself were angry over the death and desolation winter had wrought and sought to cleanse the land of its misery.

The melting snow from the gullies and cuts fed into creeks, which spilled into the river. In doing so, it revealed a site of horror no one expected. Thousands of dead cattle populated the land, their stiff carcasses bobbing down the angry Little Missouri.[8] Other bodies were found hanging in trees where they had gone to eat bark and twigs, only to die. As temperatures rose, coulees revealed hundreds and hundreds of dead cattle that had been buried in the snowdrifts. This went on for weeks as the losses to the various cattle ranches became a grim reality. Some ranchers had their cowboys gather up the carcasses and set them on fire, while others simply left them where they lay, fodder for the wolves and coyotes.

The heady dreams and days of the Badlands cattle industry had come to an end.

The newlyweds arrived in New York City on March 27.

Reporters were quick to note how happy Theodore looked as he walked off the *Etruria*'s gangplank. Edith, unbeknownst to the press, was in the early stages of pregnancy. Theodore informed the press that he intended to divide his time between writing books and ranching, not politics. This was before he received the letter from Ferris and Merrifield, still tallying the damage in the Badlands, urging him to come out as quickly as possible. During his European travels, Theodore had heard vague reports about the blizzard, but nothing substantial. Anxious now to leave for Medora, he had to wait until April 4 to handle a delicate family issue. As he and Edith settled in at Sagamore Hill, Theodore had to inform Bamie that Edith wanted Baby Lee to live with them. While Bamie accepted Edith's decision as the correct one, it left an unspoken discomfort in the relationship between the two women.[9]

"You were mighty lucky to leave when you did. This spring I should have had to rustle pretty hard to pay your fare back," Theodore wrote Bill Sewall on his way to the ranch. It was indeed fortunate that the Sewalls and Dows left when they did, especially with two young babies who may not have survived that winter. A few months later, Sewall received another letter from Theodore, describing the devastation. "Well, you cannot imagine anything more dreary than the look of the Bad Lands when I went out there. Everything was cropped as bare as bone, the sagebrush had been eaten down until the stems were as thick as my two fingers . . . In almost every coulee there was dead cattle," he noted.[10]

Losses for most ranches were devastating. Lincoln Lang stated that their losses were about 80 percent. Other ranches had losses just as high, or higher, and many investors quickly sold off whatever remained. Sir John Pender, the backer for the Langs, quickly departed. The Langs were left to fend for themselves, which they did. To their surprise, their small herd of horses had survived the winter, and so they began to raise horses, along with the small herd of cattle that remained. By the end of the 1880s, rearing horses would become a new industry within the Badlands.[11]

As for Theodore's losses, there has never been an official accounting. Records for Maltese Cross Ranch show they branded 475 new cattle in

1886, and that only 106 were counted in 1887. One reason Theodore's losses may have been lower than others was partially due to the wooded bottoms of both the Maltese Cross and the Elkhorn, which offered some shelter from the harsh winter. It is surmised that his losses were about 65 percent of his holdings, and his net loss, by 1899, was $20,292.63 (not including lost interest).[12] Even though he didn't suffer as greatly as his fellow ranchers, Theodore was emotionally disappointed. "I am bluer than indigo about the cattle," he wrote Bamie. "It is even worse than I feared; I wish I was sure I would lose no more than half the money ($80,000) I invested out here. I am planning on getting out of it."[13]

Theodore didn't get out of the cattle business right away. He turned the management of the Elkhorn herd over to Merrifield, who moved them to Maltese Cross Ranch. Theodore continued to maintain his small herd, selling stock when he could to lower the loss of his investment. The Little Missouri Stockmen's Association held a meeting on April 16, where they agreed that a spring roundup wasn't worthwhile. Theodore attended the Montana Stockmen's yearly meeting in Miles City three days later, which was an equally bleak affair. Only 100 of the 337 registered members bothered showing up.

Theodore returned to Elkhorn Ranch in November, for a month. It would now serve as a hunting lodge. However, the game he once hunted was now either gone or scarce. The harsh winter had not led to the disappearance of game, but prolific hunting. Riding alone through the Badlands and the prairie, Theodore observed firsthand what unrestricted hunting had done.

He would return every fall to the Elkhorn from 1888 to 1896 to hunt and camp, usually alone, for two to four weeks. (He never came in 1895.) In 1890, Edith and Bamie accompanied him to the ranch for four days in September before taking a side trip to Yellowstone. Returning east, the women stayed for an additional thirteen days at the Elkhorn. It was the only time Edith ever visited the ranch. Theodore made his last trip to the Elkhorn in late August 1896, camping and hunting for twenty days. He never again returned to his cabin. The emptiness of it, and the lack of game, left a void within him. On December 7, 1897, Theodore wrote Sylvane Ferris that he should sell off what remained of his cattle, and asked Pierre Wibaux to purchase his herd. (Wibaux, who had bought out many ranchers who were quick to sell, went on to own one of the biggest cattle ranches in the area for many years.)

"You spoke of bidding on them yourself, but before you do so I want you to be sure you are not undertaking something more than you can handle," he cautioned Sylvane.[14] In the end, Theodore sold the remaining herd to Sylvane.

Theodore Roosevelt's days as a Dakota cowboy and rancher had come to an end.

The blizzard of 1886–87 became known as "The Great Die-Up." The cattle ranchers and their herds were not the only ones to suffer. The blizzard spelled the end of Medora. Even before the massive storm, the small town had been showing signs of decline.

The abattoir run by the Marquis had been destined to fail. Although his plans had sounded promising, even logical, the Marquis underestimated the Chicago beef trust. The Chicago interests were not about to sit by and let some newcomer—especially a foreigner—squeeze them out. They used all their influence and connections to make it as difficult as possible for the Marquis to get ahead, including advertising. Ads depicted scrawny cows that were identified as grass-fed versus a robust cow that was labeled corn-fed.[15] That alone did more damage to the Marquis than anything else. The public, aided by a deceptive visual ad, claimed to prefer the beef that was corn-fed.

By October 1886, the Marquis had left for France. His abattoir would shut down in November for the winter, even though it had little or no business. An article in the *New York Tribune* indicated that there had been "a serious disagreement" between the Marquis and his father-in-law, Louis von Hoffman, over his investments in the beef industry, and von Hoffman had withdrawn his "financial support."[16] With the failure of the cattle business, not to mention the busted Medora–Deadwood stage line, von Hoffmann had had enough of pouring money into losing propositions. It was estimated that between them, the Marquis and his father-in-law had invested over a million dollars, with little to show for it. The chateau remained occupied by staff, who kept it ready for the return of the

Marquis in the spring of 1887. When he did arrive, it was only because he was passing through on a worldwide trip. The Marquis informed reporters that his intentions were to stay in the Dakotas, but it was a lie. He never returned. His abattoir never reopened. The chateau was closed up, with the furniture and other items left in place. John Goodall, the ranch foreman, sold off the remaining stock for the Marquis before moving to Dickinson.

Others joined in the exodus.

E. G. Paddock dismantled his buildings, including the Pyramid Park Hotel, and placed them on a flatcar to relocate in Dickinson. A. T. Packard moved the *Bad Lands Cow Boy* offices down to the cantonments, but he did not stay long. His office burned to the ground on January 12, 1887. It was the end of Medora's newspaper and its editor, who left with his new wife. Joe Ferris remained, running his general store for the few remaining ranchers, including his brother and Bill Merrifield.

The Medora many had known four years earlier was now nothing but a memory.

Only the Badlands remained.

NEW HORIZONS

We cannot do great deeds unless we are willing to do the small things that make up the sum of greatness.

No one knows when Theodore had his moment of epiphany.

It could have been one day during his long rides in the Badlands in November 1887, seeing the territory bereft of the wild game that was once so plentiful. Perhaps it was when he commented that he was sad to see sections of forests chopped down. One thing was certain: His time in the Badlands had impressed upon him that as with other resources on Earth, there was not a never-ending supply of game.

However, he himself never stopped hunting. In Montana, he took home three mountain goat heads and skins. In his defense, he easily could have killed more if he had wanted to, but Theodore was never one to hunt to excess, or for the sheer thrill of killing something, only to leave it behind. True, he did kill animals, taking the hide and head as a trophy for the walls of his home. He also took some of the animal's meat, leaving the rest for the coyotes, wolves, and other scavengers of the wild.

Returning to New York City that December of 1887, Theodore made a decision to do *something*. In typical fashion, he jumped right into action. He formed the Boone and Crockett Club, named after his two frontier heroes, to protect big game and their environment. As his father had done before him, Theodore contacted influential friends to assist. George Bird Grinnell was invited to be a cofounder, using his *Forest and Stream* magazine to help spread the word to the public. By bringing in Grinnell, Theodore displayed the talent he would use throughout his life in various efforts to achieve important goals: seeking valued help from those who were leaders in their respective fields.

The club's membership was limited to one hundred members, and Theodore served as the club's president until 1894. (The club had an associate member field which was limited to fifty.) With Theodore's influence, such notables as artist Albert Bierstadt, generals William T. Sherman and Philip H. Sheridan, author Owen Wister, Henry Cabot Lodge, and Carl Schurz joined, as did many scientists, explorers, and politicians.[1]

One of the first things the club acted upon was to provide much-needed support in protecting the nation's first national park, Yellowstone. Established in 1872, the park was a victim of poachers, souvenir hunters, and miners. The Northern Pacific Railroad was very persistent in its desire to build tracks across the park; others simply wanted to whittle down the acreage. The Boone and Crockett Club quickly set up a committee that opposed such actions, and even encouraged enlargement of the park's boundary. Naturally, Theodore came out swinging, stating that the park should be enlarged and legislation adopted to appoint the military to enforce the laws and punish wrongdoers. Theodore and Grinnell were also very vocal in demanding the protection of the herds of buffalo inside the park from hunters.[2] Passage of the Yellowstone Game Protection Act on May 7, 1894, allowed the government the ability to arrest and prosecute poachers and others in court, as well as allow the US Army to protect the park from timber harvesting and mineral extraction.[3] The club's additional lobbying efforts in Washington proved to be effective with the enactment of the Forest Reserve Act on March 3, 1891, allowing the president to set aside "any public land bearing forests . . . entirely or in part . . . whether of commercial value or not, as public reservations."

Theodore Roosevelt's crusade as a conservationist had just begun.

His plan to write a single book of Western history soon developed into a four-volume opus. In March of 1888, Theodore signed a deal with G. P. Putnam's Sons to author *The Winning of the West*, delivering the first two volumes by the spring of 1889. It is doubtful he realized, as he sat in his library at Sagamore Hill on May 1 and began writing, that his literary task would take seven years to complete. Theodore wasn't as diligent in working on this project as he should have been, due to the siren call of politics. Although he had claimed politics held no future for him, Theodore campaigned for Republican presidential candidate Benjamin Harrison. His loyalty and duty to the party caused him to fall severely behind in his writing, completing only half of the first volume by early October. After the elections, Theodore returned to his desk, finishing the first volume by Christmas. He started on volume two in January 1889, delivering it to Putnam by mid-April. The two volumes, released in June, were highly praised by critics; the first run sold out in one month.[4]

Ranch Life and the Hunting Trail, released in December 1888, was Theodore's second book based on his experiences in the West. He assembled and revised the six articles he had previously penned for *Century* magazine, adding an additional six chapters to the book, which was lavishly illustrated by Frederic Remington. Reviews were very complimentary, with *The Book Buyer* stating, "To a most readable style of writing Mr. Roosevelt adds a thorough familiarity with his subject, happily combining accuracy with entertainment."[5]

In the lore of Western fiction and in movies, a stranger rides into a lawless town and pins on the badge with the intention of bringing law and order. "A new marshal in town" became a common term in such works, eventually growing into an appellation in popular culture that continues to this day. During the next eight years, Theodore became "the new marshal" in two positions in which he did his best to bring law and order. He relished bringing forward new ideas, pitting him against a political party machine and those who benefited from its corruption.

Having actively campaigned for Benjamin Harrison, who won the presidency, Theodore was offered one of three civil service commissioner positions. It was a low-paying job, $3,500 a year, and his old friend Henry Cabot Lodge was certain he would decline it.

Theodore leapt at the opportunity.

During this period in our history, civil service jobs were often handed out as payment for a favor to political allies, friends, and relatives. Those applying for a job needed to pass a written examination that eliminated the less qualified but, in many instances, questions were given in advanced to favored candidates. Positions were bestowed on people who had minimal, if any, experience. Civil service commissioners lacked the ability to fire the incompetent or those caught breaking the law. Their only recourse was to recommend termination to the specific Cabinet officer, who held the power to either fire the person, or ignore the problem. Reforming the civil service was an issue that garnered a lot of verbal support and press, but when it came time for action, things became eerily quiet.

In typical fashion, Theodore jumped into the job with the intention of making a difference. The other two appointed commissioners were not the type of men to lead, let alone ruffle anyone's feathers. This meant that if any reform or change were to happen, it would be up to the young man from New York. Shortly after the new commissioners were sworn in, their attention was called to a case in Indianapolis, which was a prime example of corruption infesting the civil service. Three ex-employees, all corrupt lackeys, had been fired with cause by a postmaster, who happened to be a Democrat. When a new postmaster was installed—a Republican—the three were rehired solely because of their political party affiliation. Theodore went to Indiana, where he forced the three men to resign, and left the postmaster chagrined.[6]

The postmaster general, John Wanamaker, was not pleased with Theodore's action. Wanamaker actively supported the "spoils system," taking advantage of the government to further one's own purposes. To men such as Wanamaker, reform was a dirty word, and a dangerous attitude. Frank Hatton, a former postmaster general, was the current editor of the *Washington Post*, and was actively against any effort to reform the civil service. Using his position, Hatton continually castigated Theodore's reform-minded actions in the press. Ironically, one of Hatton's attacks and deceptive claims led to a congressional hearing into the allegations of abuse and corruption by the civil service commissioners, namely Theodore.

The charges against Theodore related to his securing a job in the Census Bureau for one Hamilton Shindy (known as "Shady Shindy"), despite the man's violation of his oath of office, making false certifications, and not reporting violations of the Civil Service Law.[7] Shindy admitted to approving tests without checking the answers, at the urging of his superior. After Theodore assured him his job would be protected, Shindy agreed to testify against his boss. Once he was finished testifying, Shindy was promptly fired, which angered Theodore. Despite Shindy breaking the law, Theodore felt obligated to uphold his promise. Contacting the Census Bureau, Theodore asked if they could give a position to Shindy. In Theodore's eyes, Shindy had kept his word and testified, and Theodore, who had given *his* word, could not turn his back on the man. That would have been a violation of his code of honor. It was utterly unthinkable to him to do anything else. Even though he believed Shindy was a fool to have broken the law, Theodore, like the people in the West, kept his word. The prosecutor, aided by Hatton, did his best to smear Theodore, but failed. Charges against Theodore were proven false, and he was exonerated.

Despite enforcing the law, and making some small headway in reform, Theodore quickly tired of his civil service commissioner position. Wanamaker and others did everything they could to thwart any major reform Theodore proposed. He was determined to continue in his efforts and would not give his detractors any satisfaction in forcing him out of office. However, a new job offer surfaced on April 17, 1895. Newspapers informed the citizens of New York City that Theodore, at the age of thirty-six, had been appointed as one of four new police department commissioners, taking the seat of president.

Police officers were doubtful that this young man with a wide smile, bristling mustache, and glasses would do much to eliminate corruption in the department. They soon learned otherwise. Theodore quickly instituted changes, including creating bicycle patrols (bicycling had become a new fad in America during this period), and installing telephones in every station house for faster communication. Officers were required to be able to read and write. Theodore created meritorious service medals, and instituted a policy that every officer had to display proficient use of firearms after rigorous training. (It was during this period that the NYPD established one of the first police academies in the United States.)

Theodore's biggest challenge was the department mentality of allowing corruption to taint the officers. "I have the most important, and the most corrupt, department in New York on my hands," he informed Bamie in a letter. "I shall speedily assail some of the ablest, shrewdest men in this city, who will be fighting for their lives, and I know well how hard the task is ahead of me. Yet, in spite of the nervous strain and worry, I am glad I undertook it; for it is a man's work. But I have to stop my fourth volume [of *Winning of the West*] for the time."[8]

One way Theodore rooted out corruption filled him with delight. He took "midnight walks," accompanied by friend and newspaper reporter, Jacob Riis. On these walks, usually sporting a cape or greatcoat, hat, and a cane, Theodore would prowl the streets, looking for officers not performing their duties (sleeping on the job) or, even worse, breaking the law (drinking on the job, gambling, or obtaining favors from prostitutes). His midnight prowls became so effective that the city newspapers began using Theodore's likeness in editorial cartoons. The image of a big mustache, wide, square teeth, and glasses became synonymous with Theodore for the rest of his life. "I am immensely amused and interested in my work. It keeps me so busy I can hardly think," he told Bamie. "These midnight rambles are great fun. My whole work brings me in contact with every class of people in New York, as no other work possibly could; and I get a glimpse of the real life of the swarming millions. Finally, I do really feel that I am accomplishing a good deal."[9]

The Sunday Excise Law, which began in 1857, forbade saloons from selling alcohol on Sunday; however, it was rarely enforced, or simply ignored. Theodore believed all laws, no matter how unpopular, must be enforced. The law was the law, with no exceptions. If the public was unhappy with a law, they could protest to their elected officials to have it repealed. Until then, all laws would be fully imposed. On June 10, 1895, Theodore instructed all his officers that the Sunday Excise Law would be thoroughly enforced, adding that even if they felt the law was "a bad one," the police must pursue the law "to the letter."[10]

Imposing the Sunday Excise Law did not sit well with the working-class citizens of Manhattan, who looked forward to having a drink (or two) on Sunday—their only day off. For German immigrants particularly, the thought of going without beer with their Sunday dinner was unthinkable. Saloons ignored threats of being shut down, but when officers swarmed in to serve warrants and order doors closed, it was apparent that Theodore was not bluffing. A group of Germans formed a parade to protest the enforcement of the law. The participants and viewers did not expect Theodore to show up, feeling certain that he would hide from such open dissent, like most politicians. As he had done in Medora when Eldridge "Jerry" Paddock had threatened to kill him, Theodore faced his critics head-on by attending the protest. Watching the procession, he smiled at the placards that denounced him. A chorus of voices from the crowd chanted in German "Where's Roosevelt?" Without missing a beat, Theodore replied, in German, "I am here!"[11]

One day Jacob Riis and Lincoln Steffens, a reporter with the *New York Evening Post*, walked into Theodore's office to ask him if he was planning to become president. Theodore jumped from his chair. "Never, never, you must never either of you remind a man at work on a political job that he may be President. It almost always kills him politically. He loses his nerve; he can't do his work; he gives up the very traits that are making him a possibility," he lectured them. Author Bram Stoker, of *Dracula* fame, saw Theodore at a literary dinner and in the police courts. His diary comments about Theodore sound like a description of the hero in a Western novel. "A man you can't cajole, can't frighten, can't buy," he noted.[12]

❦

Despite the ups and downs in his jobs, Theodore found happiness at Sagamore Hill and with his growing family. In addition to Alice Lee, his first son, Theodore Jr., was born on September 13, 1887. Theodore and Edith would have four additional children: Kermit (October 10, 1889), Ethel (August 13, 1891), Archibald (called "Archie"; April 9, 1894), and Quentin (November 19, 1897). Theodore loved them all, but it was apparent that Quentin was Theodore's favorite, possibly because the boy was so much like his father—curious, adventurous, and rambunctious. By all accounts, all of the children were well loved by their parents, although Alice often felt like an intruder. In later years, presidential meetings held at Sagamore Hill came to a complete halt at four o'clock in the afternoon, with Theodore announcing it was his time to play with his children. They would hike, roughhouse in the fields, climb trees, swim, row boats, and collect insects. Pillow fights would break out in any room at a moment's notice, along with anything else that delighted all of them, especially Theodore. These same adventures, and more, would also take place at the White House. One of the more-accurate, and interesting, descriptions about Theodore came from his friend, British ambassador Cecil Rice Spring, who said, "You have to remember, the President is about six."[13]

Theodore's service as New York City police commissioner eventually became more of a headache than a delight; many city politicians viewed his efforts as more troublesome than effective. When reform-minded officials were defeated in the election and replaced by Tammany Hall lackeys, Theodore lost his base of political support. Theodore's biggest headache was a fellow commissioner, Andrew Parker, who did everything possible to stymie any proposed progress. Again, however, as he had done when serving as a civil service commissioner, he refused to resign, and the mayor, at least publicly, stated he would not fire him.

When Republican William McKinley won the 1896 presidential election, Theodore hoped to be appointed assistant secretary of the navy. While his friends rallied on his behalf, this time Theodore had a big hurdle to conquer—McKinley himself. Although grateful that Theodore had spoken on his behalf during the presidential campaign, McKinley was wary of the young man's pugnacious reputation, not to mention his overly vocal support of the United States' taking military action if a situation called for it. Theodore quickly assured McKinley and Secretary of the Navy John D. Long that he would adhere to administration policies. He even offered to stay at his Washington office during the summer months. This was music to Long's ears, who preferred to spend time tending his garden at his Massachusetts home than dealing with politics. With Long's approval, on April 6, 1897, McKinley appointed Theodore assistant secretary of the navy at a yearly salary of $4,500. Secretary Long's precarious health did not always allow him to handle a majority of the details of his position, let alone show up at the office. It fell—most happily—on Theodore to run the navy department. Relishing every moment, he pored over naval maps, studied ships, ordered expansion of the naval fleet and dry docks, promoted those who earned it, and fired the incompetent.

A potential war with Spain was on many people's minds in the spring of 1897. Spain's draconian actions in Cuba and the Philippines had many concerned, but McKinley, a Union veteran of the Civil War, wanted to avoid armed conflict if at all possible. By June, calls for military action against Spain were gaining momentum over their treatment of Cubans rallying for independence. Cuba, which had been a Spanish colony for over four hundred years, was ever present in the newspapers that detailed Spain's atrocities against men, women, and children. McKinley refused to take any steps against Spain because the country had done nothing to warrant American military intervention. Support for the Cuban rebels' bid for independence was growing in many European countries, however, and it was just a matter of time before the United States would be pushed into action. When rioting escalated in Havana, President McKinley sent the battleship USS *Maine* to Cuba in January 1898. He assured Spain that the ship's visit was not a hostile act but was done only to protect "United States businesses and interests." As the *Maine* sat in the Havana harbor without incident, scuttlebutt among the sailors was that they would soon head to New Orleans in time for Mardi Gras.

Everything changed on the evening of February 15, 1898. An explosion obliterated the forward third of the *Maine*, and within minutes the ship settled to the bottom of the harbor, killing a total of 262 men. Although no one could exactly state what had caused the blast, many, including William Randolph Hearst's *New York Morning Journal*, declared a Spanish mine was the culprit.[14] Calls of "Remember the *Maine*!" filled the streets, newspapers, and offices in Washington. War fever swept the country. Hearst sent several reporters, including illustrator Frederic Remington, to cover the story, as well as promoting a $50,000 reward for the conviction of those responsible for the *Maine*'s demise.[15]

McKinley resisted calls to declare war against Spain. The president's lack of action drove Theodore to the breaking point; privately, he claimed that McKinley had "the spine of a chocolate eclair." In a final effort to avoid a military conflict, McKinley sent Spain an ultimatum, which included the demand that it accede independence to Cuba. Spain refused. On April 23, the president formally recognized Cuba's independence, and, as many expected, Spain declared war on the United States. McKinley, as Lincoln had done at the outbreak of the Civil War, called for volunteers (125,000) to supplement the regular army.

America, and Theodore Roosevelt, were going to war.

◆

Writing in his journal, Secretary Long commented about his soon-to-be-former assistant secretary:

> *My Assistant Secretary, Roosevelt, has determined upon resigning, in order to go into the army, and take part in the war . . . He has lost his head to this unutterable folly of deserting the post where he is of most service and running off to ride a horse and, probably, brush mosquitoes from his neck in the Florida sands . . . how absurd all this will sound if, by some turn of fortune, he should accomplish some great thing and strike a very high mark.*[16]

With his resignation accepted, Theodore was given the rank of lieutenant colonel in the United States Volunteers (USV) unit. He would serve under Lt. Col. Leonard Wood, a fellow Harvard graduate, who had been a contract surgeon in the army during the Apache Wars and had earned a Medal of Honor for his actions during the Indian Wars. As usual, Theodore rapidly consumed books on military procedure, actions, and attacks. He had Brooks Brothers in New York City design his dress uniform: a khaki coat with a brown high collar and epaulets and matching khaki pants. His collar bore the crossed-sabers medallion, with the number "1" resting between the sabers, along with USV. To add a dash of color, he wore a navy-blue bandana with white dots around his neck. The left side brim of his campaign hat was pinned to the crown with the crossed-sabers medallion. Theodore carried a dozen pair of glasses, some sown into his hat. The pistol he carried had been salvaged from the *Maine*.[17]

The time had come for Theodore, once again, to push himself. To prove himself against the odds. It was in this war, this fight, that he would expunge his father's sin of not going into battle. He would make things right. For Theodore, this was another fantasy come true for him. As he had tested himself in the Dakotas, he would now test himself in battle, against an enemy in mortal combat. This was a glorious moment for him. He would leave his children behind, and Edith, who was recovering from a strained childbirth and removal of an abdominal tumor. She would be fine, ultimately—but Theodore left her for the glory of the fight. Since childhood, he had harbored a fantasy of being a hero in a military action.

Theodore Roosevelt would lead men into battle, to glory—and possibly death.

The volunteers who joined came literally from all walks of life. Cowboys, Indians, Hispanics, frontier lawmen, a few outlaws on the run, and alumni from Harvard and New York blue bloods. It was an eclectic group, to say the least. Theodore was so overwhelmed with requests to sign up that he had the sad duty of notifying men when the ranks were closed, including a twenty-two-year-old veteran of the Seventh Cavalry. His name was Edgar Rice Burroughs, who later created *Tarzan*.[18]

Training for this volunteer group was set up in San Antonio. The New York blue bloods mixed with cowboys, Hispanics, and Indians (there were sixty Native Americans in the group). Their training was covered by newspapers reporters, who knighted this volunteer group "Roosevelt's Rough Riders." (One of the reporters was Stephen Crane, author of *The Red Badge of Courage*.) The Rough Riders had three mascots: Josephine, a mountain lion brought by the Arizona troops; a golden eagle, named after Theodore, came from the New Mexico contingent; and, a "rather disreputable but exceedingly knowing little dog named Cuba."[19]

Following a month of training, men, horses, and supplies boarded a train for Tampa, Florida, where they would be put on cargo ships bound for Cuba. Tampa was anything but pleasant. Many called the city a "swamp hole" filled with humidity and mosquitoes. Instead of the well-managed military departure the volunteers anticipated, Tampa was a mass of confusion. There was no organization in dispatching troops to the few ships at dockside, and even worse, there were too few ships to carry all of the men and their horses. Forced to leave their horses behind, the Rough Riders quickly became an infantry unit. (Officers' horses and pack mules were put aboard the ships.) Some units were told they would have to wait for additional transport—which never came. While troopers stood by to board a ship, Tampa's suffocating humidity and blistering sun took its toll on them. Many sought shelter by crawling under freight trains parked next to the harbor. Raw, rank sewage from the town spilled into the harbor, itching in their nostrils.

The ocean voyage to Cuba wasn't much better. Theodore commandeered a ship, and it was quickly crammed with his men. Belowdecks, volunteers were lined in cramped, hot quarters. The outside deck was equally jammed, but at least the sea breeze offered some relief—provided the fellow next to you wasn't vomiting from the rolling of the ship. The canned-meat rations went bad very quickly, and the drinking water wasn't much better. The cargo ships the military had leased—for a hefty price— lacked the facilities to cook or store food for such a large group. But there was music! A band on board played "A Hot Time in the Old Town Tonight," which became the unofficial melody of the Rough Riders.

Daiquiri, on the southern side of the Cuban island, was chosen as the landing site. It proved to be another nightmare. Lacking any form of a dock for the ships to unload the men and supplies, troopers were ferried to shore in long rowboats, while the horses and mules were simply lowered over the side of the ship and forced to swim to shore. Many drowned, including Rain-in-the-Face, one of Theodore's two horses.[20] Once on land, the Rough Riders, along with the Tenth United States Colored Troops (better known as the Buffalo Soldiers) and the First US Cavalry (dismounted), made their way through the dense jungle toward Las Guasimas.

The opaque jungle was the perfect site for an ambush.[21]

Firing came thick and fast. The Rough Riders and the other two military units quickly returned fire at an enemy that was largely unseen. Spaniards were using the new smokeless black-powder bullets, making it tough for Rough Riders to ascertain where the firing was coming from. Taking coverage in the dense foliage while Mauser bullets whined over their heads, the Rough Riders held their ground. The Spanish eventually pulled back and left. After the fighting subsided, Lieutenant Colonel Wood was ordered to take over command of Gen. Sam Young's brigade, and given a promotion to general. (Young had been stricken with malaria.) Theodore, promoted to colonel, was now in complete charge of the Rough Riders.

The march continued in the oppressive humidity. The Rough Riders sweated through their blue flannel shirts, swatting at mosquitoes as if they were the real enemy. The water in their canteens was as hot as the air, offering little relief. Many fell sick with malaria and dysentery, and a few caught yellow fever. Theodore led by example, not complaining, urging his men to keep going. A series of low ridges known as the San Juan Heights was all that separated the US Army from the city of Santiago. The navy blockaded the Spanish ships in the city's harbor, and once the army took control of the city, Spain would have little choice but to surrender. San Juan Heights, and a low knoll on the northern end of the heights, named Kettle Hill, was the focus of the army's next attack.

On July 1, Theodore was to take his command up the small ford that looked up at the Heights and Kettle Hill, and wait there for further orders. The Rough Riders, along with the Tenth USCT and the First US Cavalry, were assigned to attack Kettle Hill while the regular army units would strike the fortification on San Juan Hill.[22] As they moved up the ford, the Rough Riders encountered heavy gunfire from the Spanish, who held the high ground on both San Juan and Kettle Hills. Bodies quickly filled the passage, nicknamed "Bloody Ford." The lasting gunfire from Kettle Hill kept the Rough Riders pinned down on the left bank of the ford. Capt. Bucky O'Neill, walking up and down the line in front of his men, was warned by a sergeant that such action was dangerous. O'Neill stated that there wasn't a Spanish bullet made that could kill him. Within seconds, he was shot in the mouth. "Even before he fell his wild and gallant soul had gone out into darkness," Theodore later commented.[23]

At 1:05 p.m., Theodore and his Rough Riders were given the orders to assault Kettle Hill. Theodore called it "his crowded hour."

Riding his mount, Little Texas, out into the open field, Spanish bullets whizzing around him, Theodore yelled to his men, "Follow me!"

The Rough Riders, with a chorus of yells and whoops, advanced up the hill, returning fire at the Spanish. They were quickly joined by members of the Tenth USCT and the First Cavalry. Making their way up the hill, the guidon bearer for the First Cavalry was fatally shot and went down. A Buffalo Soldier quickly grabbed the staff and continued advancing up the hill. Forty yards from the crest of the hill, a barbed-wire fence forced Theodore to dismount Little Texas. With the Americans less than ten yards from their front line, the Spanish fighters broke ranks and fled down the backward slope. As the Rough Riders, the Tenth USCT, and the First Cavalry swept onto the top of the hill, the Buffalo Soldier carrying the guidon firmly planted it in the ground, next to the one from the Rough Riders.[24]

Securing Kettle Hill, Theodore saw the northern point of the Spanish defenses on San Juan Hill was open to an attack. Theodore led his men down the side of Kettle Hill, over the trenches, and up the northern side of San Juan Hill. The majority of Spanish soldiers fled down the other side of the bluff toward Santiago, while the few that stayed to fight paid the ultimate price.

The following day, July 2, Theodore and his Rough Riders stood on San Juan Hill with the American flag behind them, posing for photographer William Dinwiddie. That image—Theodore standing with his hands on his hips, his battered campaign hat slightly cocked on his head, and a resolute look on his face—became the iconic image of the battle—and of Theodore's crowded hour.[25]

Two weeks later, Spain surrendered.

For the military, the next big problem was evacuating the troops, including the sick and wounded, off the island and stateside, where they could get proper medical treatment. Officials in Washington had no effective plan for properly withdrawing the men, nor did they truly understand how dire conditions were on the island. Washington insiders, fearful that many of the soldiers had contracted yellow fever, would return with the disease and lead to an epidemic within the United States. In reality, very few men suffered from the "yellow jack" disease. Most suffered from either battlefield wounds, malaria, or dysentery.[26]

Theodore was in a fury at the lack of preparation to get his men, as well as the regular army soldiers, off the island quickly. He wasn't afraid to express his feelings to reporters, who liberally quoted him in their articles. Newspaper stories of men dying due to the military failing to provide an organized withdrawal caused a furor in the States. The blame rightly fell on Secretary of War Russell Alger, who had no solution; his incompetence led to his forced resignation a year later. Although Theodore's public shaming of Alger brought attention to the plight of the suffering soldiers, it likely cost him his chance at being awarded the Congressional Medal of Honor. Many felt that Theodore should have been given the distinguished medal for his action in the field, and several officers and soldiers signed documents in support. However, others, mainly in the War Department, held a different opinion of Roosevelt. It began with the uninterrupted newspaper coverage of Theodore and his Rough Riders, from their training in San Antonio to San Juan Hill. Army officers and enlisted men equally grumbled that they were all but ignored by the press in favor of his volunteers. Combined with Theodore's public attack over Alger's actions, or lack of them, it all but assured Theodore would not get the Medal of Honor. (The medal was awarded posthumously in 2000.)

Boarding the steamer *Miami* on August 8, the Rough Riders were bound for Montauk, Long Island. Unfortunately, the return trip wasn't an improvement over the first one. The food was barely edible, and the water, again, was virtually undrinkable. Seven days later, the steamer arrived at Montauk, and once again the troopers were greeted by mass confusion. The camp lacked food, medicine—even cots. By the time the Rough Riders marched ashore, those without battle wounds were suffering from malaria, dysentery, or both. Some were too weak to walk and had to be carried off the ship. Theodore, with his newfound popularity in the press, quickly took control, and by week's end, medicine, food, and sleeping arrangements were secured for all.

From that point on, life for the Rough Riders at Montauk became a paradise. Food was ample and rich, with no further concern over having enough good water or ice. Those who were physically able to do so spent their days swimming in the surf or riding horses along the beach. The Rough Rider units that were left behind in Tampa, as well as the regiment's three adopted mascots, joined the men on Long Island. One night, Josephine, the mountain lion, managed to get loose from her chain and prowl around the camp before entering the tent of a trooper from the First Cavalry. Finding a comfortable spot, she settled down next to him, much to his horror.[27]

During his stay at Montauk, Theodore signed a contract with Charles Scribner's Sons to write a book about the Rough Riders' exploits. His work would first appear as six serialized installments in *Scribner's Magazine* before being released as a book in May of 1899.[28] After a month, the men were declared sufficiently physically fit to disband the unit. The last Sunday service before they were mustered out, Theodore addressed his men.

I told them how proud I was of them, but warned them not to think
that they could now go back and rest on their laurels, bidding them to
remember that though for ten days or so the world would be willing to
treat them as heroes, yet after that time they would find they had to get
down to hard work just like everyone else, unless they were willing to
be regarded as worthless do-nothings.[29]

As a gesture of their respect for their leader, the regiment presented
Theodore with a bronze of Remington's *The Bronc Buster.* "There could
have been no more appropriate gift from such a regiment, and I was not
only pleased with it, but very deeply touched with the feeling which made
them join in giving it. Afterward they all filed past and I shook the hands
of each to say good-by[e]," Theodore later wrote.[30]

On September 15, 1898, the colors and standards were taken down
for the last time. The Rough Riders were now a part of history.

The newspaper coverage of the Rough Riders turned Theodore Roosevelt
into a bona fide hero. His image in his khaki dress uniform was everywhere, from the cover of sheet music and on cigar boxes, to highly inac-
curate, yet heroic, paintings of his leading a mounted group in a charge,
with sabers drawn. Theodore Roosevelt, the hero of San Juan Hill, was the
man of the hour. Boys looked up to him, men and women admired him.
His magnetic charm was irresistible to the American public.

Theodore's ascension to a heroic designation couldn't have come at
a better time for US Senator Thomas Platt of New York. Known as the
"easy boss" because of his smooth manner, Platt was the power behind
the Republican Party. He had the ability to make or break a political
career. The current Republican governor of New York, Frank S. Black,
was nominally linked to "improper expenditures" charges on a stalled
Erie Canal improvement project. Platt realized that supporting Governor
Black's reelection could damage his reputation and that of the Republican Party. He began to look for another person to back for governor, and
many were pushing Theodore Roosevelt as a promising alternative. Platt
had serious doubts due to the young man's reputation for independence.
The last thing Platt wanted was a loose cannon in the halls of Albany's

state capitol. When the two men finally met, Theodore assured Platt he would consult the senator on various bills and consider his choices for certain positions. However, what Theodore did *not* promise Platt was that he would always follow the old man's demands. He would act on matters based on his own conscience, nothing more. Platt, given the choice between Black or Theodore, went with the latter, feeling he could handle the young upstart.

Theodore campaigned throughout the state, often accompanied by some of his fellow Rough Riders in uniform. His arrival at train stops and halls was heralded by bugler Emil Cassi blowing "Charge." Remarks about his service with the Rough Riders brought hearty rounds of applause from young and old alike who gathered in the audiences.[31] What looked to have been a certain Democratic win was now turning into a neck and neck race. On Election Day, November 7, 1898, Theodore Roosevelt won the governor's seat by 17,794 votes.

"I have played it in bull luck this summer," Theodore wrote to Cecil Spring Rice. "First, to get into the war; then to get out of it; then to get elected. I have worked hard all my life, and have never been particularly lucky, but this summer I was lucky, and I am enjoying it to the full. I know perfectly well that luck will not continue, and it is not necessary that it should. I am more than contented to be Governor of New York, and shall not care if I ever hold another office; and I am very proud of my regiment, which was really a noteworthy volunteer organization."[32]

Right from the start of his governorship, Theodore and Thomas Platt butted heads. Platt had chosen Francis Hendricks of Syracuse as superintendent of public works. Theodore knew the man and liked him, but felt that his coming from a city along the Erie Canal improvement project was not a proper or ethical choice. When Theodore notified Platt that he had declined to appoint Hendricks, it "produced an explosion, but I declined to lose my temper." Theodore repeated that he himself must choose the man for the position. Although Platt relented, the "easy boss" began to wonder if he would be able to control the new governor.

As his term progressed, Theodore managed to push through several reforms, including strengthening the state's forest department, enlarging the Adirondack state park, strengthening state factory inspections, improving working conditions in tenement sweatshops, limiting the work hours for women and children, and imposing a maximum eight-hour workday for state employees. He hoped the latter would be adopted by various industries, but it was ignored.

Theodore's support for one bill forced a showdown with Platt. Called the Ford Bill (written by Senator John Ford), it proposed to force corporations to pay a tax on the public franchises they owned and operated, such as elevated railways and gas companies. Theodore believed it was only fair for these companies to pay a reasonable tax that would then be used for community services. Howls of protest erupted. Senator Platt got an earful of complaints from assorted corporations—the very same corporations that had amply paid Platt (in the form of campaign contributions) to halt such legislation. Platt was none too happy over the firestorm, which he expressed in a letter to the governor:

> *I had heard from a good many sources that you were a little loose on the relations of capital and labor, on trusts and combinations, and, indeed, on those numerous questions which have recently arisen in politics affecting security of earnings and the right of a man to run his own business his own way . . . I understood from a number of business men, and among them many of your own personal friends, that you entertained many altruistic ideas, all very well in their way, but which before they could safely be put into law needed very profound consideration.[33]*

Two days later, Theodore sent a calm and reasoned reply, stating his position on why the tax law was just and necessary. Platt warned him that if he pushed his support of the bill, his political career would be destroyed. Theodore ignored the threat. The tax proposal passed the Senate but was held up in the House, where Speaker S. Fred Nixon had direct orders from Platt not to pass the bill.

During his time as governor, Theodore once said, "Speak softly and carry a big stick; you will go far." The "big stick" term became as synonymous with him as his glasses, mustache, and wide grin. He had spoken softly to Platt about his reasons for seeing the tax bill become law. Now he would wield the big stick. A law, called the Special Emergency Message, allowed the governor to take a bill out of turn and force it to the floor for a vote. Theodore sent such a message to Speaker Nixon, who tore it up before having a "nervous collapse." The following morning, Theodore sent another message, demanding it be read, or he would come over and read it himself. The bill was read and passed.

Not only had Theodore gotten the law enacted, but he had also thoroughly embarrassed his own party and its boss. Republicans winced, Democrats gloated, and Platt seethed with anger. Theodore knew it was only a matter of time before Platt and his followers would take their revenge. It didn't matter. He had stood up and done what was right. He had faced down the opposition, as he had done with the drunken cowboy in Mingusville, and confronting the man who had threatened to shoot him on sight.

"I want to bury him," Platt said.[34]

The political gods answered Platt's wishes. US vice president Garrett Hobart died of a heart attack on November 21, 1899. With a new presidential campaign about to begin, Platt had the perfect running mate for McKinley. During this period in American politics, the office of vice president was considered a dead end for a political career. Largely a ceremonial position, it offered nothing else. By 1900, only three previous vice presidents had been elected to the presidency on their own.[35] For Platt, the vice presidency was the perfect place to bury the pugnacious governor.

Theodore was not in favor of taking the job, mainly because it offered few challenges. In a letter to Lodge, Theodore noted, "It seems to me that the chance of my being a presidential candidate is too small to warrant very serious consideration at present. To have been a good Colonel, a good Governor, and a good Assistant Secretary of the Navy is not enough to last four years. If McKinley were to die tomorrow I would be one of the men seriously *considered* as his successor—I mean that and just no more. But four years hence the Spanish War will be in the very remote past and what I have done as Governor will not be very recent . . . I would still like to be in the running, but I do not regard it as sufficiently probable to be worth receiving very much weight."[36]

Despite any doubts McKinley may have harbored about Theodore Roosevelt, he was keen enough to realize the young man had a name value ("the hero of San Juan Hill") which would be beneficial to the upcoming campaign. Theodore won the nomination and, setting aside any private concerns, was quickly out campaigning.

In September 1900, Theodore's travels took him to the state of North Dakota. Joe Ferris was the first of many to greet him. E. G. Paddock, the man who had once threatened to shoot Theodore on sight, greeted him warmly in Dickinson. Theodore recalled how Paddock had lent him his buffalo rifle on his first visit, ignoring Paddock's past threat. In Medora, several people came to the train station to greet the vice presidential candidate, including George Myers. Theodore kidded his old friend about his cooking, adding, "The best proof in the world, George, that I have a good constitution is that I ate your cooking and survived!"[37] Theodore was given a horse, which he quickly mounted, going for a ride up to a bluff overlooking the area.

The McKinley-Roosevelt ticket won the election in November. Mark Hanna, a US senator and McKinley's closest adviser, implored the president to remain healthy for the next four years, the most important thing he had to do. The moment Theodore was chosen as a running mate, Hanna had not been happy. Early in the campaign, he once blurted to associates, "Don't any of you realize that there's only one life between this madman and the Presidency?"[38]

Presidential swearing-in ceremonies during this period took place in March because of the milder weather. Theodore sat alone in the carriage as it made its way to the Capitol, where he'd take his oath of office. There exists brief film footage of this moment, Theodore sitting stoically and alone, looking ahead, not acknowledging the crowd. He doesn't wave, tip his hat, or smile broadly. It reminds one of a funeral procession.

Another custom was for the Senate to meet for one week in March before adjourning, returning in October. This was done to avoid the oppressive heat and humidity that filled Washington in the late spring and throughout the summer. Once his four-day duty in the Senate was over, Theodore and his family would return to Sagamore Hill. For the next six months, Theodore enjoyed his days at the rambling home with

Edith and the children, which helped to soothe the problems that came with his new job. Not only was the vice president basically a ceremonial figurehead, but he also could not publicly speak out on any issue without first considering how it would reflect on the administration. Anything Theodore said or did was now fodder for newspaper reporters looking to make something out of nothing. The Democratic press loved to point out his slightest mistake, taunting him. Theodore was forced to remain silent, growing to dislike the position more and more. He told Leonard Wood that the vice presidency was an "abnormal job" and felt it should be abolished. "The man who occupies it may at any moment be everything; but meanwhile he is practically nothing."[39]

The Pan-American Exposition in Buffalo, New York, opened in May 1901. It was a world's fair covering 350 acres, celebrating the "commercial well-being and good understanding among the American Republics." A grand canal more than a mile in length surrounded the ornate buildings, which were illuminated at night with electric power. Patrons could marvel at new machines to make life easier, as well as take a "trip to the moon." This was the first "dark ride" attraction; for the unheard-of price of fifty cents, thirty visitors would board an "airship-ornithopter" and blast off for the moon. Along the way, they'd see views of Niagara Falls and then Earth before landing on the moon. Exiting the airship, visitors could explore the moon's surface (a large papier-mâché set), before visiting the Man in the Moon's palace, complete with dancing "moon maidens."[40]

President McKinley had spent September 5 touring the grounds with his wife, and gave a public speech. The following day, the president returned to the exhibition and greeted the public in the Temple of Music building. The line moved through without incident, people happily shaking the hand of the president. Among those in the line was Leon Czolgosz, a disgruntled anarchist and the son of Polish immigrants. Approaching McKinley, the president noticed the man's right hand was bandaged with a handkerchief. Reaching out to shake the man's left hand, Czolgosz shoved his right hand toward McKinley's body and fired twice from a .32 pistol concealed in the handkerchief.[41]

McKinley was rushed to a nearby hospital where surgeons found that one bullet had simply gashed McKinley's ribs. The second bullet hit the president in the stomach but had gone through. Theodore was in Vermont attending a luncheon of the state's Fish and Game League when he was informed of the news; he immediately left for Buffalo. Upon his arrival, Theodore was told that the doctors had managed to stabilize the president's condition. With McKinley showing signs of improvement over the next few days, Theodore was urged to take his planned family trip in the Adirondacks.

The cabin was located in Camp Tahawus, a remote resort location within the park. Although several family members had planned to accompany Theodore on a hike to the top of a nearby mountain, inclement weather left only Theodore and a few friends to trudge on. Mist and clouds forced the group to move down to a small lake. As the group sat by the lake eating their lunch, Theodore saw a man running up the trail, holding a piece of paper.

Even before he read the telegram, Theodore knew it was serious.

Family portrait in 1903. (Left to right: Quentin, Theodore, Theodore Jr., Archie, Alice, Kermit, Edith, and Ethel.) AUTHOR'S COLLECTION

Theodore (left) in camp during his days exploring Yellowstone National Park in 1903, with his old friend John Burroughs (standing, with white beard) and guide Billy Hofer (seated). AUTHOR'S COLLECTION

Visiting Yosemite in 1903: John Muir (left), Theodore (right), and guides Charles Leidig and Archie Leonard ride to Bridalveil Meadows. Half-Dome can be seen in the background. THEODORE ROOSEVELT COLLECTION, HOUGHTON LIBRARY, HARVARD UNIVERSITY

Theodore traveled to Frederick, Oklahoma Territory, in 1905 to witness Jack Abernathy's unique ability at catching wolves and coyotes. (Left to right, standing: Lee Bivins, William MacDonald, Jack Abernathy [holding a live coyote], S. M. B. Young, Burk Bennett, Theodore and Ed Gillis; seated: two unidentified men, Guy Waggoner, Quanah Parker, Cecil Lambert, Alexander Lambert [Theodore's physician], and D. P. Taylor.) THEODORE ROOSEVELT COLLECTION, HOUGHTON LIBRARY, HARVARD UNIVERSITY

Theodore sharing a story with other cowboys during his time in Oklahoma Territory. THEODORE ROOSEVELT COLLECTION, HOUGHTON LIBRARY, HARVARD UNIVERSITY

Taking a break during his Colorado 1905 bear hunt, Theodore reads a book while Skip keeps him company. The two became very close during this hunt, and Skip traveled to the White House, where he became part of the Roosevelt menagerie.
THEODORE ROOSEVELT COLLECTION, HOUGHTON LIBRARY, HARVARD UNIVERSITY

Seth Bullock (left of Theodore, with large mustache and hat) was one of Theodore's closest friends. When Bullock was asked how long he had known Theodore, he replied, "From the tail of a chuck wagon to the Court of St. James."
THEODORE ROOSEVELT COLLECTION, HOUGHTON LIBRARY, HARVARD UNIVERSITY

Old friends from Medora gather around their choice for the 1912 presidential campaign at the Progressive Party Convention in Chicago. (Left to right: Bill Merrifield, Sylvane Ferris, Theodore, Joe Ferris, and George Meyers.)

"Ding" Darling's quickly sketched editorial cartoon, "The Long, Long Trail," at the time of Theodore's death. Many newspaper cartoons paid homage to Theodore using a Western theme. AUTHOR'S COLLECTION

Above: Theodore's Maltese Cross cabin now resides at the South Unit of the Theodore Roosevelt National Park, outside of Medora, North Dakota. Inside the cabin are items Theodore used during his time in the Dakotas, including a canvas trunk, writing desk, bookshelf, and rocking chair. AUTHOR'S COLLECTION

Left: Dedicated in October 2011, the statue *Young TR Enters the Arena* commemorates Theodore's July 4, 1886, speech. The sculpture, by Tom Bollinger, stands in front of the Stark County Courthouse in Dickinson, North Dakota, the same location where Theodore gave his speech. AUTHOR'S COLLECTION

As part of the US Mint series honoring the National Park Service, Theodore's cowboy likeness was chosen to represent Theodore Roosevelt National Park.

Where Theodore led, others followed. He once said, "Life is a great adventure, and I want to say to you, accept it in such spirit."

THAT DAMNED COWBOY!

What a place the Presidency is for learning to keep one's temper.

THE LAST OF TWO TELEGRAMS THEODORE RECEIVED AT THE CABIN
informed him that President McKinley was sinking fast and that the vice
president was to waste no time in coming to Buffalo. It was raining when
he left by buckboard, enduring a rough and bumpy ride along a dark trail
that, fortunately, the horses knew by memory. Even so, he urged the driver
to go faster.

As the sun was breaking over the horizon, the buckboard pulled up
to the North Creek train station. A train was waiting, the engine quietly hissing, holding its steam to rush its very important passenger to
Buffalo. Climbing aboard, a telegram informed Theodore that President
McKinley had died at 2:15 a.m. Arriving in Buffalo at 1:25 p.m., he was
taken directly by carriage to the two-story home of an old friend, Ansley
Wilcox. Theodore, who chose to be sworn in at Wilcox's home instead of
the residence where McKinley's body was lying in state, took the oath of
office at 3:30 p.m. on September 14. He spoke briefly with Cabinet members, later announcing to gathered reporters that all six officers agreed to
remain in their positions, "at least for the present."

"It is a dreadful thing to come into the Presidency this way; but it
would be a far worse thing to be morbid about it. Here is the task, and I
have got to do it to the best of my ability; and that is all there is about it,"
Theodore wrote to Lodge. "I believe you will approve of what I have done
and of the way I have handled myself so far. It is only the beginning, but
it is better to make a beginning good than bad."[1]

Mark Hanna, who was stunned by McKinley's death, not to mention his recollection of the eerie request he had made of McKinley on Election Night, reportedly lashed out in private, "Now we've got that damned cowboy as President!"

Hanna was correct about one thing: Theodore would often be referred to as "The Cowboy President" by the press and the public. The earliest political cartoon portraying Theodore as a cowboy appeared in the *New York World* on October 31, 1886, during his campaign for mayor. Theodore is portrayed wearing chaps, boots and spurs, a bandana, and a cowboy hat, while throwing a lasso around a steam train with the face of Democratic candidate Abram Hewitt on the front of the engine. A political cartoon during Theodore's tenure as a civil service commissioner showed the young man, clad in buckskin clothing, sitting astride a bucking horse, looking calm as his quirt, labeled "Reform Law," is raise above his head. The saddle is labeled "Civil Service Reform," while the haunch of the horse is branded "Spoilsman." His hat, which has flown off his head, has a piece of paper coming out from under the brim on which appears "The Commission Means Business. T. R." When he was governor of New York, the *Denver Post* illustrated Theodore, in full cowboy regalia, riding a tiger with a collar that read "Tammany" (for Tammany Hall, the Democratic Party), firing his gun. The caption read, "The Champion Rough Rider of the World."[2]

For political cartoonists, Theodore's background in the West, and his role as leader of the Rough Riders, provided them with a profusion of material. From the time of his governorship through his presidency, cartoonists usually portrayed Theodore in either Western or Rough Rider attire, a pistol on his hip or a rifle in hand. Artist Bernard Partridge of the British humor magazine *Punch* paid tribute to Theodore as he took over the presidency mounted on a horse, with an American flag as the saddle blanket, sporting cowboy attire. He is looking to the horizon, his right hand shielding his eyes. The caption reads "The Rough Rider."[3]

Because of these cartoons and the press's constant mention of Theodore's days in the West, the public was quickly drawn to their new leader. His magnetic charm and down-to-earth attitude—suffering no fools—appealed to the American citizen. Many in the Midwest and West claimed him as "one of us," even though his total time residing in Medora between 1884 and 1887 was just north of 365 days. But he was *one of them*. Theodore Roosevelt's blue-blooded mentality, apparent during his early adulthood, was quickly shed when he went west to live among the cowboys and cattlemen. His Harvard degree meant nothing to the people of the land. His political career up to that point was irrelevant to them. Who he was as a man mattered. People would judge him by how he conducted himself. They originally regarded him as a dude, something of a joke. Yet he persisted. He stayed with them, much like riding a bucking horse. Theodore came to earn their respect and trust, until they considered him one of their own. He talked a good fight, and his previous actions in other positions demonstrated he could be counted on. Now, more than ever, he had to prove to the American people that he *was* truly one of them.

Theodore, although publicly stating that he would carry on the plans of the McKinley administration, quickly made it apparent that it was now *his* administration. One of his biggest steps, which left the pro-business Republicans aghast, showed the public where this administration, and its leader, stood on behalf of the people.

Corporations at the turn of the century were the biggest employer within the United States, and some of the wealthiest. They controlled the country and the politics. When two (or more) corporations merged, they were, during this period, referred to as *trusts*. Trusts held monopolies on many goods and services, whether raw materials (such as sugar, cotton, and coal) or transportation. These monopolies controlled every aspect of American life and were free to charge for their products whatever price they could get away with. Without competition for goods and services in the open marketplace, the public had almost no opportunity to do business with anyone but the trusts.

In 1901, Jerome Hill, president of the Great Northern Railway, struck a deal with E. H. Harriman, of Union Pacific Railroad, to join J. P. Morgan's Northern Pacific. Together, the trio would form the largest trust in the country, and the second largest in the world. Purchasing enough stock of Burlington and Quincy Railroad, the three men held the controlling interest, which gave them ownership of rail lines across most of the Western half of the United States. They created the Northern Securities Company, a "holding company" that would serve as a channel for the company profits, which were estimated to be $100 million a year. J. P. Morgan's own newspaper, the New York *Sun*, did not release the news of the company's formation until the stock market had closed on November 13. As word spread about the major merger, the newspapers and the public were aghast. Headlines in competing newspapers screamed that if no other merger violated the Sherman Antitrust Act, this one did, by a mile.[4]

Theodore was against the alliance. Contrary to common belief, Theodore was not an all-consuming buster of trusts. He was far more in favor of regulating instead of busting them, believing they were, in many cases, necessary for the good of the economy. However, this one he would not approve, seeing it as a simple power grab. Theodore realized that such a merger would hurt small farmers and businesses because railroads gave price breaks to companies that shipped large amounts of material. Businesses and farmers shipping smaller quantities received no reduction in fees. With this major merger, only higher rates could be expected for shipping, as well as higher ticket rates for passengers. Theodore instructed Attorney General Philander Knox to file a suit against the Northern Securities Company for violation of the Sherman Antitrust Act. The case moved its way through the various courts until 1904, when the Supreme Court, in a five-to-four vote, ruled that the trust violated the law and ordered it be broken up. Theodore believed that going after the Northern Securities Company would serve as a warning to other trusts to act within reason or face legal challenges.

Coal, the black, dirty mineral, was the source of power for almost everything in the United States in 1902—trains, ships, machines. Coal was used to cook food and provide heat in the winter. It was as essential to the way of life in America then as oil is today. A labor dispute in May 1902 caused anthracite coal miners to walk off their jobs, shutting down 147 Pennsylvania mines. Mine owners refused to discuss the workers' demands, which included a pay increase, shorter working hours, and union representation. The life of a coal miner meant hard, backbreaking work, deep down in the mines where cave-ins were common. If a tunnel collapse didn't kill a man, then slow death by "black lung" was certain. Men contracted asthma or emphysema, which aged them greatly before they were thirty—if they lived that long. Children worked in the mines for six dollars a month, straddling chutes that moved along chunks of coal at a rapid rate. Their job was to pull out the rocks, and the children often suffered serious accidents.

As the summer months of 1902 came to an end, the last of the coal reserves were delivered. Fall and winter were fast approaching; people needed coal to keep their homes and apartments warm. Trains had to move goods across the country. As fall progressed, schools were forced to close. Mobs looted any remaining coal cars.

Theodore had no constitutional right to intervene; neither would any law on the books allow him to step between the miners and the owners. Only his moral law told him he had to act for the good of the country. He summoned representatives for the miners and the owners to a meeting.[5] He suggested that the workers return to the mines while submitting to the arbitration of a board chosen by the president and agreed upon by the mine owners. John Mitchell, representing the mine workers, readily agreed. The owners flatly refused. The stalemate and strike continued. It looked as if it would be a bleak winter.

"Well, I tried and failed," Theodore wrote to Mark Hanna. "I feel downhearted over the result, both because of the great misery made necessary for the mass of our people, and because the attitude of the operators will beyond a doubt double the burden on us who stand between them and socialistic action. But I am glad I tried anyhow. I should have hated to feel that I had failed to make any effort. What my next move will be I cannot yet say."[6]

His next moved involved Secretary of War Elihu Root holding a discreet meeting with J. P. Morgan. Morgan used his influence to get the mine owners to agree to an arbitration panel, while the workers went back to the mines. The mine owners were adamant that no one from labor be part of the arbitration panel. In addition, they demanded that the panel consist of an officer of the engineer corps (with military or naval service), an expert mining engineer who had coal-mining experience, a judge of the United States Court of the Eastern District of Pennsylvania, a man of prominence ("eminent as a sociologist"), and, finally, a man active in mining and selling coal.

At first Theodore bristled at the demands, but then he saw a silver lining in this gray cloud. He proposed E. E. Clark, chief of the Brotherhood of Railway Conductors, as the "eminent sociologist." Theodore argued that as a union leader, Mr. Clark had to have "thought and studied deeply on social questions." Mine owners agreed, and the workers went back to work. The arbitration panel's decision was to cut a worker's day from twelve to nine hours, and to provide them a 10 percent pay increase. Union recognition would have to wait for another day. The strike ended just before the cold winter set in.

"I shall never forget the mixture of relief and amusement I felt when I thoroughly grasped the fact that while they would heroically submit to anarchy rather than have Tweedledum, yet if I would call it Tweedledee they would accept it with rapture; it gave me an illuminating glimpse into one corner of the mighty brains of these 'captains of industry,'" Theodore wrote in his autobiography.[7]

With the coal strike resolved, Theodore shook off the formalities of political life and jumped back into the clothes of a hunter. He traveled in early November to Smedes, Mississippi, for a black bear hunt. Theodore had the worst luck during the next five days in finding a bear to shoot, which no doubt reminded him of his first buffalo hunt. With his inability to bag a bear, reporters were quickly painting "the great hunter" as an inept, laughable figure in their columns. Frustrated at not shooting a bear, the newspaper coverage left him chagrined.

Holt Collier, the main guide for this trip, eventually caught a black bear, lassoing it around the neck and tying it to a tree. Theodore rushed to find a muddied, scrawny animal—a mere 235 pounds, and almost as big as Theodore himself. He flatly refused to shoot the bear, which was in very poor shape, stating it wasn't sportsmanlike to shoot an animal that was tied up. He ordered the animal be put out of its misery.[8]

Reporters quickly grabbed on to the story of Theodore refusing to shoot a bear tied to a tree. The public went wild with approval, especially after *Washington Post* cartoonist Clifford Berryman produced a sketch of a black bear with a rope around its neck held by a hunter. Theodore's back is turned on the animal, his gun lowered and waving a hand in disgust. Titled "Drawing the Line in Mississippi," it became very popular. In his subsequent editorial cartoons of the president, Berryman always had Theodore accompanied by a small, cute bear cub.[9]

Legend has it that Morris and Rose Michtom of Brooklyn were so taken with Theodore's compassion for the bear that they made two small stuffed bears, which they put on display in their stationery and novelty store. Both bears quickly sold. Morris Michtom reportedly wrote to Theodore asking his permission to name the bears they planned to sell after him. The president supposedly gave his blessing, although expressing doubts that his name would help sales. (There is no record of Michtom's letter, or Theodore's response, in the voluminous Roosevelt collections.) The couple sold the toy bears, dubbed "Teddy's Bears," for $1.50 each. Business was very brisk, and by 1907, the Michtoms formed the Ideal Novelty and Toy Company, which went on to become one of the biggest toy companies in the country for nearly eighty years.

At the same time, in a small town in Germany, Margarete Steiff made plush dolls, including a bear. In 1903, an American buyer saw Steiff's bears at the Leipzig Fair and placed an order for three hundred of them. (In 1903, Steiff's produced 12,000 stuffed bears. By 1907, they had sold 974,000.[10]) More than a hundred years after its inception, the teddy bear is still popular, and provides comfort and joy to young and old alike.

Theodore's contact with the bear wasn't limited to editorial cartoons or stuffed dolls. The infant motion picture industry also found Theodore's bear incident, and hunting in general, material for a good-natured spoof. *Terrible Teddy, the Grizzly King* was released in 1901, before he assumed the presidency. Produced by Edison Manufacturing Company under the direction of Edwin S. Porter,[11] the film was based on a series of cartoon panels that appeared in the *New York Journal and Advertiser* on February 4, 1901. The Edison Company's catalog described the one-minute-long film as a "burlesque" of Theodore hunting mountain lions in Colorado.

The scene opens in a very picturesque wood. Teddy with his large teeth is seen running down the hill with his rifle in hand, followed by his

photographer and press agent. He reconnoiters around a large tree and
finally discovers the mountain lion. He kneels on one knee and makes
a careful shot. Immediately upon discharge of his gun, a huge black
cat—a domestic breed—falls from the tree, and Teddy whips out his
bowie knife, leaps on the cat, and stabs it several times, then poses
while his photographer makes a picture and the press agent writes up
the thrilling adventure. A side-splitting burlesque.[12]

The "Teddy" Bears (Edison, 1907), also directed by Porter, was advertised as "a laughable satire on the popular craze." The fourteen-minute
film begins as a variation of *Goldilocks and the Three Bears*. One would
assume the film would be suitable for children; however, the movie
abruptly shifts from the inside of the cabin to an exterior snow-covered
landscape, with the three bears (adults in costume) chasing the young girl,
with the intention of harming her. Suddenly, like the cavalry coming to
the rescue, an actor resembling Theodore shows up with his rifle, kills the
two adult bears, and captures the baby bear.

The trade paper *Variety* commented that the film begins as an enjoyable piece, but noted that the ending, with Theodore's character killing
the bears, would cause children to "rebel against this position." Stating
there was "considerable comedy" in the chase through the snow, "the live
bears seemed so domesticated that the deliberate murder . . . left a wrong
taste of the picture as a whole,"[13] Oddly, *The "Teddy" Bears* proved to be
very popular with audiences, doing great business in the bigger cities.

◆

Despite his popularity with the public, Theodore had his doubts about
winning a second term when he ran in 1904. His worries were for naught,
as he received 56 percent of the popular vote, while his opponent, Alton
Parker, managed a weak 38 percent. (Theodore won the Electoral College vote by 336 to 140.) His daughter, Alice, noted in her diary, "An
unprecedented landslide. It is all colossal."[14] Addressing reporters late in
the evening, Theodore announced he would not seek another term.

It was a statement he would live to regret.

One of many people who actively campaigned on his behalf was William Masterson, better known as "Bat" Masterson, an Old West icon. As a

buffalo hunter he took part in the famous standoff with the Comanche at Adobe Walls in 1874, and later served as sheriff of Ford County, Kansas (which included Dodge City), for three years. He was friends with Wyatt Earp (a Dodge City deputy marshal at the time), Luke Short, Bill Tilghman, and other notable Western icons. By the mid-1880s, he was working as a gambler in Colorado, eventually running a saloon in Denver. An avid fan of boxing, he became involved with a boxing association in Colorado.

Bat's popularity as a true Westerner attracted Theodore like a moth to a flame. Newspapers were always quick to exploit Bat's handiness with a gun, leaving a slew of bodies in his wake. Of course, it was all hyperbole, but the public ate it up, and it made Bat a celebrity. During Theodore's time as police commissioner, Jay Gould, one of the original "robber barons," had asked that his son, George, be given protection after receiving death threats. Theodore contacted Bat in Denver, asking if he'd like to serve as the young man's bodyguard. Bat quickly jumped at the offer and headed east. While watching over Gould's son, he also fraternized with the wealthy and engaged in high-stakes gambling. Once the man who had threatened George Gould was arrested, Bat returned to Denver, but soon saw his prestige as a gambler lose its luster due to reform-minded civic leaders. He moved to New York City in 1902, where he found employment as a sportswriter for the New York *Morning Telegraph*.

In 1904, Bat was invited to the White House. Theodore asked him about his days in the West, and shared their mutual interest in boxing. "I guess the President was glad to see me," Bat told reporters, "knowing that I had no politics to talk about and no favors to ask."[15] Theodore offered Bat the position of US marshal in the Indian Territory, but Masterson turned it down. Citing his personal history, Bat said that some kid wanting a reputation would "crawl around to a gun play and I'd have to send him over the jump."[16] Another reason, which he didn't reveal to Theodore, was that Bat simply had no interest in leaving New York City.

Bat's close friend, Alfred Lewis, suggested to Theodore that he appoint Bat as a deputy US marshal in New York City. Theodore was receptive but cautious. His assigning Ben Daniels to a federal position had caused him some public embarrassment, and he wanted to be certain not to repeat that headache with Bat. He asked Lewis if Bat could read and write. Lewis quickly forwarded a letter that Bat had written, noting "that the education of our homicidal friend has not been neglected."[17]

After his 1904 election, Theodore asked his attorney general, William H. Moody, if he could find a deputy marshal's position for Bat in New York City. William Henkel, the US marshal for the Southern District of New York, agreed, and requested permission for an additional office of deputy US marshal with a salary "not to exceed $2,000 per annum." The new position, assigned to the US Attorney's office, required the appointee to take charge of the grand jury room when it was in session. Henkel nominated W. B. Masterson for the position, noting he was "most highly endorsed and in every way worthy to fill this office in a most credible manner."[18]

On February 2, 1905, Theodore wrote to Bat with some fatherly advice relating to his new job:

> *It was a pleasure to get you the appointment as Deputy Marshal. Now you have doubtless seen that there has been a good deal of hostile comment upon it in the press. I do not care a snap of my fingers for this; but I do care very much that you shall not by any act of yours seem to justify this criticism.*
>
> *I want you not only to be a vigilant, courteous and efficient officer, always on hand, always polite to everyone, always ready for any duty that comes up, but I also want you to carry yourself so that no one can find in any action of yours cause for a scandal or complaint.*
>
> *You must be careful not to gamble or do anything while you are a public officer which might afford opportunity to your enemies and my critics to say that your appointment was improper.[19]*

Bat's appointment was announced in the *New York Times* on February 7, 1905, noting that Masterson "gave up killing for the sake of orderly government." The article was quick to add that he had killed "a dozen or more lawless characters." No doubt this kind of press made Bat groan with weariness. He was tired of being labeled a "man-killer" with a gun that had notches on the grip. He later told the *New York Times*, "I haven't done anything like what's been printed. I can't say I like it much either; it seems a little like ridicule to me, and no man likes ridicule."[20]

As far as his duties as a deputy marshal, it seems all Bat did was show up to collect his paycheck and little else.

Another Westerner Theodore held in high esteem was Ben Daniels. Born in Illinois and raised in Kansas, Daniels had headed to Texas as a teenager to work on cattle drives before taking up buffalo hunting on the Southern Plains. Drifting to Montana Territory in 1879, Daniels fell in with the notorious horse thief "Dutch Henry" Born, and was arrested for stealing US Army mules. Taken into custody by the military, he managed to escape, shooting two soldiers in the process. (One of them, a lieutenant, later died.) Daniels landed in Dodge City, Kansas, where an arrest warrant caught up with him, and Ford County sheriff Bat Masterson took him into custody in early September 1879. Sentenced to three and a half years in the Wyoming Territorial Prison, Daniels was released four months early because of his good behavior.[21]

Between 1883 and 1898, Daniels served as a lawman in such Western towns as Dodge City, Lamar, and Cripple Creek, as well as working as a gambler. When the call went out for volunteers to fight in the Spanish-American War, Daniels, like other Westerners, quickly joined up. This is how Daniels and Theodore came to know each other. In *The Rough Riders*, Theodore described Daniels as "a very large, hawk-eyed man," noting his lower right ear lobe was missing, which Daniels claimed was "bitten off" in a fight. "Naturally, he viewed the dangers of battle with a philosophic calm," Theodore wrote. "Such a man was, in reality, a veteran even in his first fight, and was a tower of strength to the recruits in his part of the line."[22] The two men remained friends through the years, and once Theodore took over the president's office, Daniels approached him about the position of US marshal in Arizona Territory.

A Secret Service memo indicated that Daniels may have had a questionable background relating to his gambling interests; however, Attorney General Philander Knox gave Theodore a positive recommendation. Stories quickly circulated, real and concocted, about Daniels's background. His profession as a gambler and saloon owner was quickly condemned by religious leaders, as were the lurid tales (which were untrue) of his deeds as a deadly lawman in the old days of the West. After his Senate confirmation on January 21, 1902, Theodore reminded Daniels that his approval had come about because Theodore had given his personal word that Daniels was an honest and courageous man. As he had done with Bat Masterson, Theodore cautioned Daniels that he must "feel to the fullest extent the weight of your responsibility, not only to the Government and yourself, but to me. You are bound by honor to make my judgement good. You have been my comrade in days of risk and hardship and danger against a violent criminal, against an anarchist or mob leader; I know I can count on you always."[23]

Not every man can escape the shadows of his past.

In early February 1903, newspapers began to detail Daniels's criminal background. When it became obvious that some senators wanted to remove Daniels from his post, Theodore quietly asked him to resign. "You did wrong in not being frank with me," Theodore wrote to Daniels. "You put me in the position of unwittingly deceiving my friends in the Senate ... I am more sorry than I can say to write you this letter."[24] Despite the setback, Theodore remained loyal to his friend, getting him appointed warden at the Arizona Territorial Prison in Yuma. Daniels attended Theodore's swearing-in ceremony for his second presidential term in March 1905, and during a private lunch, Theodore said that he intended to nominate Daniels again for US marshal of Arizona Territory. Armed with letters of support from many notable citizens, judges, and law officers, Daniels's appointment was approved by the Senate on April 25, 1906, ten months after he had already pinned on the marshal's badge.[25]

Seth Bullock, the former lawman of Deadwood, was another Westerner who was very close to Theodore. The two men first met around 1892, when Theodore was a civil service commissioner. Crossing the Belle Fourche River, Theodore and his party were spotted by Bullock, who thought they might be gamblers. (Having visited Medora and his old ranch, Theodore was making his way through Deadwood to the Sioux reservations.) Exchanging greetings, Bullock learned of Theodore's profession, and stated, "Well, anything civil goes with me."[26] It was the beginning of a lifelong friendship between the two men. During Theodore's vice presidential campaign trip of 1900, Seth joined his express train in Yankton, South Dakota, and traveled with Theodore through South Dakota, North Dakota, and Montana. At a stop in Butte, Montana, Theodore spoke to a group of miners who were strong Democratic Party supporters. Bullock, expecting the audience to be hostile, sent advance word that if anyone in the audience was rude, he would kill them. Backing up his words, Bullock sat on the stage behind Theodore, his pistols very much in evidence. No one did a thing.[27]

In 1897, President Grover Cleveland used the power of executive order to create the Black Hills Forest Reserve, which closed the area to loggers, cattlemen, and homesteaders. In 1901, the position of forest supervisor of the Black Hills Forest Reserve became vacant, and interested parties hoped a local man would be appointed to the position, thus easing the tight regulations. Bullock's name was sent to McKinley, and with Theodore's strong lobbying, the former lawman was given the position. Once in office, Bullock managed to persuade Washington to allow him to hire men from the West as rangers instead of a bunch of Eastern dudes. Although Bullock's administration issued more grazing and timber permits than his predecessor's, they were carefully monitored to keep things in balance.

In 1902, before it was granted national park status, Theodore appointed Bullock as custodian of Wind Cave in South Dakota.[28] Three years later, Bullock assembled a contingent of cowboys that he led during Theodore's inaugural parade. One young cowboy was Tom Mix, who went on to become one of the biggest Western stars in motion pictures. (Both Geronimo and Quanah Parker also rode in the parade.) When the ceremonies were over, Theodore nominated Bullock for US marshal for the state of South Dakota, which the Senate quickly approved. Bullock held the position until he resigned in 1914 at the age of sixty-four.

Bullock, more than any other Westerner, appealed to Theodore in many ways. He was a man of the West, had enforced the law, and was as practical, no-nonsense, and honest as the day is long. He was also a living link to the West Theodore had just missed. Friendships with men such as Bullock, Daniels, and Masterson allowed him to get as close to those days as possible.[29] Theodore sent his son, Ted Jr., and his nephew, George, to Deadwood for a two-week stay with his old friend in 1903, where Bullock introduced the teenagers to the West, teaching them to ride, shoot, hunt for game, and fish. In a letter to Ted Jr., Theodore mentioned that Bullock had complimented the young man, stating he was "hard as nails," and that there was "good leather in you, and that he believed you might make a good citizen in time if you were allowed to complete your education out west!"[30] (Theodore also sent Kermit and Archie to visit Bullock in subsequent years.)

Pat Garrett, the lawman who shot Billy the Kid in 1881, was one Westerner who ultimately proved to be a headache for Theodore. General Lew Wallace had introduced Garrett to Theodore and had "vouched for him most warmly."[31] Unlike Masterson, Daniels, and Bullock, Theodore did not have a personal relationship with Garrett, who relied on his influential friends to lobby on his behalf for a federal position. Garrett was appointed collector of customs in El Paso, Texas, in January 1902, which ignited a firestorm of protest from Texans who wanted one of their own appointed, not a nonresident. (Garrett was living in New Mexico at the time.) After assuming the job, Garrett racked up several complaints (mainly citing his poor attitude), and a street fight with a former employee in 1903 did little to help his reputation. However, Garrett's fate was sealed by his actions when he attended the 1905 Rough Riders reunion in San Antonio, and brought along his friend Tom Powers, known as the owner of El Paso's most notorious saloon. Introducing his friend to Theodore, Garrett stated Powers was a "cattleman."[32] A photo of Theodore, Garrett, and Powers sitting at a table with other guests appeared in numerous newspapers, and Garrett's detractors quickly pointed out to Theodore the true profession of Tom Powers. It was an embarrassment Theodore did not forget.

Learning he was likely not to be reappointed to his position, Garrett made a trip to the White House in December 1905, hoping to change Theodore's mind. In a move that can only be described as imbecilic, Garrett brought along Tom Powers! The two men received an icy greeting to rival a Dakota winter. Theodore made it perfectly clear to Garrett that Powers was not welcome at the White House, and his days as collector of customs were finished.

Who would have expected that a woman's wardrobe accessory would have created the first Federal Bird Reservation? At the turn of the century, the newest fashion for women's hats was to adorn them with large plumes. The larger and more colorful the plume, the better. Women loved the fashion, and milliners loved the profits.

No one bothered to ask the birds what they thought.

By the end of the 1890s, upwards of five million birds from fifty species had been killed for the millinery trade.

In March 1903, William Dutcher and Frank Bond of the American Ornithologists Union (AOU) secured a meeting with Theodore to inform him about the situation at Pelican Island in Florida. Hundreds of birds, especially egrets, were being slaughtered for their feathers, with the carcasses carelessly tossed aside. The AOU had tried to purchase the island from the federal government, with little success. Theodore, the self-taught ornithologist, was disgusted by the news. He asked those assembled if there was *any* law that would prevent him from claiming Pelican Island as a Federal Bird Reserve. Informed that there was no law that could stop him, he slapped the table with his hand. "I so declare it!" he announced.[33]

In that moment, Theodore Roosevelt had taken a major step as president to protect the land and the animals for the people of the United States. If Congress would not support his ideas, he would find a way around them by an executive order. Too impatient to wait for Congress to make a decision, Theodore initiated action and let others debate his efforts afterwards.

When he assumed the office of president, over half of the virgin forests were gone. Ten times more trees were being cut down than were planted for regrowth. Theodore put a stop to that and saved what he could. His future decrees would infuriate the pro-business side of the Republican Party and its financial contributors, but Theodore did not care. He carved out sections of the country that would forever be safe from the hands of developers, allowing generations of families to appreciate this country's natural wonders. "There's nothing lower than somebody that wants to develop this land for their own personal gain without concern about how the land will be for the next generation," he once stated.[34]

There was an interesting dichotomy in Theodore Roosevelt's conservation efforts. He would save thousands of acres of land, yet he also built huge dams, such as the Roosevelt Dam in Arizona, for water reclamation. He believed the parched desert areas of the Southwest, with proper water projects, could be used to sustain the area for growing crops, thus making the country self-sustaining, as well as providing goods for trade. Just as he was adamant in saving wild game from destruction but continued to hunt, Theodore's conservation beliefs were often something of a paradox. Actually, Theodore wanted to take both paths. He saw nothing wrong in carving out an area for a dam that would provide irrigation for hundreds, if not thousands, of acres for growing crops. However, where those dams were built was just as important to him. He would not allow a dam in, or near, an area that would spoil natural beauty. It may seem self-serving on his part as to where he approved dams to be located, but in Theodore's mind, he felt he knew best, rarely altering his opinion. He wanted farmers to thrive, to grow fields of wheat, corn, fruits, and vegetables. Theodore embraced the vision of the spring planting, a wide wheat field shimmering in the summer sun, and the fall harvest of crops. It was one of the things he believed was best about America—that a man could plant crops in a field and see his efforts pay off with a healthy harvest, allowing him to be independent.

Just as he wanted farmers and cattlemen to thrive, he also wanted to protect the land from developers, who were interested only in immediate profit and not the future. To allow a railroad to traverse through Yellowstone National Park was unthinkable to Theodore, just as it was to cut the trees down in the area for profit, or hunt the animals for only their hides. Developers didn't care about the potential damage their projects would bring decades later. It wasn't their land; they didn't live there. To the lumbermen, trees were simply a means to an end. Cut them down and collect the money. They cared little about the environment or the animals that needed forests to survive. Where was the immediate, practical profit in protecting trees for birds, ground squirrels, or a doe and its fawn?

The same mentality was found in the mining companies that wanted to dig in what they called the "Big Ditch" in northern Arizona Territory. To them, the minerals in the rocks of the Grand Canyon were all that mattered. Majestic beauty? It was a wide hole in the ground. The minerals would make them money. The land above what became Wind Cave National Park could be useful for lumber, farming, or building a town. What was a cave worth? What could it possibly provide for this country? Who cared about the cliff dwellings of some long-forgotten tribe? What did a petrified forest matter, except to chip and sell the remains as souvenirs?

The land became one of Theodore's biggest battlegrounds. He would lead the fight to protect American lands and native animals. It is interesting that, during his first term, he took small steps in creating forest reserves and national parks. Knowing that he had stepped into the presidency by default, he was cautious about taking big strides in preserving lands. The majority of his preservation actions happened after he was reelected on his own terms.

The first forest reserve he chose was not within the United States but rather Puerto Rico. In January 1903, he created the Luquillo National Forest Reserve, setting aside 28,000 acres of rain forest. (In 1907 it was renamed Luquillo National Forest.) Some historians have speculated that Theodore chose this location for his first forest reserve so as not to panic the pro-timber Republicans and their contributors. He created another national forest, White River, in Colorado in May 1904, prior to his reelection. Crater Lake in Oregon and Wind Cave in South Dakota became national parks in May 1902 and January 1903, respectively.

❖

The "Great Loop Tour of 1903" was an affirmation of Theodore's desire to carry out his plan to protect the land and its wildlife. The expansive train trip, the first by any sitting president, made many stops where he delivered speeches on various subjects, including conservation. (After all, he was running for reelection the following year.)[35] After a two-week rest in Yellowstone, Theodore's schedule had him stopping at St. Louis (dedicating the Louisiana Purchase Exposition Grounds), then crossing the prairies of Nebraska and Kansas to the Grand Canyon, and on to California and Yosemite.

Theodore wanted to shoot a mountain lion in Yellowstone, hoping to reduce the population, but came to realize that mountain lions were valuable in thinning out the park's elk herds to reasonable numbers. On this trip, the only shooting of animals would be done with his camera.[36] Close friends since 1889, John Burroughs, the noted naturalist, and Theodore shared a love for the outdoors and birds. Invited by Theodore to come "see" Yellowstone, Burroughs quickly accepted. He later stated, "I knew nothing about big game, but I knew there was no man in the country with whom I should so like to see it as Roosevelt."[37]

Burroughs recalled that as the train made its way across the country, they saw a small schoolhouse not far from the train tracks, with the teacher and her students lined up to see the president go by. Spotting the group, Theodore jumped from the lunch table and rushed to the rear platform, waving to the children as the train passed them. Theodore told Burroughs the children wanted to see the president and he couldn't disappoint them. "They may never have another chance. What a deep impression such things make when we are young," he said.[38]

Reporters, Secret Service agents, Theodore's physician, and his secretary were all left behind in Gardiner, Montana. Theodore wanted none of the trappings that went with the office of the president around him. As Burroughs noted, the president "craved once more to be alone with nature." Theodore wanted to walk alone in the park, refusing Maj. John Pitcher's request to send an orderly along with him. After an eighteen-mile hike by himself, Theodore walked briskly back into camp.[39]

With only a few guides accompanying them, Theodore and Burroughs spent hours walking through the fields and along the riverbanks, soaking up the vastness and majesty that is Yellowstone. From April 8 to 24, Theodore and Burroughs observed buffalo and elk herds, the various geysers and mud pots. They kept themselves busy identifying the various birds by their songs or colors. "I found his interest in bird life very keen," Burroughs wrote, "and his eye and ear remarkably quick."[40] As impressed with Yellowstone as he was, Burroughs was equally impressed by Theodore's encyclopedic knowledge of the area's flora and fauna. "Nothing escaped him, from bears to mice, from wild geese to chickadees, from elk to red squirrels; he took it all in," the naturalist commented. He was also impressed by the way Theodore treated the men and women of the West, giving himself "very freely and heartily" to people wherever he went. Burroughs observed Theodore easily matched their "Western cordiality and good-fellowship."[41]

On the last day of their visit to Yellowstone, April 24, Theodore laid the cornerstone for the archway at the park's northern entrance, known today as the Roosevelt Arch. Standing thirty feet tall, the inscription above the archway reads "For the Benefit and Enjoyment of the People." Speaking to a crowd of 3,500 people, Theodore commented, "The Yellowstone Park is something absolutely unique in the world, so far as I know. Nowhere else in any civilized country is there to be found such a tract of veritable wonderland made accessible to all visitors, where at the same time not only the scenery of the wilderness, but the wild creatures of the Park are scrupulously preserved . . . The creation and preservation of such a great natural playground in the interest of our people as a whole is a credit to the nation."[42]

Reluctantly bidding good-bye to Yellowstone and Burroughs the following day, Theodore continued on the train for St. Louis. Traveling through South Dakota, he and Seth Bullock managed to find time to ride horses over some of the Black Hills Forest Reserve, as well as share a chuck-wagon meal with locals before heading east. In St. Louis, he was reunited with former president Grover Cleveland, where the two men participated in the World's Fair ceremonies. As his train headed west, Theodore made stops in Iowa, Nebraska, and Kansas, where a young girl gifted him with a baby badger she named Josiah. The child and the gift delighted Theodore no end, and Josiah became part of the expanding White House menagerie.[43]

Its length is 277 miles, it is up to 18 miles wide, and it has a depth of more than 1 mile. It is estimated that the Colorado River, which runs through it, began its course nearly 17 million years ago. The river has, over time, exposed nearly 2 billion years of the Earth's geological history. The oldest human artifact found in the area dates back 12,000 years, and the region has been continuously inhabited and occupied since then. Many describe it as massive, grand, majestic, or beautiful; some locals sarcastically call it "the Big Ditch." Others say nothing—they simply stare at its expanse.

It is the Grand Canyon.

Theodore arrived on May 6, 1903, and was instantly left speechless by his first glimpse. The Grand Canyon is so vast that no one can grasp all of its wonders in a day, or even a week. There is nothing like it in the world. Prior to this visit, Theodore had only heard of the Grand Canyon, or read about it (especially John Wesley Powell's trips down the Colorado River), or seen Thomas Moran's paintings. Now the child in him was filled with delight, awe, and fascination. Theodore's ever-inquisitive thirst for knowledge filled him with hundreds of questions dying to be answered. He later called the Grand Canyon "the most wonderful scenery in the world."

His visit to the canyon was brief, about twelve hours, which did not allow him the time he wanted to truly inspect it. However, it made an impression upon him that he never forgot. He would take steps to see that the Grand Canyon became a national park. Speaking to a group of local people on the south rim of the canyon, Theodore urged them to do their duty in preserving this place of wonderment:

In the Grand Canyon, Arizona has a natural wonder which, so far as I know, is in kind absolutely unparalleled throughout the rest of the world. I want to ask you to do one thing in connection with it in your own interest and in the interest of the country—to keep this great wonder of nature as it now is . . . I hope you will not have a building of any kind, not a summer cottage, a hotel or anything else, to mar the wonderful grandeur, the sublimity, the great loneliness and beauty of the canyon. Leave it as it is. You cannot improve on it. The ages have been at work on it, and man can only mar it. Keep it for your children and your children's children and all who come after you as one of the great sights which every American if he can travel at all should see.[44]

His train headed west to California, through the Mojave Desert and the citrus-filled San Bernardino Valley. He spoke in Redlands, Los Angeles, and then made his way up the Pacific Coast. Stopping in Santa Cruz, he gave a short speech before heading to the Big Tree Grove of sequoias. Gazing at the massive growths that lifted to the sky, he was disturbed that name placards (such as "Uncle John," "Old Fremont," and "Giant") had been placed on the trees. He felt it demeaned them, and made his feelings quickly known, even when it was announced that a tree would be named after him. Theodore would accept the tribute under one condition: that no sign *ever* be posted on it. He believed the sequoia grove was one of God's great cathedrals, and asked to be left alone, walking among these giants in isolation. When he returned, all the placards had been removed from the trees.[45]

After speaking in Berkeley (where he gave the commencement speech at University of California, Berkeley), Oakland, and San Francisco, Theodore's train arrived on May 15 in the small town of Raymond, the nearest location with a rail line for anyone wishing to visit Yosemite. Before giving a brief speech to the waiting crowd, Theodore and the Sierra Club's John Muir met in his private car. Muir, realizing he had an opportunity to do "some good in talking freely around the campfire" with Theodore, postponed a trip abroad to accompany Theodore "out in the open."

Boarding a passenger stage (travel by stagecoach or horseback was the only way into Yosemite from Raymond), Theodore sat up front with the driver, while Muir sat behind the president, pointing out various sites. After a lunch at the Wawona Hotel, the group traveled to the Mariposa Grove of sequoia trees, home to some of the oldest redwoods in the state. Posing with Muir and other dignitaries next to the "Grizzly Giant," Theodore bade farewell to the cavalry officers who had accompanied him from Raymond, as well as other dignitaries, his staff, and the press. While others expected Theodore to return to the Wawona Hotel for a dinner in his honor, he had other plans. Accompanied by guides Archie Leonard and Charles Leidig, he and John Muir disappeared into the Mariposa Grove, where they camped for the night under the Grizzly Giant, much to the frustration of visiting dignitaries waiting at the hotel. "We lay down in the darkening aisles of the great Sequoia grove. The majestic trunks, beautiful in color and in symmetry, rose round us like the pillars of a mightier cathedral than [was] ever conceived even by the fervor of the Middle Ages," Theodore recalled in his autobiography.[46] (The Grizzly Giant, the oldest tree in the area, is estimated to be between 1,900 and 2,400 years old.)

As the sun broke over their camp, Theodore instructed Charles Leidig to "keep away from civilization." Saddling up, they left Mariposa Grove and headed down Lightning Trail, then crossed the South Fork at Greeley's before switching to the Empire Meadows Trail, where they had lunch. The group encountered snow as they crossed toward Sentinel

Dome, with each man taking turns carving a trail through the heavy snow, which at times was nearly five feet deep. Reaching Glacier Point, they were greeted with blowing wind and snow. Once they got their camp set up, Muir built a bonfire and talked endlessly about his glacial theory.[47] (The bonfire was needed, as it snowed five inches overnight, much to Theodore's delight.) The following morning, as they were about to pose for what has become an iconic photograph of the duo, Theodore told Muir that he believed the Yosemite Valley should become part of the park.[48]

Making their way down from Glacier Point, they encountered a crowd of women who lined the road waiting to see the president, effectively blocking the group's passage. Theodore, clearly not happy at the crowd, asked Leidig for help. His guide tapped the spurs into his horse's flanks and the animal took off at a gallop, quickly parting the group. Theodore doffed his hat and waved at the ladies as he rode by. Muir suggested a campsite in Bridalveil Meadows, not far from the falls.[49] Onlookers followed and Leidig asked them to please leave the president alone, as he was very tired. As the sightseers quietly left, Theodore told Leidig he was "hungry as hell."[50] (During the trip, Theodore consumed healthy amounts of chicken-fried steak and strong black coffee.) A stage arrived in the morning, collecting Theodore and Muir for the ride back to his train. Anyone within earshot of Theodore was regaled with stories of his grand time in the outdoors, even sleeping in a snowstorm. ("We were in a snowstorm last night, and it was just what I wanted.") As his train slowly made its way back to Washington, he waxed on about the wonders of Yellowstone and Yosemite.

Theodore and Muir may seem to be an odd couple if there ever was one, but the two men got along famously, despite Muir's disinterest in animals and birds. One interesting story from the three-day trip happened up on Glacier Point. Sitting before the bonfire, Muir took a burning branch and placed it on a dead pine tree. The lifeless timber was quickly engulfed and lit up the area like a huge candle. Muir broke out into a jig, dancing around the flaming tree, and Theodore quickly joined him. They were like two little boys on an adventure, sharing their joy of the land in a childlike manner. Theodore commented that the dead tree was a candle that took five hundred years to make, adding "Hurrah for

Yosemite!"[51] The love they had for the land was obvious, and Theodore's first visit to the famous park did more than open his eyes. It spurred his desire to conserve more land for the public and the wildlife.

In addition to establishing federal bird and forest reserves, national parks, and national monuments, Theodore helped to create the Bronx Zoo. Theodore and William Hornaday, a noted zoologist and author, sponsored a program to breed buffalo in captivity at the zoo to save the species from extinction. (By 1889 only 1,091 buffalo remained either in the wild or in captivity.[52])

In the spring of 1905, Theodore traveled to San Antonio, Texas, for a reunion with his beloved Rough Riders. (This was the reunion that Pat Garrett and Tom Powers attended.) From there, he traveled to Oklahoma Territory for two reasons: to scout an area for a future buffalo reserve, and to visit Jack "Catch 'em Alive" Abernathy.

The Wichita Mountains are located in the southwestern portion of what is now the state of Oklahoma. About 330 to 290 million years ago, an upheaval occurred, establishing mountains that eventually were worn down by erosion to their current height (400 to 1,000 feet). The land is a combination of forest, rock outcroppings, and mixed grassland, and was an area the buffalo had once called home.[53] After inspecting the mountains firsthand, Theodore believed the region could support a herd for reintroduction onto the Southern Plains. His administration set aside 60,800 acres in the Wichita Mountains, officially protecting all wildlife from hunters.

Jack Abernathy was an authentic Texan, having worked as a cowboy and a bronc buster. He was plainspoken, direct, and just the type of man Theodore would gravitate to. Abernathy gained notoriety by jumping off his horse and tussling a wolf to the ground bare-handed, earning him the nickname "Catch 'em Alive Jack." Abernathy would jam his fist (wearing a glove, of course) into the back of the wolf's jaw, which would make the animal perfectly passive. He would then wire its muzzle closed and tie its feet. It was something Theodore had to see in person.

Theodore's train arrived in Frederick, Oklahoma Territory, on April 5, 1905, to an appreciative crowd. He appealed to the audience not to follow him on his adventure. "Give me a fair deal to have as much fun as even a President is entitled to," he requested.[54] Abernathy had chosen Deep Red Creek, fifteen miles from Frederick, for the campsite, which boasted fifteen tents. After dinner, a large fire was built outside the tents where Theodore told others of his days in the Dakota Territory, where he'd "gained a lasting respect for western life. I was amazed at the President's knowledge of wild animals, snakes, and even the smallest of reptiles and insects," Abernathy recalled.[55]

Watching Abernathy catch a wolf for the first time, Theodore was like a child at Christmas, uttering "Bully!" numerous times. When he asked the Texan how he got his hand behind the wolf's teeth, Abernathy replied, "By practice, Mr. President."[56] Theodore was astonished by the actions of Abernathy in countless chases and catches. Recalling one of Abernathy's catches, Theodore commented, "I was not twenty yards distant at the time, and as I leaped off the horse he was sitting placidly on the live wolf, his hand between its jaws . . . It was as remarkable a feat of the kind as I have ever seen."[57]

While Theodore did not attempt to catch a wolf himself, the closest he came to danger was when a six-foot rattlesnake lunged at him four times. He killed it by thrashing it with his eighteen-inch quirt.[58]

During his stay, Theodore met with Quanah Parker, the famous Comanche chief, about his plans to repopulate the Wichita Mountains with buffalo. Quanah had long held the dream that the buffalo would come back to the Plains. The two men enjoyed a close friendship, riding around the land, sharing stories. Both shared a love of the buffalo, which they had hunted earlier in life. Now they would see them reborn.

In Colorado Springs, Colorado, Theodore once again asked his well-wishers to give him some privacy as he started another bear hunt. "You cannot combine bear hunting with a brass band," he noted.[59] While Theodore did manage to shoot some bears on his trip in the Rockies, he also gained a new friend. "There was also a funny little black and tan [dog], named Skip, a most friendly little fellow. . . . Skip adopted me as his special master, rode with me whenever I would let him, and slept on the foot of my bed at night, growling defiance at anything that came near. I grew attached to the friendly, bright little fellow."[60] Like Josiah the badger from his previous trip, Skip went home to join the Roosevelt menagerie and became a favorite with Archie.

In addition to their buffalo project at the Bronx Zoo, Theodore, William Hornaday, and Charles "Buffalo" Jones founded the American Bison Society (ABS) in December 1905.[61] The society's mandate was to increase the numbers of buffalo and return them eventually to the Great Plains and northern Rocky Mountain regions. Fifteen buffalo left the Bronx Zoo on October 18, 1907, traveling in individual padded compartment cars to their destination of Cache, Oklahoma. Waiting for them was Quanah Parker. His steely eyes watched as the buffalo were offloaded from the train onto wagons bound for the Wichita Mountains, where they were released. (The Wichita Mountains Wildlife Refuge now boasts a herd of 650 buffalo.)

On May 23, 1908, Theodore signed into law legislation creating the National Bison Range, with the specific intention of maintaining a buffalo refuge.[62] For the first time in American history, the US Congress purchased over 18,000 acres for the sole purpose of providing shelter for wildlife. The original herd was donated by the ABS, with additional buffalo coming from the legendary Texas rancher, Charlie Goodnight.

The American buffalo had begun its comeback.[63]

The 1906 Act for the Preservation of American Antiques gave Theodore the freedom to set aside historic landmarks, historic and prehistoric structures, and other objects of historic or scientific interest under the title "National Monument." The law gave the president nearly unfettered discretion in choosing what to protect, as well as determining the size of these locations. It was just the type of decree Theodore needed when Congress was too slow to act. Between 1906 and 1909, Theodore created eighteen national monuments, including the Grand Canyon, Devils Tower in Wyoming, Petrified Park in Arizona, Jewel Cave in South Dakota, Natural Bridges in Utah, and Mount Olympus in Washington. (The Grand Canyon was granted national park status in 1919, seven and a half weeks after Theodore's death.)

By the end of Theodore's time in office, he had done more for the land and wildlife than any other US president, past or present. In addition to national monuments, Theodore established six national parks and fifty-one federal bird reserves, and created or expanded 150 national forests.

It is estimated that Theodore preserved 230 million acres during his presidency, equaling half of the land size of Thomas Jefferson's Louisiana Purchase in 1803.

◆

Like a cowboy, Theodore's word was his bond. Despite the emotional pains, he honored his promise not to seek a third term. Friends and supporters urged him to reconsider, and even the majority of the public wanted him to run again. (Historians believe that had Theodore run for a third term, he would have easily won.) Tempting as it was, he wouldn't go back on his word.

He convinced his friend, Secretary of War William Howard Taft, to take up where he had left off, carrying on his ideals and policies. Taft was an agreeable sort who honestly had no real desire to be president. His personal desire was to serve as Supreme Court chief justice.[64] Between Theodore's cajoling, and the prodding of Taft's ambitious wife, he agreed to run, and easily won the presidency.

Snow blanketed Washington on March 4, 1909. Actually, it was a blizzard. It made the carriage carrying Theodore and Taft from the White House to the Capitol move ever so slowly. People cheered Theodore, and he responded; despite the blowing snow, he lowered his carriage window to wave to the crowd. Because of the weather, the swearing-in ceremony at the Capitol took place inside the Senate chamber.

Once Taft took the oath of office, Theodore shook the new president's hand and wished him well. After a few minutes of people expressing their feelings to Theodore, he left the chamber to return to his waiting carriage. Outside the Capitol, the crowd would not let their beloved former president go quietly. Among cheers and well wishes, Theodore made his way to the carriage that took him to the train station where Edith and Quentin were waiting. As his carriage left the Capitol, a band began to play "Auld Lang Syne," leaving many a face tear-streaked.

The presidency of Theodore Roosevelt had come to an end.

THE OLD LION'S AUTUMN

Every feat of heroism makes us forever indebted to the man who performed it.

"AMERICA EXPECTS EVERY LION TO DO HIS DUTY," J. P. MORGAN STATED as Theodore headed to Africa, three weeks after leaving office.[1]

While Theodore kept up the appearance of his usual "bully" attitude, leaving the presidency left him depressed. For a man used to action and jumping into the fray (and usually, emerging victorious), the sedate life of a former leader all but made him doleful. (He was only fifty when he left the White House.) In typical fashion, when losing something he greatly cared about, Theodore fled into the wilderness. This time, however, he would not go west. He would not return to Medora, Yellowstone, or the Rocky Mountains. On this occasion, he chose the most remote wilderness possible.

Africa.

What began as a private hunting trip soon became a massive trek, thanks to the sponsorship of the Smithsonian Institution and Andrew Carnegie. The Smithsonian, wanting to enlarge its collection of wildlife specimens, asked Theodore to bring back as many big-game carcasses as he could shoot, as well as collect as much flora as possible.[2] He would be accompanied by his son, Kermit, on the yearlong expedition that would start in Mombasa (coastal town in Kenya). The three-hundred-man expedition would make its way to the Belgian Congo (now the Republic of the Congo) and on to the Nile River, before concluding in Khartoum. On the vast African plains a huge tent city rose, with the Stars and Stripes prominently displayed near Theodore's tent, which included a rubber bathtub and sixty books.

The interior of Africa in 1909 was as far from civilization as one could get. The remoteness delayed news of the world, especially from Washington, from reaching Theodore and his party in a timely manner. When letters and newspapers finally did arrive, they detailed a dismal picture of Taft as an executive. Privately, as frustrating as it was for him, there was little Theodore could do. He told a reporter traveling with the caravan that he was "only focusing" on the current expedition. Between hunting trips, Theodore was busy taking notes and writing a series of articles for *Scribner's Magazine*.[3]

By February 1910, as the safari was winding down, the various flora and fauna were packed and sent back to the United States. Theodore felt the pangs of homesickness. "I am homesick for my own land and my own people! Of course it is Mrs. Roosevelt I most want to see; but I want to see my two youngest boys; I want to see my own house, my own books and trees, the sunset over the Sound from the window in the north room," he confessed to Andrew Carnegie in a letter.[4]

In another letter to his friend Seth Bullock, Theodore noted how well Kermit had done on the trip, as well as showing his fatherly concern.

He is not quite as careful as he should be, and keeps my heart in my mouth, but he is a good boy, and although he does not shoot very well, he rides hard, fears no risk, cares nothing for fatigue, and is as keen as mustard. The day before yesterday he killed a charging Leopard in fine style, which had already mauled one of our men.[5]

Theodore's homesickness was eased when their ship arrived in Khartoum on March 14, 1910, as he and Kermit were reunited with Edith and Ethel. The Roosevelts then traveled on to Alexandria and viewed the Great Pyramids. Crossing the Mediterranean Sea, they visited Naples and Rome. Everywhere Theodore went, he was followed by reporters anxious for his opinion about the Taft administration, but Theodore refused to be drawn into a public debate. Privately, the letters continued to paint a grim picture of Taft ignoring, or curtailing, the progressive agenda Theodore had established. Taft was friendlier than Theodore had been to the pro-business side of the Republican Party, often playing golf with many industry executives. Before he'd left office, Theodore had warned Taft to limit his golfing, as it was perceived as a "rich man's sport," and would give the wrong impression to the public.

The Roosevelts' trip across the European continent was nonstop, with almost every nation and monarch wanting at least a day with the former president. For the next three months, they visited several cities, including Paris (where Theodore gave his famous "Man in the Arena" speech at the Sorbonne), Vienna, Copenhagen, Stockholm, Berlin, and London.

In Norway, on May 5, he belatedly accepted his Nobel Peace Prize for his 1904 mediation in ending the Russo-Japanese War. "Peace is generally good in itself," he stated, "but it is never the highest good unless it comes as the handmaid of righteousness."[6] When he was awarded the Nobel Prize, he kept the medal, but he gave the $40,000 to a foundation for industrial peace. Addressing the Nobel Prize committee, Theodore stated that in most situations, the recipient should keep the money. "In this case," he noted, "while I did not act officially as President of the United States, it was nevertheless only because I was President that I was enabled to act at all; and I felt that the money must be considered as having been given me in trust for the United States. I therefore used it as a nucleus for a foundation to forward the cause of industrial peace, as being well within the general purpose of your committee."[7]

With the death of England's King Edward VII, Theodore accepted President Taft's request to represent the United States at the funeral. Every head of Europe attended the funeral, but Theodore had had enough of royalty. He needed to be with his own kind of people. From Nairobi, he sent a letter to Seth Bullock, inviting his friend and his wife to come visit him. "There are few things I should like quite so much as meeting you in London, when I get back from this trip. We shall have a great time together. . . . Do try to come over, Seth."[8]

Bullock sensed that Theodore had sent for him to "help him laugh." His friend did not let him down. One day, as the two were walking along the Thames River, Bullock strolled up to a pompous-looking Englishman. Pointing to the Thames, Bullock asked "What's the name of this creek?" It gave Theodore a chuckle that lasted all day. When a reporter asked

Bullock how long he had known the former president, he replied, "From the tail of a chuck wagon to the Court of St. James."[9]

It was a true hero's welcome when Theodore's ship arrived in New York Harbor on June 18, 1910, escorted by a battleship, five destroyers, and a plethora of smaller vessels. Crowds cheered and waved flags at their beloved Theodore's return. When he and his company moved to a smaller boat, there was a reunion of the entire family, including Bamie and Corinne, as well as his distant cousin, Franklin Delano Roosevelt. Coming ashore at Battery Park, the loud cheers from the crowd moved him to tears, which he quickly covered up by cleaning his glasses. After giving a brief speech, there was a five-mile ticker-tape parade, escorted by many uniformed Rough Riders. Theodore, standing in the mayor's carriage, acknowledged the adoring crowd.[10]

Settling in at home at Sagamore Hill, Theodore told a reporter that he looked forward to some privacy. He also kept his silence relating to President Taft's administration. He was deeply disappointed in Taft dismissing Gifford Pinchot as chief forester, scaling back many conservation programs, and simply ignoring others. He was invited by Taft to the White House, but the former chief executive was less than responsive. "I don't think it well for an ex-President to go to the White House, or indeed go to Washington, except when he cannot help it," he wrote to Taft.[11]

Theodore was reluctant to publicly criticize Taft, wishing to give him the benefit of the doubt as he started out in office. Yet more and more disgruntled progressive members of the Republican Party kept complaining to Theodore, some even suggesting that he should run for the presidency again. Brushing off the hints, Theodore met briefly with Taft near Boston. It was obvious the old friendship had dimmed.

It was soon to get darker.

The drumbeats for Theodore to run against Taft began quietly as 1911 started. By the end of the year, those drumbeats were louder, and a strong movement to nominate Theodore had formed. Privately, Theodore became more and more critical of the president and his actions, yet he was conflicted about running against Taft. It was more than exasperating for him to sit idly by and watch the advances he had made be dismantled or weakened. The lion paced his cage, his roars growing louder with his dissatisfaction.

Theodore sought the opinions of political friends about launching a 1912 campaign. Edith was completely against it. His old friend and closest confidant, Henry Cabot Lodge, urged him to wait until 1916. Lodge told Theodore that if he ran against Taft in 1912, it would split the party in two and allow a Democratic victory. A group drafted a petition to nominate Theodore as the Republican candidate, which he privately indicated he'd accept. Edith, tired of the nonstop visits by politicians to Sagamore Hill, left with Ethel for a trip to Panama and Costa Rica. She knew Theodore's mind was already made up and whenever he made his announcement, Edith wanted to be far from the circus.

At the end of February 1912, Theodore stated, "My hat is in the ring. The fight is on and I am stripped to the buff."[12] Theodore wasted no time in criticizing Taft, his actions, or his inertia. Taft fought back, publicly calling Theodore a dangerous egotist. Privately, Taft was deeply hurt by Theodore's attacks. He could not understand how his best friend could turn on him so viciously. Others questioned why Theodore had chosen to run. Did he truly believe he was fighting the fight for the people, or was his ego running unchecked? The disparity between rich and poor had greatly increased since Theodore had left office, and he knew such a wide gulf could lead to revolt and anarchy. By taking up the cause, he was prepared to risk everything he had accomplished for the good of the people. He would see that the regular people had a voice, a man who would fight for them. Some historians have likened his 1912 political campaign to a quixotic experience.

In 1912, not all states held primaries, but of those that did, Theodore won all but two, even taking Taft's home state of Ohio. In order for Theodore to secure the nomination, his delegates had to carry the convention, something the old guard of the Republican Party would fight to the bitter end. As the Republican convention opened in Chicago, 250 delegates were up for grabs. Theodore needed only 70 to secure the nomination, but the credentials of delegates were determined by a committee that favored Taft, who easily won the nomination.[13] Theodore's supporters claimed that the nomination had been stolen, and quickly bolted from the party. They formed a third-party ticket, with Theodore as their candidate.

They called themselves the Progressive Party, but it was commonly referred to as the Bull Moose Party after Theodore stated he was as "strong as a bull moose." His old friends from Medora, Joe and Sylvane Ferris, Bill Merrifield, and George Myers served as delegates at the first Progressive Party convention held in August in Chicago. Dr. V. H. Stickney, who had treated Theodore's near-frostbitten feet after the capture of the boat thieves, worked as a county chairman for the party. Bat Masterson, Ben Daniels, and Seth Bullock joined the party. The Progressive Party's platform supported women's rights, abolishing child labor, providing a minimum wage for workers, and establishing workers' compensation. Its goals were lofty, which scared conservative Republicans. The Bull Moose Party believed many progressive Democrats would join them to elect Theodore, but that hope was dashed when Woodrow Wilson, a liberal progressive, won the Democratic nomination. At that point, Theodore knew it was, at best, an uphill battle for the White House.

October 14, 1912, found Theodore on the campaign trail in Milwaukee, Wisconsin. Before heading to an auditorium to deliver a speech, he stood up in his seven-seat vehicle to wave at the crowd, which included a man named John Schrank. Standing next to the car, Schrank raised his hand that held a pistol and fired. The bullet hit Theodore in the right breast, causing him to fall back into the seat without uttering a word. Police and Secret Service agents quickly pounced on the young man. Getting up from his car seat, Theodore asked to see him. Looking at Schrank's face, he saw nothing but the dead eyes of an insane person. He told those around him to turn the man over to the police.[14] Aides believed Theodore was unhurt, but still examined his overcoat for any bullet hole. Looking at his shirt, Theodore found blood. Refusing to be taken to the hospital, he ordered his driver to take him to the auditorium. The audience was told of the attempt on Theodore's life, and many believed it to be a prank until Theodore came onstage and displayed his bloody shirt. Bellowing "It will take more than that to kill a bull moose," he asked the audience to remain quiet while he gave his speech. He spoke for ninety minutes before going to the hospital.

The .38 caliber bullet had gone through Theodore's heavy overcoat, into his suit-jacket pocket, through the folded fifty-page speech, into the vest pocket that held his steel eyeglass case, through suspenders, shirt, and undershirt, before piercing the skin. The bullet was embedded adjacent to his fourth right rib, pointing straight to the heart. Doctors decided not to operate, and the bullet was never removed.

Luck was with him that night.

What Henry Cabot Lodge predicted became a reality on November 5. Woodrow Wilson received 6.3 million popular votes. Theodore earned 4.1 million, and Taft, a distant third, had 3.5 million. Not since 1897, when Grover Cleveland left office, had a Democrat sat in the White House. Republicans were furious, blaming Theodore for their defeat. Within weeks, visits and phone calls from politicians and loyal party members dwindled, then eventually stopped at Sagamore Hill.

Theodore Roosevelt had become a pariah to the Republican Party.

◆

When asked why he undertook the arduous South American river trip in late 1913, Theodore replied that it was "his last chance to be a boy."

Once again, Theodore sought an escape after a loss. This time he went to South America to navigate a waterway in Brazil known as the River of Doubt. Unlike his African safari, this trip was not well planned or provisioned. The river itself was problematic from the beginning. Merciless rapids forced the canoes to be hauled over land, requiring those on the expedition to hack through thick, dense jungles. The river also hid rocks and palms that could easily overturn a canoe. Piranha fish, known for their vicious attacks on man and beast, called the river home, as did mosquitoes, flies, and other bugs. Rain and humidity were unrelenting, and the density and deafening silence of the jungle were equally fascinating and intimidating. Before the canoes were launched, Theodore, who was again accompanied by Kermit, updated his last will and testament—a harbinger of things to come.

As the expedition moved on, one canoe sank, while another split open, but was repaired. The expedition began confronting several sets of rapids on a daily basis, forcing the canoes to be hauled through a quickly hacked-out path in the jungle. One set of rapids took the group three days to bypass.[15] Provisions began to run low, a few more canoes were lost to the river, and Kermit nearly drowned going over a fast-moving falls, which killed another man. One member of the group went mad, killing another man before fleeing into the dense jungle. He was never found.

On March 27, 1914, one of the canoes overturned and jammed against some boulders. Jumping into the river with other men to save the canoe, Theodore cut his right leg on a rock. By evening, he was limping and the leg had turned red. Hiking over rough terrain the following day wore Theodore out, leading Kermit to privately worry about his father's heart. Two days later, malaria fever, which Theodore had caught in Cuba in 1898, returned. His fever soared to 104 degrees, and he grew delirious. The doctor in the group gave him quinine, and by the following morning Theodore's fever had dropped, but he was still weak. Not only did fever wrack his body, but he also now suffered from dysentery. If that weren't enough, the gash on his right leg showed signs of infection. Theodore made the decision the group should leave him behind, but none of the men, especially Kermit, was about to let that happen.[16]

The bedraggled group pushed on, and by April 14, it was apparent the rapids were behind them. Twelve days later, they reached the confluence of the River of Doubt and the Aripuana, as well as their relief party.

The River of Doubt was renamed Rio Roosevelt in Theodore's honor.

When he returned home, it was obvious that Theodore was not the same man he had been eight months previously. He had lost a considerable amount of weight, which he eventually gained back, but the robust, energetic man of action was now slower and looking older. Many believe Theodore's health was never the same after the South American river trip. During the trip, not only had he suffered from previous maladies, but he had developed a serious abscess that had to be operated on in the jungle. For the rest of his life, Theodore would suffer recurring abscesses that quelled his strength, often incapacitating him for days or months at a time.

In the summer of 1914, the world went mad. Archduke Ferdinand and his wife were assassinated in Sarajevo, Bosnia, by a nineteen-year-old student. Within weeks of the archduke's murder, Austria and Germany went to war against Serbia. By August, Europe was involved in what would be called the Great War. Carnage that had been unseen since America's Civil War would now be played out in the ruined fields of France, Germany, and elsewhere. Tens of thousands upon thousands of men would be killed or wounded.

As President Woodrow Wilson preached neutrality, Theodore was beside himself with rage that Wilson would simply sit on the sidelines as the country's allies died in battle. Some historians, playing the "what-if" game of speculation, wonder whether the war would have started at all had Theodore been president, since he had a strong relationship with Kaiser Wilhelm II. During his visit to Germany in 1910, Theodore privately expressed concerns that a conflict with Germany in Europe would sooner or later arise. (He also believed that the United States could someday be involved in an armed conflict with Japan.) Rumors in 1915 began to circulate that Theodore might lead an American peace commission to reach a diplomatic end to the conflict, but Wilson rebuffed any overtures, especially those involving Theodore.[17]

The conflict and body count continued to rise as 1915 gave way to 1916, yet the United States remained on the sidelines. Theodore, fed up with Wilson's lack of action, began to publicly criticize the president, calling him a "coward" and "yellow." Theodore's rhetoric, in his public speeches, and in his monthly column for *Outlook Magazine*, was heartily endorsed by the public, but the Republican Party ignored him when it came to the 1916 presidential campaign. The wounds from 1912 were too fresh to warrant a truce. Progressives tried to lure Theodore back into the race, but he declined. The Republican nominee, the moderate Charles Evan Hughes, could not dislodge Wilson from office, who campaigned on the slogan, "He Kept Us Out of War."

That soon changed. As 1917 dawned, German submarines commenced attacks on US merchant ships, carrying supplies for England and France, as they crossed the Atlantic Ocean. President Wilson was forced to take action, and on April 2, 1917, asked Congress to declare war on Germany.

Theodore was quick to join the mobilization, already drafting plans to assemble another volunteer army.[18] His four sons joined the army, taking front-line duty. Ted Jr. and Archie went into the infantry. Kermit served with the British Army in Iraq, while Quentin, who loved anything mechanical, became a pilot. Theodore went to Washington on April 9 to speak to President Wilson. Regarding his criticism over the past few years, Theodore called them "dust in a windy street," then requested to form another volunteer unit. Wilson listened patiently, saying that he would consider his proposal. Wilson later told associates, "I think the best way to treat Mr. Roosevelt is to take no notice of him. That breaks his heart, and is the best punishment that can be administered."[19]

Theodore realized Wilson had no intention of giving him what he so desperately wanted. He was a warrior without a fight. His sons would have to carry the Roosevelt name into battle. Theodore, forced to remain stateside, helped raise war bonds, supported the Red Cross, and preached preparedness. On July 17, 1918, a reporter showed up at Sagamore Hill with a telegram no parent wants to receive. Quentin, Theodore's youngest and favorite child, had been killed when his plane was shot down by a German pilot. Looking at the telegram, he was lost in thought. "Mrs. Roosevelt. How am I going to break it to her?" he quietly asked, before walking into the house.[20] Quentin's death left a great emotional hole in his heart. The nobility of war, dying for the grand cause, was to have been his final stand. He did not expect it from one of his children.

Ironically, on November 11, 1918, as peace was declared, Theodore entered a New York hospital, suffering from severe rheumatism. As the weeks wore on, signs of a pulmonary embolism required round-the-clock care. Edith, who had taken a room next to his, would sit next to his bed and read to him. By Christmas morning, he was deemed healthy enough to return home to Sagamore Hill.

On New Year's Day, 1919, Theodore was ailing again, but a few days later showed signs of improvement. On Sunday, January 6, he and Edith spent time sitting next to each other, watching the sun settle. Later in the evening, Theodore complained to his nurse that he felt his heart and lungs were about to give in. His physician, Dr. George Faller, came at once. After examining him, the doctor told Theodore that his lungs were clear and his pulse was normal.

In the early hours of January 6, 1919, Theodore Roosevelt, at the age of sixty, quietly gave up the strenuous life.

Archie telegraphed his brothers in Europe: "The Old Lion is dead."

Two days later, Theodore was buried in Young's Cemetery in Oyster Bay. According to the tradition of the time, Edith did not attend the funeral. After the graveside services ended, the crowd slowly dispersed. One of the last mourners to leave was William Howard Taft. He stood at Theodore's grave, crying.

Tributes flowed in. People cried. The man who had been viewed as a pariah by his party seven years earlier was, at the time of his death, being talked up as the leading candidate for the 1920 election. Books were written by friends, and even his enemies paid tribute to his memory. His deeds as president were honored: the building of the Panama Canal, securing a peace treaty between Russia and Japan, conserving the land and the wildlife for future generations.

At the time of his passing, cartoon editorialists expressed their remembrances of Theodore. Clifford Berryman, whose drawing of Theodore's bear hunt in Mississippi launched a stuffed doll, drew the bear cub, who always accompanied Theodore in his cartoons, in pajamas, standing on a chair and turning off a gas lamp. Billy Ireland, of the *Columbus Dispatch*, showed Theodore riding in a buckboard, pulled by two horses and driven by a cowboy. Theodore sits in the back, with his ever-present rifle and other Western gear, as the wagon makes its way toward the mountains. He looks back on the trail, smiling, and doffing his cowboy hat. The cartoon simply says, "Good-bye!"

J. N. "Ding" Darling hastily sketched out an image of Theodore on his horse, his hat raised above his head, smiling. Ahead of him is a winding path of wagons making their way through the mountains. Titled "The Long, Long Trail," it became one of the most famous editorial cartoons in America. Most editorial cartoonists found the best way to depict Theodore's passing was in true Western fashion—riding into the sunset.

◆

Edith remained at Sagamore Hill until her death in 1948, at the age of eighty-seven. She is buried next to Theodore at Young's Cemetery.

Ted Jr., who was honorably decorated for his service in World War I, went on to serve as a New York assemblyman and assistant secretary of the navy before losing a bid for New York governor. He was appointed governor of Puerto Rico, and then of the Philippines. With the outbreak of World War II, he was given a brigadier general's commission and ably served in Europe. Despite his suffering from arthritis, he landed with his men on Utah Beach in Normandy on D-Day (the only general to do so), and his heroism on the beach earned him the Medal of Honor. He died of a heart attack on July 12, 1944.[21] Kermit enlisted in the British Army in 1917, serving as an Arabic translator. Resigning from the British forces in April of 1918, he joined the US Army as a captain of an artillery unit, fighting in the Battle of the Argonne Forest. After the war, Kermit founded the Roosevelt Steamship Line, working for the company until 1939, when he enlisted in the British Army. Medically discharged in 1941, mainly due to heart problems, he was overwhelmed with depression. Kermit sought relief from his emotional issues with alcohol, and was ultimately institutionalized. Franklin, his cousin, liked him greatly and used his presidential powers to appoint Kermit as a major in the US Army. Stationed in Alaska, he committed suicide on June 4, 1943.

Ethel married Dr. Richard Derby in 1913, and worked alongside him as a nurse in a French hospital during World War I. She continued her efforts with the Red Cross for many years, eventually earning the association's sixty-year service pin. An ardent supporter of civil rights, she helped build the first low-income housing for blacks in Oyster Bay. She passed away in 1977. Discharged from the army after being wounded during World War I, Archie became an executive for Sinclair Oil Company for several years. He resigned from the company when the Teapot Dome scandal broke, eventually testifying before a Senate committee. (Archie was never implicated in the scandal.) He then worked at Roosevelt and Son until the outbreak of World War II. In New Guinea, commissioned as a lieutenant colonel, Archie was wounded in the same leg that had been badly injured in World War I. After the war, he formed an investment firm and was very active in many right-wing causes, and was a fervent anti-Communist. He died from complications of a stroke in 1979.

Alice, Theodore's first child, was the most impulsive. During her White House years, she wore a small green snake around her neck (called Emily Spinach), and smoked in public, a major social taboo for a woman in the early 1900s. Theodore once told his friend Owen Wister, "I can either run the country or attend to Alice, but I cannot do both." In 1905, she married Senator Nicholas Longworth III, but the marriage was shaky from the start. Alice's only child, Paula, was fathered by Senator William Borah, with whom she had a long-term affair. In later years, she was a well-known Washington socialite, acknowledged for her stinging wit. Alice died in 1980.

In 1949, Sagamore Hill was purchased by the Roosevelt Memorial Association (later renamed the Theodore Roosevelt Association), with plans to turn the home and land into a museum. In 1962, Congress established the home as a National Historic Site, and the following year, the property became part of the National Park Service.

Bamie, Theodore's oldest sister, married naval lieutenant commander William Cowles in 1895, and they had one son, William Jr. She was plagued in later years by deafness and crippling arthritis before her death in 1931. Elliott married Anna Hall in 1883 and had three children, including his eldest daughter, Eleanor. His engaging personality helped to mask his growing attachment to alcohol. A horseback-riding accident left him addicted to opiates, and his life began to spiral downward. He would disappear for weeks at a time, leaving no idea of his whereabouts. A family trip to Europe proved to be a disaster, as Elliott drank profusely and, at times, was violent toward his now-pregnant wife. Bamie traveled to Austria, where she got Elliott admitted into a sanatorium; shortly after that, his affair with a household servant, which had left her pregnant, surfaced. (The woman was paid an undisclosed sum to remain silent.) Elliott agreed to seek further treatment in the United States, and for a while seemed to be conquering his demons. Things deteriorated when his wife, Anna, died in December 1892 of diphtheria, and his second child, Elliott Jr., died the following May from scarlet fever. Elliott returned to his old habits, and his tragic end came on August 14, 1894, at age thirty-four, when he suffered a seizure and collapsed. Corrine, Theodore's youngest sibling, was a writer of poetry, her first book being published in 1911.

She eventually published five books of poetry, as well as a book about her famous brother. Corrine married Douglas Robinson in 1882, and they had four children. She died in 1933.

Joe Ferris, who guided Theodore on his first buffalo hunt, remained in Medora with his wife, running his general store even when almost everything else in the town had disappeared. He was elected postmaster in 1887. When Theodore became president, he reappointed him to the position, and he served until 1908. In 1909, Joe moved to Sidney, Montana, where he ran another general store. In 1922, Ferris and his wife moved to Santa Paula, California, where he died in 1937. Sylvane Ferris became the auditor of Billings County, and later, a bank president in Dickinson. Like his brother, Sylvane moved to California, passing away in 1933. Bill Merrifield eventually moved to the Flat Head Lake area in Montana where, in 1907, Theodore appointed him US marshal. Merrifield died in Kalispell, Montana, in 1929.[22]

Bill Sewall and Theodore maintained their close friendship until Theodore's death. Theodore invited the Sewalls to visit him at the White House in 1903, where he showed him the presidential house. Afterwards, he asked his old friend what he thought of the White House. "Why, it looks to me as how you've got a pretty good camp," Sewall stated. "It's always a good thing to have a good camp," Theodore replied. When reporters asked Sewall what he thought of his visit, he said he liked it, but would rather go fishing.[23] In 1905, Theodore appointed Sewall collector of customs for Aroostook County in Maine. They saw each other one last time in 1918, when Theodore came to Portland, Maine, to give a speech. After Theodore's death, Sewall wrote a small book about his memories and friendship with Roosevelt. Sewall passed away in 1930 at the age of eighty-five. Wilmot Dow, Sewall's nephew, died in 1891 at the age of thirty-six, possibly of Bright's disease. His passing was quick and a shock to everyone, including Theodore. Months later, Theodore recalled Wilmot in a letter to Sewall:

I think of Wilmot all the time. I can see him riding a bucker or paddling a canoe, or shooting an antelope; or doing the washing for his wife, or playing with the children. If there ever was a fine, noble fellow, he was one.[24]

Bat Masterson continued as a sportswriter for the *New York Morning Telegraph*. He had just finished his column when he died at his desk of an apparent heart attack on October 25, 1921. He was sixty-seven. Ben Daniels, despite all the controversy over his appointment as US marshal for the Arizona Territory, was a dedicated lawman and served nobly until he was asked to resign by President Taft in August 1909. After two failed election attempts, Daniels won the position of Pima County sheriff in Arizona in 1920. He was sixty-eight years old. Two years later, at the age of seventy, Daniels led a manhunt for some killers, resulting in their capture. Defeated in 1922 when he ran for reelection, Daniels suffered a stroke and died on April 20, 1923. Seth Bullock continued to live in Deadwood, South Dakota, and after Theodore's death, he came up with the idea of a memorial in Theodore's honor. With the help of the Black Hills Pioneers, a thirty-two-foot castle-styled tower was built on a mountaintop that was renamed Mount Roosevelt. Bullock helped dedicate the structure (which is still open to the public) on July 4, 1919. Bullock died of cancer at the age of seventy on September 23, 1919. He is buried in Mount Moriah Cemetery in Deadwood, along with the remains of Wild Bill Hickok and Calamity Jane.

Gregor Lang and his wife remained at their ranch, even after Pender withdrew his financial support following the disastrous winter of 1886–87. After a while the ranch succeeded, and Lang went on to become a county commissioner. He died in 1900 while visiting his native Scotland. Lincoln, his son, went on to work as an engineer, developing an apparatus for braking and reversing locomotives. In 1926, his memories of Theodore and the Badlands were published, entitled *Ranching with Roosevelt*.

The Marquis de Morès never returned to Medora after 1887. His dreams of wealth and successful businesses in the Badlands disappeared. He returned to France, where he was involved in politics for a while, including a plot to overthrow the French government. He attempted to start a railroad in Indochina but failed. A rabid anti-Semite, he came up with a ridiculous idea to unite all of Islam against the English and the Jews. He traveled to Libya to help mount a resistance to British colonialism, and on June 9, 1896, was killed in the Sahara Desert by a Tuareg tribe. He was thirty-seven.

Dutch Wannegan, who had survived the Marquis's ambush and later worked for Theodore, moved to Montana, living out his days as a hermit. Frank O'Donald, who had fueled the fire between himself and the Marquis, left Medora and is lost to history. The body of Riley Luffsey, who was killed in the ambush, is buried in the Medora cemetery. Eldridge "Gerry" Paddock, the man who instigated the ambush and later threatened Theodore's life, remained in Dickinson, operating his Pyramid Park Hotel. In 1890, he was appointed sheriff of Billings County before moving, in 1900, to California, where he died twelve years later.

A. T. Packard, editor of the *Bad Lands Cow Boy*, left Medora after the newspaper office burned to the ground in 1887. He went to Montana before eventually settling in Chicago, where he continued to work in the newspaper business. He died in 1931.

Henry Gorringe, who had envisioned the Badlands area as a retreat for hunters, died on July 7, 1885, from injuries suffered when he jumped from a train the previous year.[25]

The town of Medora limped along over the years, with a few businesses offering services. In the early 1960s, the streets were still dirt and the town had no sewer lines, no hotels, and only one restaurant. The Metropolitan Hotel, built in 1884, closed its doors in 1886. Reopened in 1901, it was renamed the Rough Riders Hotel in 1905, in honor of Medora's most famous resident. The hotel survived countless owners until it closed in 1943. It reopened a year later, but closed for good in 1960. By 1962, the building was about ready to fall down when Harold Schafer, founder and CEO of the Gold Seal Company, stepped in. A lover of the Badlands area, Schafer rebuilt the hotel and the Joe Ferris general store, as well as paving the streets and installing a municipal water and sewer system. The Rough Riders Hotel reopened in 1965 and was extensively remodeled in 2009. The extension of Interstate 94 across the western portion of the state gave Medora new life.[26]

Today, Medora attracts numerous tourists during the summer. Visitors flock to see the national park named after Theodore, and to ride horses, fish, and camp. In 1965, *Old Four-Eyes*, a stage show about Theodore's days in the Dakotas, came to an end after a six-year run at the nearby Burning Hills Amphitheater. Since then, *The Medora Musical* has performed nightly during the summer season to appreciative audiences.

In front of the post office on Third Avenue stands a tall cottonwood tree, jutting out into the street. It was there before the town of Medora was ever built. Since it has seen so much history over the years, it is known as a "witness tree."

The tree, like Medora and the Badlands, has endured and survived.

A LASTING MEMORIAL

*It is not what we have that will make us a great nation; it is the way
in which we use it.*

As early as 1920, the Roosevelt Memorial National Park Association (RMNPA) launched a campaign to honor Theodore's memory with a park in North Dakota. With the growing popularity of the automobile as an easy way to see much of the country, several entrepreneurs believed a way to attract tourism within the state should include a national park. Who better to honor than the late former president? Pitching the idea to the National Park Service (NPS) proved to be an uphill battle, however, because existing national parks were very much in need of improvements, and budgets were tight. Adding an additional park would only strain resources, not to mention the fact that some officials in the Park Service disagreed in regard to the scenic beauty of the Badlands.

When the proposed national park was first suggested around Medora, the local ranchers were quick to support the idea. However, their endorsement was not completely altruistic, as they believed tourists visiting the park would need to stay at their ranches and rent their horses. However, ranchers hastily changed their tune after learning the park would encompass 1.3 million acres. (Had it been approved, it would have been the third-largest national park then existing.) They opposed closing that much grazing land, and even when a smaller park was suggested in 1927, a coalition of ranchers defeated that proposal.[1]

In 1934, a cooperative agreement to kick off a Roosevelt Regional Park Project was signed by the Resettlement Administration, the Civilian Conservation Corps (CCC), the National Park Service, and the State of

North Dakota. The CCC immediately began constructing roads, trails, picnic areas, campgrounds, and buildings. (Today, at the North Unit, a CCC stone overlook still stands.) When the State of North Dakota announced that it did not want the responsibility of managing a state park in 1941, North Dakota congressman William Lemke stepped in. (The state felt the park should be administered by the National Park Service, which had a larger budget for maintenance.) Lemke lobbied to establish a national park, but his efforts were met with heavy resistance by the National Park Service. With the outbreak of World War II, many politicians felt a new national park was a waste of needed resources. Newton Drury, head of the National Park Service since 1940, held the opinion that the Badlands area could not sustain a national park. It didn't help matters that Drury's budget had been slashed by 85 percent since he'd taken charge.[2]

In September 1944, the National Park Service revived a plan to turn the land into a wildlife refuge under the supervision of the Fish and Wildlife Service. Congressman Lemke, however, would not give up on his goal to establish a national park, introducing a bill in November 1945 to create a national park from 36,000 acres. The bill was defeated, but Lemke returned in January 1947 with another bill, which would include the area of Theodore's Elkhorn Ranch. The National Park Service flatly informed Lemke they really did not want the South Unit of the park, and had zero interest in the North Unit of the park.[3] Finally, on April 25, 1947, President Harry Truman signed bill PL-38, creating the Theodore Roosevelt National Memorial Park. (The North Unit was added on June 12, 1948, with additional revisions made in later years.) At the time, it was the only memorial park within the National Park Service.

Theodore Roosevelt National Memorial Park was dedicated on June 4, 1949, with a crowd of about forty thousand in attendance, parking their cars as far as three miles along both sides of US Route 10. (It was renamed Theodore Roosevelt National Park on November 10, 1978.)

Today, the Theodore Roosevelt National Park covers 70,448 acres, separated into three sections: North Unit, Elkhorn Ranch site, and South Unit. It is home to a variety of plants, geological formations, and wild animals. The Little Missouri River flows along the banks, providing a major water source for animals that call the park their home, as well as serving as a migratory stop for various birds. The river also offers recreation activities for park visitors; and until 2014, visitors could mount a horse and ride along some of the same trails that Theodore had once traversed.[4]

The park is a haven for numerous animals, including many prairie dog "towns" in both the North and South Units. These furry rodents, which Theodore described as "noisy and inquisitive," provide visitors with continuous amusement. The air is filled with their high-pitched squeaks, warning fellow prairie dogs of visitors, or predators, who may get too close. Despite these towns' being far from a source of water, the prairie dogs thrive due to the various grasses surrounding their burrowed holes. The land is also home to the white-tailed jackrabbit, eastern cottontail rabbit, fox squirrel, least chipmunk, deer mouse, and a half-dozen other mammals. The river offers shelter for five species of frogs, and the snapping and western painted turtles. Five different snakes can be found in the park, including the bull snake and the prairie rattlesnake, as well as the sagebrush and short-horned lizards. When it comes to birds, 185 species visit the area on a migratory route. Only a few birds call the area home on a full-time basis due to the harsh winter weather.[5] At any given time of the year, a visitor will see a variety of birds, including the Canadian goose, golden eagle, turkey vulture, great horned owl, black-billed magpie, spotted sandpiper, barn swallow, yellow warbler, eastern bluebird, ring-necked pheasant, sharp-tailed grouse, and white pelican. For a devoted ornithologist like Theodore, having such an array of birds in his park would give him great delight.

The park also hosts a herd of elk, although they are one of the hardest animals to spot during a visit. Forty-seven elk were introduced into the park in 1985 and continue to thrive. Equally hard to spot are bobcats and mountain lions. Coyotes, on the other hand, are always around, their melancholy howls filling the night air. They can often be seen near prairie dog towns, as well as badgers. Beavers still live along the banks of the Little Missouri River in the South and North Units, as well as on Squaw Creek in the North Unit. Pronghorns are rarely, if ever, sighted in the park's North Unit; however, they are quite common in the open fields alongside Highway 85 and around the northern section of the South Unit.[6] Small herds of mule deer and white-tailed deer can be found in the park, while the North Unit boasts about a dozen longhorn cattle, which were first established in 1967.

The South Unit has about 136 wild horses that roam freely. The National Park Service tried to remove all wild horses from the park in the early years, but dropped that policy in 1970 when preservationists convinced them the wild horses were very much part of the park's historical backdrop. They maintain a strict number of horses to avoid overgrazing, holding a roundup every few years, with the extra horses sold to the public. Next to the buffalo, the wild horses are the most popular animal with visitors.

The buffalo herd at Theodore's park has increased over the years, making a strong but conservative comeback. Knowing how these magnificent creatures were nearly pushed to extinction on the very land they now roam reminds us that their survival is nothing short of a miracle. Today, an estimated 500,000 buffalo survive on public and private lands. In 1956, Theodore's park introduced 29 buffalo to the South Unit, and by 1962, the herd had increased to 145. The park relocated 10 bulls and 10 cows culled from the South Unit herd and established a second herd in the North Unit that same year. Although the park could easily handle a much larger herd, park managers choose to limit the herd's total number to 600, since they have no natural predators at either unit. (Approximately 200 buffalo are located in the North Unit, with the larger herd residing in the South Unit.) To maintain a reasonable total, the park holds a buffalo roundup every three to five years. Each buffalo is weighed and given a blood test to check for diseases by a veterinarian and park biologist. Based on the age and sex of the buffalo, the biologist determines whether to release it back into the park, or cull it from the herd. The culled buffalo are given to zoos, other national parks, and various Native American tribes.

While other national and state parks have their own buffalo herds, it is altogether fitting that Theodore Roosevelt National Park has its own buffalo herd. When Theodore arrived in 1883, buffalo were nearly extinct from the Badlands area. Despite his penchant for hunting, Theodore quickly became aware that if action was not immediately taken, the American buffalo would cease to exist. Thanks to the efforts of a few determined people, including Theodore, steps were taken to rescue them from extinction. Watching these massive, shaggy beasts roam among the hills and coulees of the park, roll in a buffalo wallow, or hold up vehicle traffic as they walk along the roadway (much to the delight of visitors), one cannot help but feel emotional at the herd's recovery. This is exactly what Theodore had envisioned, allowing future generations to view them in the wild.

In the early days, the national park lacked anything tangible that had been connected to Theodore himself. The land that he'd ridden across was there, but there was no building that park personnel could point to and say that he'd actually lived in it during his years in the Dakota Territory.

The Maltese Cross Ranch cabin remained on the land where it was built. Both the ranch and cabin were sold in 1901 to Jack Snyder, who removed the pitched roof. In 1903, the State of North Dakota purchased the cabin from Snyder and displayed it as part of the state's exhibition at the 1904 World's Fair in St. Louis. Under Snyder's ownership, the cabin had fallen into a state of disrepair over the years. Windows and doors had disappeared, and one man, Harry Roberts, recalled "seeing cattle standing inside watching you go by."[7] The cabin was dismantled and taken to Medora, where it was shipped by train to St. Louis. At the World's Fair, the cabin was rebuilt, windows and doors restored. During the year it was on display, it was estimated that over a million people viewed the cabin, making it one of the biggest attractions at the fair. Theodore even paid a visit, pointing out the Maltese cross that had been etched into the end of one log. The exposition's program claimed that, at the conclusion of the fair, the cabin would be moved to Sagamore Hill, but there is no evidence Theodore even considered it.

With the conclusion of the exposition, the cabin was once again dismantled and shipped to Portland, Oregon, where it became part of the North Dakota exhibit at the 1905 Lewis and Clark Expo. At the conclusion of that event, the cabin found a new home in Bismarck, North Dakota, on the grounds of the state capitol in 1908, where it remained for eleven years. By 1919, the cabin was once again in sorry shape, displaying severe signs of decay. The local chapter of the Daughters of the American Revolution petitioned the state to allow them to restore and maintain the cabin. When it comes to government—be it federal, state, or local—elected officials will wax on and on about the importance of a historical building, yet when it comes to supplying the money to fix such a structure, they quickly sing a different tune. In many cases it falls to an individual, or to a private organization, to raise the needed funds for restoration. This is exactly what the local chapter of the Daughters of the American Revolution did, holding teas, lunches, and other forms of fund-raising events. Their tenacity paid off, and the cabin was reopened to the public (charging a ten-cent admission) in 1923.[8]

The North Dakota Assembly, in March 1949, approved moving the Maltese Cross Ranch cabin from the state capitol to the newly established Theodore Roosevelt National Memorial Park. While the National Park Service agreed to take over care and control of the cabin, no action was taken. The cabin remained on display in Bismarck until 1958, the centennial year of Theodore's birth, when it was finally moved to the National Memorial Park, where the logs were again repaired and the high-pitched roof restored.

Today the Maltese Cabin resides behind the park's visitor center.[9] The interior of the cabin has been restored to give visitors an accurate idea of what it looked like when Theodore lived there. The traveling trunk he brought with him on his trips to Medora, complete with his initials (T. R.), sits in what was his bedroom. In the main room, the white hutch that was originally in the cabin, along with the writing desk where Theodore labored over his letters and books, are on display. (The writing desk was originally used at Elkhorn Ranch.) It is believed the rocking chair either belonged to Theodore, or came from the upstairs room he frequently stayed in at the general store owned by Joe Ferris.

❖

The year 1892 marked the last time Theodore visited Elkhorn Ranch. (Sylvane Ferris bought the cabin in 1898.) After assuming the presidency, there was talk of moving and displaying the Elkhorn Ranch cabin; however, by then it had been stripped, leaving only a few rotting logs and the foundation stones laid by Sewall and Dow.

Today, the area where Theodore's Elkhorn Ranch once stood is surrounded by a wire-and-wood-post fence, with only the foundation stones remaining. One can walk into the fenced area, but it's easy to miss the stones hidden in the grass. To experience Elkhorn Ranch, one must drive forty-five minutes over a graded dirt road to a parking area, and from there walk a mile, escorted by grasshoppers and dragonflies. Once one arrives at Elkhorn Ranch, it is immediately clear why Theodore chose the area. The remoteness leaves a visitor alone with nature. It is easy to imagine Theodore sitting in his rocking chair on the piazza, listening to the wind as it rustles the leaves of the cottonwoods, the melodious chirping of a meadowlark mixed with the plaintive calls of a mourning dove, and the muffled movement of the Little Missouri River. It was here that Theodore found peace, here that he let his heart heal from a tragic loss. Here is where the asthmatic dude from New York was transformed into a robust cowboy.

One can sit in the shade of the cottonwoods, some of the very same ones he viewed from his porch, and contemplate what this land meant to Theodore. It was here that his birth as a conservationist began. Here is where he learned how important the land, the trees, and the water are, not just to humans but also to wildlife. He learned that the land did not offer an unlimited supply of material, that there would be a price for overuse. Theodore knew that without careful management, the land—and ultimately those that live on it—would suffer greatly.

In his 1907 message to Congress, Theodore said that "to waste, to destroy, our natural resources, to skin and exhaust the land instead of using it so as to increase its usefulness, will result in undermining in the days of our children the very prosperity which we ought by right to hand down to them amplified and developed."[10]

Today, the Elkhorn Ranch area is one of the most endangered national parks in the United States. In 2012, the National Trust for Historic Preservation named Elkhorn Ranch a National Treasure, and placed it on their list of America's Eleven Most Endangered Historic Places.

What caused the area to gain such an egregious title? The North Dakota Bakken oil boom.

Known as the Bakken formation, it is a rock unit that is roughly 200 to 350 million years old, covering 200,000 square miles of subsurface that includes western North Dakota, eastern Montana, and southern Saskatchewan and Manitoba in Canada. Oil was first discovered in the region in 1951, but technology to withdraw it was not then available. By 2000, the use of a highly debatable drilling technique—hydraulic frac- turing (commonly called "fracking")—opened the area to a massive oil boom. A US Geological Survey report in 2008 estimated that the Bakken area could produce about 3.65 billion barrels of oil. In April 2013, the USGS revised their survey, stating the Bakken area could yield 7.4 billion barrels of oil.[11]

Thanks to the advancement of technology, the area roughly produced 1.2 million barrels of oil as of 2014. Fracking is a well-stimulation tech- nique in which rock (which holds the oil) is broken by using a hydrauli- cally pressurized liquid composed of water, sand, and chemicals. (Some fractures within the rock are natural, such as a vein or a dike.) Injecting this high-pressure fluid into a wellbore creates cracks in the deep-rock formations, allowing natural gas, petroleum, and brine to discharge more freely.[12] Supporters of fracking point to the ability to remove oil from areas that otherwise would not yield the material, thereby providing eco- nomic benefits to the local community, as well as the nation. Opponents point out environmental impacts ranging from risks of contaminating groundwater, depletion of freshwater, degraded air quality, increased noise and surface pollution, and consequential hazards to public health and the environment. Another impact is an increase in seismic activity. Although it is yet to be established scientifically, many fracking areas are experienc- ing seismic action that had previously been nonexistent, or extremely lim- ited. Many countries have seriously restricted, or outright banned, the use of fracking. However, in the United States, it continues while controversy swirls around the subject.

What has happened in the western end of North Dakota has been called a modern-day oil boom. Small towns such as Watford City, which lies ten miles north of the Theodore Roosevelt National Park North Unit, has changed literally within months. What was once a small town has seen an explosion in population and growth. Open fields are now outdoor shop- ping malls. Housing for the increased population of migrant workers has doubled, in some places tripled, straining local services. New apartment buildings have been quickly erected, and a two-bedroom apartment rents at the unheard-of price (for a town such as Watford City) of $1,200 to $1,400 a month. Workers who bring their own RVs can park in a vacant field for $800 a month. (Oil workers can earn $90,000 a year working an eighty-hour week—which includes the harsh Dakota winters.) Tourists planning a summer visit to western North Dakota are advised to check in advance on hotel availability because many oil workers take over hotel or motel rooms. A local restaurant in Dickinson that had been in business for nearly thirty years was forced to close when employees left to take higher-paying jobs with the oil companies. In one year's time, the number of oil wells doubled alongside Interstate 94, from Dickinson to Medora. At night, driving to Medora, one sees the flames from the wells burning off natural gas, reminiscent of the burning oil wells in the Gulf War of 1990.

Farmers and cattle ranchers that surround Elkhorn Ranch have seen portions of their land taken over by oil wells, as well as by large oil trucks throwing up clouds of dust in their wake on the graded dirt roads. Cattle graze within twenty feet of the wells. Yet the farmers and ranchers can do little to stop the drilling. True, they are paid a one-time fee of $10,000 to $15,000 for the "inconvenience," but they have no rights to stop an oil company from coming onto their land and setting up shop. Why? It is the tangle of ownership rights that dates back to 1909. The Homestead Act of 1862 provided hardy individuals 160 acres as long as they lived and harvested the land for five years. In addition to being given the ownership of the land, they were also assigned the mineral rights. By 1909, the act was enlarged to 320 acres, but Congress came to realize that the mineral rights were far more valuable than the land rights. In 1910, the government sold the land and mineral rights separately, and by 1914, they held most, if not all, the mineral rights. The government auctioned the mineral rights off to the highest bidder, usually oil companies.

Today, an oil crew can drive up on the land of a farmer or rancher and begin drilling. The landowner cannot stop them. In courts, mineral rights trump land rights. Unless a landowner maintains both, it is impossible for them to stop an oil company from drilling on their land if the company holds the mineral rights. Many of these wells are estimated to be in service for upwards of twenty, possibly thirty, years.[13]

The 218-acre Elkhorn Ranch site is surrounded by land that is privately owned. The enveloping area could at any time, and has in many places, been besieged by oil-well crews or other development. Valerie Naylor, the former superintendent of the Theodore Roosevelt National Park, was a watchdog for the park, keeping oil wells from destroying the view of this pristine area that has remained almost exactly as it was the first day Theodore chose the land for his new ranch. While driving to the Elkhorn site, one sees numerous oil wells pumping, but, so far, there is only one well, on a ridge, that intrudes into the view from Theodore's ranch. However, the encompassing ridges could easily become full of pumping oil wells, surrounding the acreage like Custer at the Little Bighorn.

Jim Arthaud, chairman of the Billings County Board of Supervisors, and owner of a truck company, claimed that a proposed bridge over the Little Missouri River would not be within earshot or view of the Elkhorn site. (Valerie Naylor stated in 2012 that no study had been conducted to support Arthaud's claims.) The bridge's main function would be to provide access for oil trucks that make stops at the various wells. It has been estimated that about one thousand trucks would use the bridge *every day*. Arthaud claims the bridge would be good for visitors wanting to see Elkhorn Ranch. "The whole public would be able to use that place, not just the elite environmentalists. That lousy 50-however-many acres it is—200?—where Teddy sat and rested his head, and found himself," he stated. (It should be noted that Arthaud's county receives nearly 100 percent of its revenue from oil and gas businesses.)[14]

One battle against the incursion against Elkhorn Ranch appears to have already been lost. Roger Lothspeich, who owns the mineral rights near the Elkhorn Ranch site, wanted to develop a twenty-five-acre gravel pit that was roughly a mile northwest of the Elkhorn on the other side of the Little Missouri River. Both Lothspeich and the US Forest Service had signed an agreement to exchange land, or mineral rights, in another location, leaving the area near the Elkhorn alone. However, the two parties could not come to terms. The Forest Service conducted a draft environmental assessment that found the gravel pit would be of "no significant impact."[15] Unfortunately, the Forest Service ignored the objections raised by the National Historic Preservation Trust and others and granted approval of the twenty-five-acre gravel pit in January 2015.[16] This was done despite the Forest Service's lack of complying with the National Historic Preservation Act, and holding an "incompetent discussion of numerous alternatives that would highlight the adverse impacts of the Elkhorn Ranch area."[17]

In February 2012, Tweed Roosevelt, Theodore's great-grandson, met with President Obama, urging him to use the Antiquities Act of 1906 to designate the 4,400 acres surrounding the Elkhorn as a national monument. (This is the same law Theodore used on many occasions to preserve areas.) After the meeting, Mr. Roosevelt reported that he'd had a courteous hearing with the president, but to date, nothing has happened.

In a 2012 op-ed piece for the *New York Times*, Theodore's biographer, Edmund Morris, keenly noted:

> *One thing that distinguishes a great president is the ability to see through such legalistic thickets and discern the moral daylight beyond. That, and the will to do what is right for future generations of Americans. Our current raging thirst for oil, not to mention private appetites for gravel, will one day abate, either because of depletion or new technologies. Long before that, today's political issues, endlessly droned on the evening news, will become "dust in a windy street," to use one of Roosevelt's favorite metaphors. Unless Mr. Obama acts to preserve at least some threatened parts of our inventory of natural resources, he is not likely to be remembered, as Roosevelt is, as somebody who cared about how future generations live and breathe.[18]*

The irony that a portion of a national park, named for the US president who did so much for our country's conservation, is now threatened by developers and oil companies is not lost on most people.

THE ROMANCE OF HIS LIFE

It was here that the romance of my life began.

THEODORE ONCE STATED THAT IF HE HADN'T LIVED IN THE DAKOTAS, HE never would have been president. Some think this was an exaggeration on his part; however, the Dakotas, and the American West, did transform Theodore Roosevelt.

Think of the ancestors of the Native Americans coming across the Bering land bridge onto the North American continent, and consider the conquistadores from Spain, the settlers of Jamestown and Plymouth Rock, and the mountain men. All have had a natural curiosity to see what lies beyond the stand of trees or over the next mountain ridge. The people that made up America were always on the move, whether it was following a trail blazed by others or creating a new one. They sailed down rivers to see where they ended. Land rich in soil and game were not that far away, just through a gap in the mountains, beyond a forest, or across the Mississippi River. Stories, real or fictional, filled an adventurous people with a hopeful dream. The harsh reality would come later; it was the dream that mattered. The chance to see something few others could experience excited many a man and woman to pack up and move west. The land and the elements would transform those who dared to act on their dreams.

Theodore Roosevelt was one of them.

What if there had never been a Dakota period in Theodore's life? It would be absurd for anyone to think a sickly boy could later lead a charge up Kettle Hill without that intervening period in the West. For that matter, would his leadership as police commissioner, assistant naval secretary, and governor have been as effective, or even existed at all, had he not gone to the West? What would have become of his massive push for conservation, by which he created national monuments, federal bird sanctuaries, and a buffalo preserve? One cannot ignore the extensive influence the West had on all of these elements in Theodore's life. The West was a romantic fantasy to him, from the days of his boyhood. When he arrived in Medora in 1883, it entered his life. The West made him live on its terms and conditions. Unlike others, Theodore thrived in those surroundings. The tougher it was, the better he liked it. Who else would have said, "By Godfrey, but this is fun!" while sitting in several inches of water, soaked to the bone, in the middle of the night? The West dared Theodore, and he happily took up the challenge.

At first, it may have been a game for him. He was able to become the great hunter of the mighty buffalo, sleeping out in the open in all conditions. That first visit to the Badlands allowed him to live like his heroes, Crockett and Boone. But something happened during that hunt. The West cast its spell on him. The people he met, the land he rode across—they appealed to him greatly. Out in the West he was greeted with an honesty that was lacking in many circles back east, especially in the dismal halls of the New York Assembly. Western people were plainspoken. Their handshake was their contract. You lived up to a deal, or you didn't.

One may make an argument that Theodore's appreciation for conservation began on his first buffalo hunt. In his quest to shoot a buffalo, he saw how few of the shaggy beasts remained, and the image of a once-mighty herd now whittled down to a paltry few began to shape his ideals. Had he not gone to hunt the buffalo, would Theodore have formed the Boone and Crockett Club? Had it not been formed, would the regulations they helped to pass ever have become laws? Would any buffalo still survive in our country? Or would they be limited to paintings and old photographs? The beginning steps Theodore took in his first trip to the Dakotas were the first droplets of water on the seed that blossomed into his strong conservation beliefs. He would learn, albeit the hard way, about resources. The Dakotas proved to be his real education for becoming a leader, a conservationist, and a man to respect.

In his autobiography, Theodore said, "I owe more than I ever can express to the West, which of course means to the men and women I met in the West."[1] The men and women with whom he came into contact in the West, especially in the Badlands, not only influenced him but also left him with many long-lasting friendships. Bill Sewall and Wilmot Dow. Joe and Sylvane Ferris. Bill Merrifield. Gregor and Lincoln Lang. Later came such men as Seth Bullock, Ben Daniels, and Bat Masterson. They all held a special place in his life, a place that few in Washington (with the exception of his old friend Henry Cabot Lodge) ever occupied.

John Burroughs recalled the delight Theodore had in sharing memories with his Medora friends during his 1903 trip:

> *He was as happy with them as a schoolboy ever was in meeting old chums. He beamed with delight all over. The life which those men represented, and of which he had himself once formed a part, meant so much to him; it had entered into the very marrow of his being, and I could see the joy of it all shining in his face as he sat and lived parts of it over again with those men that day. . . . It all came back to him with a rush when he found himself alone with these heroes of the rope and the stirrup. How much more keen his appreciation was, and how much quicker his memory, than theirs! He was constantly recalling to their minds incidents which they had forgotten, and the names of horses and dogs which had escaped them. His subsequent life, instead of making dim the memory of his ranch days, seemed to have made it more vivid by contrast.[2]*

In several typed letters to Sylvane or Joe Ferris during his years in the White House, Theodore scribbled in his own hand, "I wish I could see you." That statement speaks volumes regarding how important their friendship was to him. In few, if any, of his personal letters to others does he share such a sentiment. His Western friends were always welcomed as guests at the White House. He once told the editor of the *Saturday Evening Post* that his closest friends were the men "I met in the mountains and backwoods and on ranches and the plains."[3] They were the people whom he could count on. When they spoke, they shared memories of times in their lives when they relied on each other in a place where their trust was highly valued. All of them influenced Theodore in some way, and, in turn, he influenced them. Their friendship was a loyalty that never wavered.

Unlike some politicians who adopted a certain look or hobby to appeal to the public, Theodore was an original. He loved the outdoors, the horses, the mountains and rivers. The public sensed this and adored him for it. When early film cameras photographed him chopping wood at Sagamore Hill, it wasn't an act; it was the real thing. It was the same with his riding a horse. A photographer set up his camera to capture Theodore jumping a hedge with one of his horses. Not certain he had caught it properly, Theodore happily said he and his horse would jump the hedge again—and did. The people of the Western lands claimed him as "one of our own," even though he was the first US president born in New York. Despite hailing from the East Coast, Theodore was definitely a man of the West. He naturally looked as though he belonged there, just like a well-worn pair of chaps on a cowboy from Texas. Numerous photographs taken from his various outdoor trips show a man completely at home in his environment. Whether he is on the back of a horse, leading it up a rocky incline, or sitting on the ground talking with other cowboys, Theodore is a man in his element. The outdoors was his drug of choice. It restored his soul, blessed him with peace, and filled him with a never-ending fascination.

Looking back over all the chapters in his life, he once said that if he could only retain one memory and have all of his other experiences erased, "I would take the memory of my life on the ranch with its experiences close to nature and among the men who lived nearest her."[4]

During a September 1900 campaign swing as the vice presidential candidate, Theodore made whistle-stop after whistle-stop on a train across Western parts of the country. Crowds came out to hear his speech and shake the hand of the man who led the Rough Riders to glory. Theodore was his usual gregarious self, making sure to step out on the train's rear platform as it crossed the land to wave at small bunches of children wanting to get a brief glimpse of him.

As his train made its way into the Badlands, heading toward Medora, he asked the porter to shut the door behind him and make sure no one would bother him. As the train rolled on, the Badlands stood silently, filling the landscape. Theodore sat on the rear platform, alone with his memories and his thoughts.

A year later, Theodore Roosevelt would become "The Cowboy President."

It is not the critic who counts: not the man who points out how the strong man stumbles or where the doer of deeds could have done better. The credit belongs to the man who is actually in the arena, whose face is marred by dust and sweat and blood, who strives valiantly, who errs and comes up short again and again, because there is no effort without error or shortcoming, but who knows the great enthusiasms, the great devotions, who spends himself for a worthy cause; who, at the best, knows, in the end, the triumph of high achievement, and who, at the worst, if he fails, at least he fails while daring greatly, so that his place shall never be with those cold and timid souls who know neither victory nor defeat.

—Theodore Roosevelt, 1910

ACKNOWLEDGMENTS

FOLLOWING THEODORE ROOSEVELT'S ODYSSEY IN THE AMERICAN WEST wouldn't have been as fruitful without the help of many people along the way.

A huge thank-you to Sharon Kilzer, project manager, and Pamela Pierce and Marlo Mallery Saxon at the Theodore Roosevelt Center at Dickinson State University in Dickinson, North Dakota. They were a tremendous help to me, as is their digital library, which is a repository of all material relating to Theodore.

Heather Cole, curator of the Theodore Roosevelt Collection at Houghton Library, Harvard University, was tremendously helpful and kind in answering my questions. Mary Hargert, at Houghton Library, was aces in guiding me to obtain some outstanding photos of Theodore that help to illustrate this book.

The staff at Theodore Roosevelt National Park were most helpful, especially rangers Michael Irving and Andrew Slotkin, who patiently answered numerous questions.

Doug and Mary Ellison, generous hosts of the Amble Inn in Medora, made me feel right at home. Their Western Edge bookstore provided me with plenty of research material, and Doug was extremely generous with his knowledge about Medora, and its citizens.

When it came to understanding the geology of the Badlands area, no one could have a better teacher than Robin McQuinn. She allowed me to see the land from a completely different perspective, and made it so damned interesting.

The staff and docents at the Marquis de Morès Chateau filled in blank spots about the Marquis and his home in Medora.

Erin Turner at TwoDot Press listened to my pitch for this book, and her interest resulted in the book you now hold. The legacy and history of Theodore Roosevelt, not to mention this author, owes her a huge thank-you.

Lynn Zelem, production editor at TwoDot Books, and copy editor Melissa Hayes were both top-notch in bringing this book to fruition. Thank you, ladies.

Terry Shulman, Kevin Kenney, and David C. Smith were most helpful with their comments, suggestions, and encouragement. They assured me that I was doing justice to TR's memory with this effort. Deepest thanks to three good friends.

A most grateful thank-you to those who helped and encouraged me along the way: John Allen, Donna J. Anderson, Marie Behar, James Benesh, Johnny D. Boggs, Sue Cabral-Ebert, Abagail Cannon, Judy Carey-Silvera, Tony and Tina Chong, Brian and Jennifer Dame, Kim Dame, Bruce Dettman, John Driscoll, the late Emil Franzi, George Gold, Richard Day Gore, Tamie Groves, Lolita Jerigan, Lisa Kelly, Robert Knott, Robert Kokai, Kathy Krause, Michael Kriegsman, Terry and Nancy Lamfers, Karla LaRive, Sam LaRive, Jenny Lerew, Craig Lindberg, William Malin, Geri Mars, Lydia Milars, Keith Palmer, Carrie Renfro, Dan Richmond, Todd Roberts, Stuart Rosebrook, Celeste Rush, Rosemary Schiano, Robert Semler, Winter Stezaker, Steve Tanner, Mitch Trimboli, and Teresa Vest.

I wouldn't be anywhere if it weren't for my wife, Linda. Through the peaks and valleys, she has always been by my side, with the patience of a saint. When I needed to visit TR's national park several times, she was a willing companion, and listened to endless discussions about TR.

Lastly, I want to thank Theodore Roosevelt. Since the age of eight, he has been my favorite US president, and has long been an inspiration. On those occasional difficult days while working on this book, Theodore's words and actions were a lighthouse beacon for me. His words are still fresh, vibrant, and meaningful today. By Godfrey, it has been fun writing about you!

NOTES

PREFACE

1. *Teddy Roosevelt: An American Lion*. Greystone Communications, Inc. / History Channel, 2002.
2. H. Paul Jeffers, *The Bully Pulpit: A Teddy Roosevelt Book of Quotations*. Lanham, MD: Taylor Trade Publishing, 2002, p. 51.
3. "Ride for the brand" meant a cowboy was loyal to the outfit he worked for and that paid his wages. His loyalty could not be bought by another outfit with a higher salary; he only rode for one brand.

A YOUNG MAN IN MOTION

1. Theodore's digestive problems were described by the family as *cholera morbus*. Today, it would be diagnosed as Crohn's disease.
2. Theodore Roosevelt, *Theodore Roosevelt: An Autobiography*. Norwalk, CT: Easton Press, 1996, p. 19.
3. Mayne Reid, an Irish national who had fought in the Mexican-American War, found a niche in writing adventure novels centered in the American West, South Africa, or Mexico. *The Boy Hunters*, which Reid called his "juvenile scientific travelog[ue]," followed three boys living with their father, who is a collector of natural history specimens. He tells his sons that he would give almost anything for the hide of a white buffalo; the boys decide to launch an expedition to find the rare buffalo, and return with the much-desired hide. Born in Ireland, Reid gave up studying to be a minister and hopped a ship bound for New Orleans in December 1839. He later worked as a journalist in Pittsburgh, Philadelphia, and then in New York City, where he joined the First New York Volunteer Infantry as a second lieutenant to fight in the Mexican-American War in 1846. Wounded during the Battle of Chapultepec, Reid was discharged and made his way to London, where his first novel, *The Rifle Rangers*, was published in 1850. A free spender, he went bankrupt in 1866, and lived off a military pension until his death in 1883 at the age of sixty-five.
4. Jack Willis with Horace Smith, *Roosevelt in the Rough*. New York: Ives Washburn, 1931, p. 55.
5. Roosevelt, *Theodore Roosevelt: An Autobiography*, p. 22.
6. Caffeine, a prime component found in the coffee plant, is considered as something of a weak bronchodilator, a substance that can dilate the airways, allowing air to flow freely. Another supposed cure of the time was to rub chloroform liniment on the person's chest.
7. As the financier of covert Confederate operations in England, James received a letter from Confederate Navy Secretary Stephen Mallory in late 1864 to send a check to Patrick Martin, a blockade runner operating out of Canada. Martin, who was working on a plan to kidnap President Lincoln, died in December 1864 when the ship he was taking to Maryland (to meet with John Wilkes Booth) was lost at sea.

8. During the Civil War, this action of paying another to serve in their place was quite common among rich Northerners. The usual fee was $300, which would amount to what an average laborer made in one year. Some enterprising fellows agreed to the bounty, taking the money and then skipping town. One man was finally caught and forced to serve, after pocketing seven bounties. By 1863, the resentment felt by the poor (mainly the Irish) began to build. Claiming they were forced to fight a "rich man's war," along with the freeing of blacks and a Federal draft, sparked the New York City draft riots in July 1863.

9. Roosevelt, *Theodore Roosevelt: An Autobiography*, p. 17.

10. Ibid., p. 33.

11. H. W. Brands, *T. R.: The Last Romantic*. New York: Basic Books, 1997, p. 33.

12. Letter dated January 26, 1876. H. W. Brands, *The Selected Letters of Theodore Roosevelt*. New York: Cooper Square Press, 2001, p. 6.

13. Letter dated February 9, 1876. Ibid.

14. Theodore Roosevelt, *The Wilderness Hunter*. New York: G. P. Putnam's Sons, 1893, p. xv.

15. Roosevelt, *Theodore Roosevelt: An Autobiography*, p. 29.

16. Ibid., pp. 29–30.

17. Brands, *T. R.: The Last Romantic*. pp. 61–62.

18. Brands, *The Selected Letters of Theodore Roosevelt*, p. 6.

19. Theodore Sr. experienced a brief reprieve during Christmas, but the tumor grew so quickly that it was literally strangling his intestines. The pain was so intense that his dark hair went gray, and his children had to hold him down as he thrashed in unimaginable pain. Edmund Morris, *The Rise of Theodore Roosevelt*. New York: Random House, 1979, pp. 69–70.

20. Ibid., p. 70.

21. Ibid., p. 5.

22. Interestingly, like Theodore, Sewall was also sickly as a child. He developed a cold after falling into a snowbank, which led to suffering chronic ear trouble. Diphtheria nearly took his life. Sewall took up logging when he was sixteen to help the family coffers. It also proved to be his cure.

23. Carleton Putnam, *Theodore Roosevelt: The Formative Years, 1858–1886*. New York: Charles Scribner's Sons, 1958, p. 157.

24. Theodore Roosevelt private diary, assorted papers, Library of Congress.

25. Letter dated October 10, 1880. Brands, *The Selected Letters of Theodore Roosevelt*, p. 16.

26. Interestingly, both Choate and Root would later serve in Roosevelt's presidential administration. Choate was ambassador to England (appointed by McKinley in 1899) until 1905, and later served as one of the US representatives at the 1907 Hague Peace Conference. Root was secretary of war (also appointed by McKinley in 1899), and he was named secretary of state by Theodore in 1905. Like Theodore, Root won a Nobel Peace Prize in 1912 for his efforts in bringing nations together through arbitration and collaboration.

27. Letter dated November 1, 1881. Brands, *The Selected Letters of Theodore Roosevelt*, p.

28. Putnam, *Theodore Roosevelt: The Formative Years, 1858–1886*, p. 247.

29. Letter dated November 12, 1882. Brands, *The Selected Letters of Theodore Roosevelt*, p. 27.
30. Putnam, *Theodore Roosevelt: The Formative Years, 1858–1886*, p. 251.
31. Brands, *T. R.: The Last Romantic*, pp. 130–31.
32. Roosevelt, *Theodore Roosevelt: An Autobiography*, p. 80.
33. Brands, *T. R.: The Last Romantic*, pp. 134–35.
34. While it was called Cleopatra's Needle, the obelisk was 1,500 years older than its namesake. It was erected on January 21, 1881, in Central Park.

THE BADLANDS

1. Alfred Sully's 1864 campaign was in response to the 1862–63 Sioux uprisings in Minnesota, where they attacked and killed 600 civilians and military personnel in the south-central area of the state. In September 1862, over 480 Sioux were captured and given military trials; while 300 were found guilty of murder and rape, President Lincoln commuted the death sentences of 264. The remaining 36 Sioux were hanged in what was the largest mass execution in the United States, on December 26, 1862. The Sioux were expelled from the Minnesota area and relocated in the southern Dakota Territory, and later in Nebraska.

Some warriors linked up with the other tribes of the Sioux Nation and continued to attack settlers and the US Army. Sully, leading two brigades (approximately 2,200 men) routed the Sioux in the Killdeer Mountains (twenty miles south of Theodore Roosevelt National Park) on July 28, 1864. On August 5, Sully and his men engaged in small-scale combat with the Sioux in the Badlands, near Square Butte (between present-day Medora and Sentinel Butte, North Dakota). This fighting continued for three days, until Sully left the Badlands and reached the Yellowstone River on August 10.
2. In the 1800s the name "Bad Lands" served as a moniker for any area that was desolate, offering little shelter, water, or land to survive. Other locations of Badland formations include Toadstool Geologic Park in the Oglala National Grassland of northwestern Nebraska, Dinosaur National Monument in Colorado, Hell's Half-Acre in Natrona County, Wyoming, El Malpais National Monument in western New Mexico, Big Muddy Badlands in Saskatchewan, Canada, as well as one in Alberta, Canada. Badland formations can also be found in New Zealand, Spain, and mid-western Argentina. Southern Taiwan has the *only* Badlands area in a tropical climate.
3. Albert Bushnell Hart and Herbert Ronald Feleger, eds., *Theodore Roosevelt Cyclopedia*. Westport, CT: Theodore Roosevelt Association and Meckler Corporation, 1989, p. 33.
4. Letter dated August 24, 1884. Ibid., p. 34.
5. In the Pliocene Epoch, the Little Missouri River flowed northward, merging with the Yellowstone River (near present-day Williston, North Dakota), eventually connecting with the Missouri River. That river flowed northeast, through Saskatchewan and Manitoba, to Hudson Bay. Looking at a current map that shows the flow of the Little Missouri River, one can see it takes on a switchback formation. This is caused by *anastomosis*, where one side of the riverbank is carved away by the flow of the water, which takes the sediment downriver, often depositing it on the opposite side. Robin McQuinn, interview with author, Medora, North Dakota, September 16, 2014.

6. These rocks are called *erratics*, because they are out of place for the area (i.e., nonindigenous).

7. The rate of erosion at Theodore Roosevelt National Park is a half-inch per one hundred years. Erosion in the park is 99 percent caused by water. Robin McQuinn, interview with author.

8. A coal vein close enough to the surface could be ignited by a lightning strike, but such incidents were infrequent. Theodore Roosevelt National Park had one coal vein that burned from 1951 to roughly 1970. Robin McQuinn, interview with author.

9. Hoodoos can also be found in Taiwan, Turkey, New Zealand, France, Spain, Serbia, Alberta, Canada, and Bryce Canyon in Utah. They can range in height from that of an average human to a ten-story building.

10. The Hell Creek Formation includes portions of Montana, North Dakota, South Dakota, and Wyoming. Numerous dinosaur remains have been found in this region. The discovery of "Dakota" was near the Badlands.

11. Most of the tribes mentioned passed through the Badlands on their way to Fort Union, where they would trade for various goods. Fort Union was built by John Jacob Astor's American Fur Company in 1828, at the juncture of the Yellowstone and Missouri Rivers. It is now a national park.

12. The Bering land bridge was an ancient land bridge that was roughly six hundred miles wide, connecting Asia with North America during the Pleistocene ice ages. Dale F. Lott, *American Bison: A Natural History*. Berkeley, CA: University of California Press, 2002, p. 62.

13. The correct term for the animal that populated the North American continent is *bison*. Predominantly located in North America, bison are recognized by their large head, short horns, and a dense hairy coat that they shed in the late spring and summer seasons. Buffalo, found mainly in Africa and Asia, have long horns and a coat that never sheds, and its head size is considered average. *Bison* comes from a Greek word meaning "ox-like." French fur trappers called them *boeufs*, which translates to ox or bullock. The first use of *buffalo* in North America dates back to 1625, while the first record for *bison* dates to 1774. Ibid., p. 69.

14. Tom McHugh, *The Time of the Buffalo*. New York: Alfred A Knopf, 1972, pp. 71–72.

15. Today, malignant catarrhal fever and brucellosis are deadly diseases to buffalo herds. As of now, no vaccination has been developed for catarrhal fever, but there is one for brucellosis. Ibid., p. 318.

16. Theodore Roosevelt, *Hunting Trips of a Ranchman*. Birmingham, AL: Palladium Press (reprint), 1999, p. 259.

17. Lincoln A. Lang, *Ranching with Roosevelt*. Philadelphia, PA: J. D. Lippincott, 1926.

18. Douglas Brinkley, *The Wilderness Warrior: Theodore Roosevelt and the Crusade for America*. New York: Touchstone / Simon and Schuster, 1994, pp. 150–51.

19. Ibid., pp. 154–55.

20. Gregorio de Villalobos brought over six heifers and a bull by way of Spain to Vera Cruz. They soon grew into a larger herd, mixing with other cattle brought over from Spain. Dee Brown, *The American West*. New York: Touchstone / Simon & Schuster, 1994, p. 42.

21. Howard Lamar, ed., *The New Encyclopedia of the American West.* New Haven, CT: Yale University Press, 1998, p. 175.

22. Brown, *The American West*, p. 43.

23. Between 1866 and 1885, it is estimated that 5,700,000 cattle were driven north. Ray H. Mattison, "Roosevelt's Contemporaries Along the Little Missouri River," Theodore Roosevelt National Park. Theodore Roosevelt Digital Library, Dickinson State University, 1950.

24. This same trail was originally used by a Delaware scout named Black Beaver when escorting exploration parties in the 1840s. Brown, *The American West*, p. 51.

25. Three other well-known cattle trails were the Shawnee Trail (1840–66), Western Trail (1876–84), and the Goodnight-Loving Trail (1866–82). The Shawnee Trail (also known as the Texas Trail) was used as far back as 1840 to move cattle, going through Austin, Dallas, and crossing the Red River at Preston, before entering the eastern half of Indian Territory (present-day Oklahoma) to Baxter Springs in Kansas, before moving east into Missouri and then north to the towns of Sedalia, Kansas City, and St. Joseph. The Western Trail began north of the Nueces River, passing through Fort Griffin, then Indian Country, and eventually, to Dodge City, Kansas. It later was continued north to Ogallala, Nebraska. The Goodnight-Loving Trail left from Fort Belknap, Texas, heading south along the old Butterfield Stagecoach route that ran through central Texas. It then moved north along the Pecos River into New Mexico Territory, ultimately arriving in Denver, Colorado. It was later extended into Wyoming Territory.

26. Longhorns vary in color, from a bluish-gray to assorted yellowish hues, to browns, black, and ruddy and white (bright or dirty-speckled).

27. Hart and Feleger, eds., *Theodore Roosevelt Cyclopedia*, p. 121.

28. After the Civil War, there was a boom in railroad construction. Between 1868 and 1873, the railroad industry laid nearly 33,000 miles of track and was the largest employer in the United States.

29. Lamar, ed., *The New Encyclopedia of the American West*, p. 179.

30. Although the Open Range Policy was started after the Civil War, its peak years were between 1880 and 1885.

31. Even today it is still a problem where there is not a management plan. Overgrazing led to the 2010 famine in the Sahel region in Africa, while the Australian government ordered the culling of 1,455 kangaroos due to overgrazing in 2013.

32. Skirmish line formation basically assigned a small number of soldiers (perhaps eight to twelve) who were deployed in a loose line of about ten to twenty feet, depending on what was needed. Use of skirmish lines had its beginnings with Napoleon battle tactics in the early nineteenth century.

33. Built and completed by Christmas of 1879, the buildings were abandoned by the army in 1883. An 1887 fire destroyed many of the buildings, and the remaining structures were salvaged for other construction. Rolf Sletten, *Medora: Boom, Bust, and Resurrection.* Medora, ND: Theodore Roosevelt Medora Foundation, 2013, pp. 32–33.

34. The Marquis was of French and Spanish heritage. His grandfather, Vincent Manca, was granted two villages on the island of Sardinia for service to the king of Spain. Failing to prevent a revolt within the palace against King Felix Albert of Spain, the

Marquis's grandfather was exiled to France in the 1820s. In 1831, he married Claire de Galard de Grassac de Béarn, an heiress related to King Henry IV of France. The Marquis's father, Richard, took the title of Duc de Vallombrosa when he reached legal age. He eventually earned the rank of lieutenant general in the French Army, and was one of the top commanders in the conquest of Algiers. Donald Dresden, *The Marquis de Morès: Emperor of the Bad Lands*. Norman: University of Oklahoma Press, 1970, pp. 16–17.

35. The military academy was France's equivalent to West Point. One of the Marquis's classmates, Henri-Philippe Pétain, rose to the rank of general in the French Army during World War I. He later served as the head of the Vichy French government during World War II until the liberation of Paris in 1945. Ibid., p. 19.

36. The Marquis's debt was 500,000 francs, which roughly translated to $110,000 in US currency. Curt Eriksmoen, "How the Marquis de Morès Got Started in Medora," *Bismarck Tribune*, December 8, 2013.

37. Dresden, *The Marquis de Morès: Emperor of the Bad Lands*, p. 35.

38. The Marquis bought sections of land on either side of the Little Missouri River, ranging from twenty to twenty-five miles long and five miles inland from the river, which was the utmost distance cattle would walk for water. Ibid., p. 42.

39. The Chateau de Morès was hardly what any European would consider a chateau. It was a two-story, twenty-six-room ranch house, more elaborate in size and decor than any other residence in the area. It is now a museum, operated by the State Historical Society of North Dakota.

40. Dresden, *The Marquis de Morès: Emperor of the Bad Lands*, pp. 42–44.

41. Lang, *Ranching with Roosevelt*, p. 73.

42. *Bismarck Daily Tribune*, July 28, 1883.

43. Carleton Putnam, *Theodore Roosevelt: The Formative Years, 1858–1886*, p. 356.

44. Dresden, *The Marquis de Morès: Emperor of the Bad Lands*, p. 61.

45. *Bismarck Daily Tribune*, June 27, 1883.

46. Putnam, *Theodore Roosevelt: The Formative Years, 1858–1886*, p. 357.

47. Lang, *Ranching with Roosevelt*, p. 74.

48. Dresden, *The Marquis de Morès: Emperor of the Bad Lands*, p. 71.

49. The Marquis's lawyer, George Flannery, used the influence of the territorial governor and attorney general to persuade Judge Collins to drop the charges. Ibid., p. 77.

THE DUDE GOES WEST

1. So serious was this attack that Theodore's doctor sent him to Richfield Springs in the Catskill Mountains in early July to recuperate. When he arrived in Chicago, on his way to the Badlands, Theodore sent his mother a postcard reassuring her that he was "feeling like a fighting cock."

2. Theodore's trip west took him five days by train. From Chicago to St. Paul, he endured a twenty-hour trip. After arriving there, he had a layover that was nearly twelve hours long. On September 7, he departed Bismarck in Dakota Territory at six in the evening, headed for Little Missouri. Donald Dresden, *The Marquis de Morès: Emperor of the Bad Lands*. Norman: University of Oklahoma Press, 1970, p. 6.

3. During Theodore's Dakota trip, Alice was staying with her parents near Boston, Massachusetts. Letter to Alice Roosevelt, dated September 8, 1883. Rolf Sletten, *Medora: Boom, Bust, and Resurrection*. Medora, ND: Theodore Roosevelt Medora Foundation, 2013, pp. 58–59.

4. The Red River Valley region is located in central North America, covering parts of North Dakota, Minnesota, and Manitoba, Canada.

5. Theodore Roosevelt, *Theodore Roosevelt: An Autobiography*. Norwalk, CT: The Easton Press, 1996, p. 110.

6. Theodore Roosevelt, *Hunting Trips of a Ranchman*. Birmingham, AL: Palladium Press (reprint), 1999, p. 34.

7. This is the rifle Roosevelt poses with in the series of photos taken in 1884, where he is dressed in buckskins. One of these photos appears in the frontispiece of his book, *Hunting Trips of a Ranchman* (1885). Curt Eriksmoen, "TR Had Three Good Friends in Dakota Territory," *Bismarck Tribune*, April 6, 2014.

8. Ibid.

9. Hermann Hagedorn, *Roosevelt in the Bad Lands*. New York: Houghton Mifflin, 1921, p. 17.

10. Western custom dictated that anyone approaching a campsite or home had to hail the occupants, usually with a "Hello in the camp!" One had to wait to be asked to dismount and invited in. Doing so without proper overture was not just bad manners, but could get one shot.

11. Lincoln A. Lang, *Ranching with Roosevelt*. Philadelphia, PA: J. D. Lippincott, 1926, p. 101.

12. Ibid., p. 102.

HUNTING THE SHAGGY BEAST

1. Hermann Hagedorn, *Roosevelt in the Badlands*. New York: Houghton Mifflin, 1921, p. 24.

2. Lincoln A. Lang, *Ranching with Roosevelt*. Philadelphia, PA: J. D. Lippincott, 1926, p. 113.

3. Hagedorn, *Roosevelt in the Badlands*, p. 37.

4. Lang, *Ranching with Roosevelt*, p. 113.

5. Letter from Theodore Roosevelt to Alice Lee Roosevelt, September 14, 1883. Theodore Roosevelt Collection. MS Am 1541.9 (101). Houghton Library, Harvard University.

6. Theodore Roosevelt, *Hunting Trips of a Ranchman*. Birmingham, AL: Palladium Press (reprint), 1999, p. 280.

7. Letter from Theodore Roosevelt to Alice Lee Roosevelt, September 14, 1883, Houghton Library.

8. Hagedorn, *Roosevelt in the Badlands*, p. 36.

9. Roosevelt, *Hunting Trips of a Ranchman*, p. 284.

10. Ibid.

11. Ibid., p. 285.

12. Letter from Theodore Roosevelt to Alice Lee Roosevelt, September 17, 1883. Theodore Roosevelt Collection. MS Am 1541.9 (102). Houghton Library, Harvard University.

13. Roosevelt, *Hunting Trips of a Ranchman*, p. 286.

14. Letter from Theodore Roosevelt to Alice Lee Roosevelt, September 17, 1883.

15. Hagedorn, *Roosevelt in the Badlands*, pp. 41–43.

16. Ibid., p. 43.

17. He earned a total of $114.75 in 1883 for his book royalties. Carleton Putnam, *Theodore Roosevelt: The Formative Years, 1858–1886*. New York: Charles Scribner's Sons, 1958, p. 337.

18. Edmund Morris, *The Rise of Theodore Roosevelt*. New York: Random House, 1979, p. 210.

19. Roosevelt, *Hunting Trips of a Ranchman*, p. 287.

20. Hagedorn, *Roosevelt in the Badlands*, p. 45.

21. Letter from Theodore Roosevelt to Alice Lee Roosevelt, September 20, 1883. Theodore Roosevelt Collection. MS Am 1541.9 (103). Houghton Library, Harvard University.

22. Lang, *Ranching with Roosevelt*, p. 119.

THE HOUSE WITH A CURSE

1. Letter from Theodore Roosevelt to Alice Lee Roosevelt, September 23, 1883. Theodore Roosevelt Collection. MS Am 1541.9 (104). Houghton Library, Harvard University.

2. Carleton Putnam, *Theodore Roosevelt: The Formative Years, 1858–1886*. New York: Charles Scribner's Sons, 1958, pp. 343–44.

3. Mike Thompson, *The Travels and Tribulations of Theodore Roosevelt's Cabin*. San Angelo, TX: Laughing Horse Publications, 2004, pp. 4–5.

4. "Gone to see the elephant" was a nineteenth-century term that meant someone who had seen things most people would never see or experience. It was a common term used among Civil War soldiers and cowboys.

5. Edmund Morris, *The Rise of Theodore Roosevelt*. New York: Random House, 1979, pp. 217–18.

6. Theodore goes on to relate how he spent the day sparring with his boxing teacher, proudly saying he bloodied his instructor's nose with an upper cut. He then mentions an "exciting debate" on his Reform Charter bill, and that he will dine the next evening at the Rathbones. "It was very kind to ask me, but I do not anticipate much fun." He signs it "Your Ever Loving Thee." Elting E. Morison, ed. *The Letters of Theodore Roosevelt: The Years of Preparation, 1868–1898*. Cambridge, MA: Harvard University Press, 1951, p. 65.

7. The family doctor was unaware that the cramps Alice complained of were related to her kidneys failing, and not a usual side effect of the pregnancy. In any case, there was nothing the doctor could have done to save her.

8. Morris, *The Rise of Theodore Roosevelt*, p. 231.

9. Inscription entered on Saturday, February 16, 1884, personal diary of Theodore Roosevelt, 1884. Theodore Roosevelt Papers, Manuscript Division, Library of Congress.

10. Morris, *The Rise of Theodore Roosevelt*, p. 235.

11. Ibid., p. 237.

12. Morison, ed. *The Letters of Theodore Roosevelt: The Years of Preparation, 1868–1898*, p. 66.

13. Morris, *The Rise of Theodore Roosevelt*, p. 238.

14. Ibid., p. 259.

15. Letter dated April 30, 1884. H. W. Brands, *The Selected Letters of Theodore Roosevelt*. New York: Cooper Square Press, 2001, pp. 30–31.

16. Theodore Roosevelt, *Ranch Life and the Hunting-Trail*. Alexandria, VA: Time-Life Books (reprint), 1981, p. 59.

17. Translation would be that a man is "all talk and no action."

18. H. Paul Jeffers, *The Bully Pulpit: A Teddy Roosevelt Book of Quotations*. Lanham, MD: Taylor Trade Publishing, 2002, p. 52.

HEADIN' WEST

1. *Bad Lands Cow Boy*, February 7, 1884. Theodore Roosevelt Center, Dickinson State University.

2. A reconstructed version of the train depot stands at the original site on Pacific Avenue.

3. *Bad Lands Cow Boy*, February 7, 1884.

4. Hermann Hagedorn, *Roosevelt in the Badlands*. New York: Houghton Mifflin, 1921, pp. 89–90.

5. *Bad Lands Cow Boy*, February 7, 1884.

6. Hagedorn, *Roosevelt in the Badlands*, pp. 76–77.

7. *Bismarck Tribune*, quoted in the *Bad Lands Cow Boy*, February 14, 1884. Theodore Roosevelt Center Dickinson State University.

8. Ibid.

9. *Bad Lands Cow Boy*, February 7, 1884.

10. Ibid. February 21, 1884.

11. Hagedorn, *Roosevelt in the Badlands*, p. 127.

12. Ibid., p.129.

13. Ibid., pp. 84–86.

14. With his mother's passing, Theodore received an additional $62,500 to add to the $125,000 he was given by his father's estate. Carleton Putnam, *Theodore Roosevelt: The Formative Years, 1858–1886*. New York: Charles Scribner's Sons, 1958, p. 453.

15. Ibid., p. 455.

16. They were also referred to as "stovepipes." Chaps made with angora hair on them were worn by some cowboys in the Northern Plains for warmth during the late fall and winter. They were known as "woolies."

17. Hagedorn, *Roosevelt in the Badlands*, p. 102.

18. Lincoln A. Lang, *Ranching with Roosevelt*. Philadelphia, PA: J. D. Lippincott, 1926, p. 157.

19. A quirt is a rider's whip. Made out of leather or rawhide, it was braided and had a weighted handle. Quirts were about a foot long with two or three thongs made from leather, buffalo, or cowhide. Ibid., p. 154.

20. Theodore Roosevelt, *Theodore Roosevelt: An Autobiography*. Norwalk, CT: The Easton Press, 1996, p. 123.

21. This is the same buckskin suit Theodore wears in a series of photographs taken in a New York City photo gallery around 1885. The publisher used one of the pictures in Theodore's book, *Hunting Trips of a Ranchman* (1885).

22. Lang, *Ranching with Roosevelt*, p. 157.

23. Ibid., p. 159.

24. Elting E. Morison, ed. *The Letters of Theodore Roosevelt: The Years of Preparation, 1868–1898*. Cambridge, MA: Harvard University Press, 1951, pp. 73–74.

25. He began his trip on June 18, 1884. Theodore Roosevelt, *Hunting Trips of a Ranchman*. Birmingham, AL: Palladium Press (reprint), 1999, p. 209.

26. Roosevelt, *Theodore Roosevelt: An Autobiography*, p. 125.

27. Theodore eventually gave the telescope to Bill Merrifield. The telescope is now on display at the visitor center at the Theodore Roosevelt National Park. Roosevelt, *Hunting Trips of a Ranchman*, p. 211.

28. Ibid., p. 214.

29. Entry written on Wednesday, June 18, 1884. Personal diary of Theodore Roosevelt, 1884. Theodore Roosevelt Papers, Manuscript Division, Library of Congress.

30. Roosevelt, *Hunting Trips of a Ranchman*, p. 220.

31. Entry written on Wednesday, June 21, 1884. Personal diary of Theodore Roosevelt, 1884.

32. Roosevelt, *Hunting Trips of a Ranchman*, p. 228.

33. *Bad Lands Cow Boy*, June 26, 1884. Theodore Roosevelt Center, Dickinson State University.

34. Putnam, *Theodore Roosevelt: The Formative Years, 1858–1886*, pp. 461–62.

35. Interview was reprinted in the August 7, 1884, edition of the *Bad Lands Cow Boy*.

36. Donald Dresden, *The Marquis de Morès: Emperor of the Bad Lands*. Norman: University of Oklahoma Press, 1970, pp. 179–80.

37. Roosevelt, *Theodore Roosevelt: An Autobiography*, p. 124.

38. Hagedorn, *Roosevelt in the Badlands*, pp. 193–94.

DAKOTA RANCHER

1. Andrew Vietze, *Becoming Teddy Roosevelt: How a Maine Guide Inspired America's 26th President*. Lanham, MD: Down East, 2010, p. 85.

2. Ibid., p. 86.

3. Edmund Morris, *The Rise of Theodore Roosevelt*. New York: Random House, 1979, p. 272.

4. Letter from Theodore Roosevelt to Anna Roosevelt, August 17, 1884. Theodore Roosevelt Collection. MS Am 1834 (198a). Houghton Library, Harvard University.

5. Vietze, *Becoming Teddy Roosevelt*, pp. 90–91.

6. Hermann Hagedorn, *Roosevelt in the Badlands*. New York: Houghton Mifflin, 1921, p. 163.

7. Vietze, *Becoming Teddy Roosevelt*, p. 89.

8. Ibid., pp. 92–93.

9. Adding to potential problems with the Marquis, Theodore had hired Dutch Wannegan as a ranch hand at the Maltese Cross. Morris, *The Rise of Theodore Roosevelt*, pp. 276–77.

10. Ibid., pp. 822–23, n. 65.

11. The town is now known as Wibaux, Montana, thirty-five miles west of Medora. There is no marker or plaque to designate Theodore's incident.

12. Theodore Roosevelt, *Theodore Roosevelt: An Autobiography*. Norwalk, CT: The Easton Press, 1996, p. 136.

13. Ibid.

14. "Down in your boots" is a term for being afraid or cowardly. Win Blevins, *Dictionary of the American West*. Seattle, WA: Sasquatch Books, 2001, p. 126.

15. "Sand" was a favorite term among mountain men and cowboys for describing courage or grit.

16. Morris, *The Rise of Theodore Roosevelt*, p. 277.

17. Vietze, *Becoming Teddy Roosevelt*, p. 96.

18. Letter from Theodore Roosevelt to Anna Roosevelt. August 17, 1884.

19. Carleton Putnam, *Theodore Roosevelt: The Formative Years, 1858–1886*. New York: Charles Scribner's Sons, 1958, p. 474, n. 12.

20. Hagedorn, *Roosevelt in the Badlands*. New York: Houghton Mifflin, 1921, pp.175–76.

21. Putnam, *Theodore Roosevelt: The Formative Years, 1858–1886*, p. 475.

22. Ibid., p. 476.

23. Personal diary of Theodore Roosevelt, 1883–1884. Theodore Roosevelt Papers, Manuscript Division, Library of Congress.

24. Elting E. Morison, ed. *The Letters of Theodore Roosevelt: The Years of Preparation, 1868–1898*. Cambridge, MA: Harvard University Press, 1951, pp. 79–80.

25. Edward P. Kohn, ed. *A Most Glorious Ride: The Diaries of Theodore Roosevelt, 1877–1886*. Albany, NY: Excelsior Editions, 2015, pp. 232–33.

26. Ibid., pp. 234–35.

27. Diary entry dated August 30, 1884. Ibid., p. 233.

28. The Tensleep Creek is a tributary of the Nowood River, which flows into the Bighorn River.

29. Kohn, ed. *A Most Glorious Ride: The Diaries of Theodore Roosevelt, 1877–1886*. Albany, NY: Excelsior Editions, 2015, p. 236.

30. Theodore Roosevelt, *Hunting Trips of a Ranchman*. Birmingham, AL: Palladium Press (reprint), 1999, p. 336.

31. Douglas Brinkley, *The Wilderness Warrior: Theodore Roosevelt and the Crusade for America*. New York: HarperCollins Publishers, 2009, pp. 174–75.

32. Morison, ed., *The Letters of Theodore Roosevelt: The Years of Preparation, 1868–1898*, pp. 81–82.

33. Kohn, ed. *A Most Glorious Ride: The Diaries of Theodore Roosevelt, 1877–1886*, p. 239.

34. Hagedorn, *Roosevelt in the Badlands*, pp. 207–08.

A STRENUOUS LIFE

1. Edmund Morris, *The Rise of Theodore Roosevelt*. New York: Random House, 1979, p. 284.
2. Carleton Putnam, *Theodore Roosevelt: The Formative Years, 1858–1886*. New York: Charles Scribner's Sons, 1958, pp. 502–03.
3. Letter dated November 11, 1884. Elting E. Morison, ed. *The Letters of Theodore Roosevelt: The Years of Preparation, 1868–1898*. Cambridge, MA: Harvard University Press, 1951, p. 88.
4. Theodore Roosevelt, *Hunting Trips of a Ranchman*. Birmingham, AL: Palladium Press (reprint), 1999, pp. 86–89.
5. Today, all that remains of Elkhorn Ranch is the stone foundation.
6. Spearfish is a town located in what is now South Dakota.
7. Edward P. Kohn, ed. *A Most Glorious Ride: The Diaries of Theodore Roosevelt, 1877–1886*. Albany, NY: Excelsior Editions, 2015, p. 242.
8. Hermann Hagedorn, *Roosevelt in the Badlands*. New York: Houghton Mifflin, 1921, p. 98.
9. Ibid., pp. 226–27.
10. Ibid., pp. 106–07, 232.
11. Roosevelt, *Hunting Trips of a Ranchman*, p. 239.
12. Ibid., p. 249.
13. Ibid., p. 254.
14. Putnam, *Theodore Roosevelt: The Formative Years, 1858–1886*, pp. 513–14.
15. Minutes of a meeting of the Little Missouri River Stockmen's Association, December 19, 1884. Theodore Roosevelt Collection. MS Am 1541 (309). Houghton Library, Harvard University.

ROUNDUP

1. This saddle is in the collection of the Buffalo Bill Historical Center in Cody, Wyoming.
2. Hermann Hagedorn, *Roosevelt in the Badlands*. New York: Houghton Mifflin, 1921, pp. 251–52.
3. Theodore Roosevelt, *Hunting Trips of a Ranchman*. Birmingham, AL: Palladium Press (reprint), 1999, p. 11.
4. Theodore Roosevelt, *Ranch Life and the Hunting-Trail*. Alexandria, VA: Time-Life Books (reprint), 1981, p. 68.
5. Theodore's reference to the Meadowbrook hunt was to a fox hunt he participated in prior to returning to Medora. Elting E. Morison, ed. *The Letters of Theodore Roosevelt: The Years of Preparation, 1868–1898*. Cambridge, MA: Harvard University Press, 1951, p. 90.
6. Lincoln A. Lang, *Ranching with Roosevelt*. Philadelphia, PA: J. D. Lippincott, 1926, pp. 176–77.
7. Roosevelt, *Hunting Trips of a Ranchman*, p. 15.
8. Roosevelt, *Ranch Life and the Hunting-Trail*, p. 50.
9. Ibid., p. 56.
10. Carleton Putnam, *Theodore Roosevelt: The Formative Years, 1858–1886*. New York: Charles Scribner's Sons, 1958, p. 527.

11. Roosevelt, *Ranch Life and the Hunting-Trail*, pp. 50, 58.
12. Ibid., p. 62.
13. While some cattle outfits still use hot irons for branding, most ranches now use more-advanced techniques to mark cattle or horses. A numbered tag is attached to the ear of cattle. Freeze-branding is done with a coolant (dry ice or liquid nitrogen). It does not burn a scar into the skin, but the freezing causes the animal's hair to grow white where the brand has been applied. Tattooing the inner lip or ear, or using a microchip, are also new ways of branding.
14. Roosevelt, *Ranch Life and the Hunting-Trail*, pp. 52–53.
15. Hagedorn, *Roosevelt in the Badlands*, pp. 283–84.
16. Theodore Roosevelt, *Theodore Roosevelt: An Autobiography*. Norwalk, CT: The Easton Press, 1996, pp. 116–17.
17. Ibid., p. 117.
18. Putnam, *Theodore Roosevelt: The Formative Years, 1858–1886*, p. 529.
19. Ibid.

DEEDS, NOT WORDS

1. Carleton Putnam, *Theodore Roosevelt: The Formative Years, 1858–1886*. New York: Charles Scribner's Sons, 1958, p. 519.
2. Douglas Brinkley, *The Wilderness Warrior: Theodore Roosevelt and the Crusade for America*. New York: HarperCollins Publishers, 2009, p. 184.
3. Ibid., p. 186.
4. This marked the third time the Marquis had charges brought against him in regard to Luffsey's death.
5. Hermann Hagedorn, *Roosevelt in the Badlands*. New York: Houghton Mifflin, 1921, pp. 339–40.
6. Donald Dresden, *The Marquis de Morès: Emperor of the Bad Lands*. Norman: University of Oklahoma Press, 1970, pp. 163–65.
7. Ibid., p. 115.
8. Ibid.
9. Putnam, *Theodore Roosevelt: The Formative Years, 1858–1886*, pp. 539–40.
10. Edmund Morris, *The Rise of Theodore Roosevelt*. New York: Random House, 1979, p. 307.
11. Rolf Sletten, *Medora: Boom, Bust, and Resurrection*. Medora, ND: Theodore Roosevelt Medora Foundation, 2013, pp. 74–75.
12. Curt Eriksmoen, "Marquis de Morès Worked Hard, But Efforts Failed," *Bismarck Tribune*, December 15, 2013.
13. Dresden, *The Marquis de Morès: Emperor of the Bad Lands*, p. 139.
14. Dow had accompanied Theodore back east in June, traveling to Maine, where he married Lizzie.
15. Andrew Vietze, *Becoming Teddy Roosevelt: How a Maine Guide Inspired America's 26th President*. Lanham, MD: Down East, 2010, p. 102.
16. Lincoln A. Lang, *Ranching with Roosevelt*. Philadelphia, PA: J. D. Lippincott, 1926, p. 209.

17. Theodore Roosevelt, *Theodore Roosevelt: An Autobiography*. Norwalk, CT: The Easton Press, 1996, pp. 120–21.
18. Lang, *Ranching with Roosevelt*, p. 202.
19. Theodore Roosevelt, *Ranch Life and the Hunting-Trail*. Alexandria, VA: Time-Life Books (reprint), 1981, p. 102.
20. Ibid., p. 103.
21. Ibid., p. 104.
22. Ibid.
23. Ibid., p. 105.
24. Ibid., pp. 107–08.
25. Theodore Roosevelt, *Hunting Trips of a Ranchman*. Birmingham, AL: Palladium Press (reprint), 1999, p. 19.
26. Ibid., pp. 19–20.
27. Ibid., p. 20.

CHANCE MEETING

1. Corinne Roosevelt was born on September 27, 1861.
2. Sylvia Jukes Morris, *Edith Kermit Roosevelt*. New York: Modern Library, 2001, p. 16.
3. Edmund Morris, *The Rise of Theodore Roosevelt*. New York: Random House, 1979, pp. 26–27.
4. Sylvia Jukes Morris, *Edith Kermit Roosevelt*, p. 27.
5. Ibid., p. 70.
6. Ibid., p. 56.
7. Ibid., p. 59.
8. Edmund Morris, *The Rise of Theodore Roosevelt*, p. 115.
9. Sylvia Jukes Morris, *Edith Kermit Roosevelt*, p. 69.
10. Diary of Theodore Roosevelt from January 1 to July 3, 1886. Theodore Roosevelt Collection. MS Am 1454.55 (12). Theodore Roosevelt Collection. MS Am 1541.9 (104). Houghton Library, Harvard University.
11. Edmund Morris, *The Rise of Theodore Roosevelt*, pp. 310–11.
12. Diary of Theodore Roosevelt from January 1 to July 3, 1886, Houghton Library.
13. Ibid.
14. Thomas Hart Benton (1782–1858), a US senator from Missouri, was a staunch advocate of westward expansion of the United States.
15. Elting E. Morison, ed. *The Letters of Theodore Roosevelt: The Years of Preparation, 1868–1898*. Cambridge, MA: Harvard University Press, 1951, pp. 93–94.
16. Ibid., pp. 94–95.
17. Theodore's speech at Princeton was given on January 27, 1886, while the one at Morton Hall was delivered on February 12, 1886. Diary of Theodore Roosevelt from January 1 to July 3, 1886.
18. *New York Daily Tribune*, October 18, 1885.
19. Carleton Putnam, *Theodore Roosevelt: The Formative Years, 1858–1886*. New York: Charles Scribner's Sons, 1958, p. 549.
20. *Bismarck Daily Tribune*, December 1, 1885.

A MATTER OF JUSTICE

1. Hermann Hagedorn, *Roosevelt in the Badlands*. New York: Houghton Mifflin, 1921, pp. 363–64.
2. Letter from Theodore Roosevelt to Anna Roosevelt. March 20, 1886. Theodore Roosevelt Collection. MS Am 1834 (206). Houghton Library, Harvard University.
3. Carleton Putnam, *Theodore Roosevelt: The Formative Years, 1858–1886*. New York: Charles Scribner's Sons, 1958, p. 562.
4. Rolf Sletten, *Medora: Boom, Bust, and Resurrection*. Medora, ND: Theodore Roosevelt Medora Foundation, 2013, p. 94.
5. Theodore Roosevelt, *Ranch Life and the Hunting-Trail*. Alexandria, VA: Time-Life Books (reprint), 1981, p. 115.
6. Hagedorn, *Roosevelt in the Badlands*, pp. 371–72.
7. Roosevelt, *Ranch Life and the Hunting-Trail*, p. 117.
8. Ibid., p. 120.
9. Andrew Vietze, *Becoming Teddy Roosevelt: How a Maine Guide Inspired America's 26th President*. Lanham, MD: Down East, 2010, p. 106.
10. Roosevelt, *Ranch Life and the Hunting-Trail*, p. 120.
11. Vietze, *Becoming Teddy Roosevelt*, p. 107.
12. Roosevelt, *Ranch Life and the Hunting-Trail*, p. 123.
13. Ibid., p. 126.
14. Ibid.
15. Ibid., p. 128.
16. Putnam, *Theodore Roosevelt: The Formative Years, 1858–1886*, p. 568.
17. Hagedorn, *Roosevelt in the Badlands*, p. 383.
18. Quote is from a speech given to Friends of Honest Government in New York City on October 25, 1895. H. Paul Jeffers, *The Bully Pulpit: A Teddy Roosevelt Book of Quotations*. Lanham, MD: Taylor Trade Publishing, 2002, p. 83.
19. Putnam, *Theodore Roosevelt: The Formative Years, 1858–1886*, p. 569.
20. Ibid., p. 569.
21. Sletten, *Medora: Boom, Bust, and Resurrection*, pp. 96–97.
22. Hagedorn, *Roosevelt in the Badlands*, p. 457.

ENTERING THE ARENA

1. Letter dated April 12, 1886. Elting E. Morison, ed. *The Letters of Theodore Roosevelt: The Years of Preparation, 1868–1898*. Cambridge, MA: Harvard University Press, 1951, pp. 95–97.
2. Ibid.
3. Hermann Hagedorn, *Roosevelt in the Badlands*. New York: Houghton Mifflin, 1921, p. 393.
4. Theodore was elected to the executive committee, the position previously held by the Marquis.
5. Howard Lamar, ed., *The New Encyclopedia of the American West*. New Haven, CT: Yale University Press, 1998, p. 106.

6. Lincoln A. Lang, *Ranching with Roosevelt*. Philadelphia, PA: J. D. Lippincott, 1926, p. 220.

7. Hagedorn, *Roosevelt in the Badlands*, p. 395.

8. Morison, ed. *The Letters of Theodore Roosevelt: The Years of Preparation, 1868–1898*, p. 99.

9. During this period, men and women in Eastern society dressed for dinner. It was considered rude form for a gentleman to show up at the dinner table in just shirtsleeves. Ibid., p. 100.

10. John Terry Morse Jr. was the editor of the American Statesman series published by Houghton Mifflin. Ibid., p. 101.

11. Letter dated June 7, 1886. Ibid., p. 102.

12. Diary of Theodore Roosevelt from January 1 to July 3, 1886. Theodore Roosevelt Collection. MS Am 1454.55 (12). Theodore Roosevelt Collection. MS Am 1541.9 (104). Houghton Library, Harvard University.

13. Carleton Putnam, *Theodore Roosevelt: The Formative Years, 1858–1886*. New York: Charles Scribner's Sons, 1958, p. 573.

14. Sylvia Jukes Morris, *Edith Kermit Roosevelt*. New York: Modern Library, 2001, pp. 84–86, 88.

15. James F. Vivian, *The Romance of My Life: Theodore Roosevelt's Speeches in Dakota*. Fargo, ND: Prairie House / Theodore Roosevelt Medora Foundation, 1989, p. 5 (photographs).

16. Ibid., p. 5.

17. Ibid., p. 7.

18. Ibid., pp. 7–10.

19. Putnam, *Theodore Roosevelt: The Formative Years, 1858–1886*, p. 581.

20. Edmund Morris, *The Rise of Theodore Roosevelt*. New York: Random House, 1979, p. 334.

DARK CLOUDS

1. Lincoln A. Lang, *Ranching with Roosevelt*. Philadelphia, PA: J. D. Lippincott, 1926, p. 224.

2. Letter dated July 5, 1886. Elting E. Morison, ed. *The Letters of Theodore Roosevelt: The Years of Preparation, 1868–1898*. Cambridge, MA: Harvard University Press, 1951, p. 107.

3. Letter dated August 20, 1886. Edmund Morris, *The Rise of Theodore Roosevelt*. New York: Random House, 1979, p. 335.

4. This is the first time the term "Rough Riders" was used in connection with Theodore. Cooler heads prevailed and there was no war with Mexico. Morison, ed. *The Letters of Theodore Roosevelt: The Years of Preparation, 1868–1898*, p. 108.

5. Jack Willis with Horace Smith, *Roosevelt in the Rough*. New York: Ives Washburn, 1931, p. 8.

6. Ibid., pp. 6–7, 9.

7. Ibid., p. 9.

8. Ibid., p. 11.

9. Ibid., p. 16.

10. Ibid., pp. 17–18.

11. Ibid., pp. 25–26.

12. Ibid., pp. 40–41.

13. Letter from Theodore Roosevelt to Anna Roosevelt. September, 1886. Theodore Roosevelt Collection. MS Am 1834 (206). Houghton Library, Harvard University.

14. Carleton Putnam, *Theodore Roosevelt: The Formative Years, 1858–1886.* New York: Charles Scribner's Sons, 1958, p. 588.

15. Andrew Vietze, *Becoming Teddy Roosevelt: How a Maine Guide Inspired America's 26th President.* Lanham, MD: Down East, 2010, p. 111.

16. Ibid.

17. Morison, ed. *The Letters of Theodore Roosevelt: The Years of Preparation, 1868–1898*, p. 111.

18. The final vote tally was Hewitt: 90,552; George: 68,110, and Theodore: 60,435.

19. Morris, *The Rise of Theodore Roosevelt*, pp. 357–58.

20. Morison, ed. *The Letters of Theodore Roosevelt: The Years of Preparation, 1868–1898*, pp. 117–18.

21. Hermann Hagedorn, *Roosevelt in the Badlands.* New York: Houghton Mifflin, 1921, p. 431.

22. Sun dogs are halos caused by light that interacts with ice crystals in the atmosphere. They appear to the human eye as a pair of bright spots on either side of the sun. Moon dogs are similar to sun dogs, but are much rarer, since the moon must be bright (full or nearly full) to be viewed by the human eye. Lang, *Ranching with Roosevelt*, p. 242.

WISHING FOR A CHINOOK

1. Hermann Hagedorn, *Roosevelt in the Badlands.* New York: Houghton Mifflin, 1921, pp. 432–33.

2. Doug Ellison, interview with author, Medora, North Dakota, September 16, 2014.

3. Edmund Morris, *The Rise of Theodore Roosevelt.* New York: Random House, 1979, p. 365.

4. Doug Ellison, interview with author.

5. *Bismarck Daily Tribune*, November 27, 1886.

6. Hagedorn, *Roosevelt in the Badlands*, p. 436.

7. Morris, *The Rise of Theodore Roosevelt*, p. 366.

8. Doug Ellison, interview with author.

9. Morris, *The Rise of Theodore Roosevelt*, pp. 373–74.

10. Andrew Vietze, *Becoming Teddy Roosevelt: How a Maine Guide Inspired America's 26th President*, Lanham, MD: Down East, 2010, pp.137–38.

11. Lincoln A. Lang, *Ranching with Roosevelt.* Philadelphia, PA: J. D. Lippincott, 1926, pp. 252–54.

12. Carleton Putnam, *Theodore Roosevelt: The Formative Years, 1858–1886.* New York: Charles Scribner's Sons, 1958, p. 595.

13. Elting E. Morison, ed. *The Letters of Theodore Roosevelt: The Years of Preparation, 1868–1898.* Cambridge, MA: Harvard University Press, 1951, pp.126–27.

14. Ibid., p. 725.

15. Donald Dresden, *The Marquis de Morès: Emperor of the Bad Lands*. Norman: University of Oklahoma Press, 1970, p. 138.
16. *New York Tribune*, October 11, 1886.

NEW HORIZONS

1. Douglas Brinkley, *The Wilderness Warrior: Theodore Roosevelt and the Crusade for America*. New York: HarperCollins Publishers, 2009, p. 203.
2. Ibid., p. 206.
3. Ibid., p. 270.
4. Edmund Morris, *The Rise of Theodore Roosevelt*. New York: Random House, 1979, pp. 397, 417.
5. Ibid., p. 837, n. 114.
6. Ibid., p. 409.
7. Ibid., p. 428.
8. Letter dated May 19, 1895. Elting E. Morison, ed. *The Letters of Theodore Roosevelt: The Years of Preparation, 1868–1898*. Cambridge, MA: Harvard University Press, 1951, p. 458.
9. Letter dated June 23, 1895. Ibid., p. 463.
10. *New York Evening Telegraph*, June 11, 1895.
11. *TR: The Story of Theodore Roosevelt*, David Grubin Prods. / Public Broadcasting System, 1996.
12. Morris, *The Rise of Theodore Roosevelt*, pp. 528, 532.
13. *Teddy Roosevelt: An American Lion*, Greystone Communications, Inc. / History Channel, 2002.
14. In February 1898, a board of inquiry was held to determine the cause of the explosion. The findings stated it was an external explosion, possibly by a mine. Another hearing, in 1910, upheld the same theory. However, a private investigation in 1976 by Adm. Hyman Rickover claimed the battleship was sunk by an internal explosion, such as a fire in the coal bunker. In 1998, the National Geographic Society launched an investigation, which concluded that it was an external explosion, supporting the mine theory.
15. Dale L. Walker, *The Boys of '98: Theodore Roosevelt and the Rough Riders*. New York: Forge Books, 1998, p. 58.
16. Ibid., p. 87.
17. Ibid., p. 108.
18. Ibid., p. 124.
19. Only Cuba went with the Rough Riders on the ship, but the trio was reunited with the surviving Rough Riders on Long Island.
20. Walker, *The Boys of '98*, p. 161.
21. Newspaper reporters called Las Guasimas an ambush in their articles.
22. Kettle Hill was given this moniker because of a large iron kettle that was placed next to the small building on the hill. The building and kettle were used for refining sugarcane.
23. Theodore Roosevelt, *The Rough Riders*. New York: Fall River Press, 2014, p. 141.

24. Angus Konstam, *San Juan Hill 1898: America's Emergence as a World Power*. Oxford, United Kingdom: Osprey Publishing, 1998, p. 66.
25. There was a second, wider photo taken on the hill where Theodore is not wearing his campaign hat.
26. Of the 1,060 Rough Riders, 100 died, including 5 officers. Only 20 deaths were caused by malaria, dysentery, and typhoid.
27. The book proved to be an immediate success, going into a third printing by the end of May 1899. Roosevelt, *The Rough Riders*, p. 229.
28. Roosevelt, *The Rough Riders*, p. 231.
29. Ibid.
30. Ibid., p. 232.
31. Morris, *The Rise of Theodore Roosevelt*, p. 718.
32. Letter dated November 25, 1898. H. W. Brands, *The Selected Letters of Theodore Roosevelt*. New York: Cooper Square Press, 2001, p. 212.
33. Letter dated May 6, 1899. H. W. Brands, *T. R.: The Last Romantic*. New York: Basic Books, 1997, p. 379.
34. *TR: The Story of Theodore Roosevelt*.
35. The three vice presidents who won the presidential office in a direct election were John Adams, Thomas Jefferson, and Martin Van Buren. John Tyler, Millard Fillmore, Andrew Johnson, and Chester A. Arthur took over the office due to the death of the sitting president.
36. Letter dated December 11, 1899. Brands, *The Selected Letters of Theodore Roosevelt*, pp. 233–34.
37. Hermann Hagedorn, *Roosevelt in the Badlands*. New York: Houghton Mifflin, 1921, p. 467.
38. Morris, *The Rise of Theodore Roosevelt*, p. 763.
39. Brands, *T. R.: The Last Romantic*, pp. 410–11.
40. When the exposition closed, the "Trip to the Moon" attraction was moved to Coney Island's Luna Park.
41. Leon Czolgosz was found guilty on September 24, 1901, of murder after the jury deliberated for one hour. He did not cooperate with his attorneys, nor make any statement in court. Czolgosz was executed in the electric chair on October 29, 1901.

THAT DAMNED COWBOY!

1. Letter dated September 23, 1901. H. W. Brands, *The Selected Letters of Theodore Roosevelt*. New York: Cooper Square Press, 2001, pp. 269–70.
2. Albert Shaw, *A Cartoon History of Roosevelt's Career*. New York: The Review of Reviews Company, 1910, pp. 13, 47.
3. Ibid., p. 75.
4. The Sherman Antitrust Act of 1890 was created to prevent corporate monopolies of a particular product or service. This law made it illegal for any company to enter into any contract that restrained trade or to form a single company that monopolized a particular market.

5. The meeting was held in Theodore's temporary offices at 22 Jackson Place, while the White House was undergoing extensive renovations. Theodore had changed the name from the Executive Mansion to the White House shortly after taking office.

6. Letter dated October 3, 1902. Brands, *The Selected Letters of Theodore Roosevelt*, p. 285.

7. Theodore Roosevelt, *Theodore Roosevelt: An Autobiography*. Norwalk, CT: The Easton Press, 1996, p. 508.

8. The bear was not killed by a rifle shot, but stabbed to death. Douglas Brinkley, *The Wilderness Warrior: Theodore Roosevelt and the Crusade for America*. New York: Harper-Collins Publishers, 2009, p. 440.

9. Clifford Berryman's cartoon appeared in the *Washington Post* on November 17, 1902. In the first version of the drawing, Berryman had drawn a full-size black bear, but later changed it to a cuter-looking bear cub. Linda Mullins, *The Teddy Bear Men: Theodore Roosevelt and Clifford Berryman*. Grantsville, MD: Hobby House Press, 1998, pp. 32–33.

10. Brinkley, *The Wilderness Warrior*, pp. 442–43.

11. Two years later, in 1903, Porter directed *The Great Train Robbery*. Film historians consider it be the first Western narrative film—shot in the wilds of New Jersey.

12. *Edison Films*, July 1901, p. 72.

13. *Variety*, March 9, 1907, p. 8.

14. Edmund Morris, *Theodore Rex*. New York: Random House, 2001, p. 363.

15. *Denver Republican*, February 2, 1904.

16. Robert K. DeArment, *Gunfighter in Gotham: Bat Masterson's New York City Years*. Norman: University of Oklahoma Press, 2013, p. 80.

17. Jack DeMattos, *Masterson and Roosevelt*. College Station, TX: Creative Publishing Company, 1984, p. 16.

18. Ibid., pp. 22–23.

19. DeArment, *Gunfighter in Gotham*, pp. 81–82.

20. *New York Times*, March 29, 1905.

21. Robert K. DeArment and Jack DeMattos, *A Rough Ride to Redemption: The Ben Daniels Story*. Norman: University of Oklahoma Press, 2010, pp. 16–17, 19–21.

22. Theodore Roosevelt, *The Rough Riders*. New York: Fall River press (reprint), 2014, p. 37.

23. DeArment and DeMattos, *A Rough Ride to Redemption*, p. 113.

24. Ibid., pp. 117–18.

25. Ibid., p. 147.

26. David A. Wolff, *Seth Bullock: Black Hills Lawman*. Pierre, SD: South Dakota State Historical Society Press, 2009, pp. 126–27.

27. Ibid., p. 145.

28. Ibid., pp. 147, 154.

29. Seth Bullock had been a lawman in Montana, before coming to Deadwood. He arrived in the mining town one day before Wild Bill Hickok was shot in the back of the head by Jack McCall. He also was a captain in the Rough Riders, a unit that mainly sat on their heels in the summer humidity of Georgia.

30. Letter from Theodore Roosevelt to Theodore Roosevelt (Jr.). September 29, 1903. Theodore Roosevelt Papers, Manuscript Division, Library of Congress.

31. Lew Wallace, a former Union general during the Civil War, is perhaps best known as the author of *Ben-Hur: A Tale of the Christ* (1880). He knew Garrett while serving as the territorial governor of New Mexico, during the Lincoln County War. Letter from Bernard Radey to Theodore Roosevelt, December 13, 1901. Theodore Roosevelt Papers, Manuscript Division, Library of Congress.

32. Jack DeMattos, *Garrett and Roosevelt*. College Station, TX: Creative Publishing Company, 1988, p. 93.

33. Brinkley, *The Wilderness Warrior*, p. 14.

34. *Teddy Roosevelt: An American Lion*, Greystone Communications, Inc. / History Channel, 2002.

35. The Great Loop Tour would take 66 days, traveling 14,000 miles. Theodore would give 260 stump and 5 major speeches. Brinkley, *The Wilderness Warrior*, p. 509.

36. Before leaving the presidency, Theodore prohibited the killing of mountain lions in Yellowstone.

37. John Burroughs, *Camping and Tramping with Roosevelt*. New York: Houghton Mifflin, 1907, p. 6.

38. Ibid., p. 12.

39. Ibid., pp. 32–33.

40. Ibid., p. 40.

41. Ibid., pp. 8, 80.

42. Paul Russell Cutright, *Theodore Roosevelt: The Making of a Conservationist*. Chicago: University of Illinois Press, 1985, p. 225.

43. Brinkley, *The Wilderness Warrior*, p. 523.

44. Albert Bushnell Hart and Herbert Ronald Feleger, eds., *Theodore Roosevelt Cyclopedia*. Westport, CT: Theodore Roosevelt Association and Meckler Corporation, 1989, p. 217.

45. Chris Epting, *Teddy Roosevelt in California: The Whistle Stop Tour that Changed America*. Charleston, SC: The History Press, 2015, p. 69.

46. Theodore Roosevelt, *Theodore Roosevelt: An Autobiography*. Norwalk, CT: The Easton Press (reprint), 1996, p. 347.

47. Epting, *Teddy Roosevelt in California*, pp. 93–94.

48. Upon his return to Washington, Theodore quickly worked to have both Yosemite Valley and Mariposa Grove included as part of Yosemite National Park. At the request of John Muir, he also extended the forest reserves in the Mount Shasta area.

49. The area where Theodore, Muir, Leidig, and Leonard camped is now marked with a sign.

50. Epting, *Teddy Roosevelt in California*, p. 96.

51. Brinkley, *The Wilderness Warrior*, p. 540.

52. Ibid., p. 624.

53. Trees found in the Wichita Mountains include red cedar and post and blackjack oaks. The grasslands are dominated by little bluestem, but also include switchgrass, Indian grass, and blue grama.

54. *Frederick Enterprise*, April 15, 1905.

55. John R. Abernathy, *Catch 'em Alive Jack: The Life and Adventures of an American Pioneer*. Lincoln: University of Nebraska Press, 2006, p. 102.

56. Ibid., p. 103.
57. Theodore Roosevelt, *Outdoor Pastimes of an American Hunter*, Birmingham, AL: Palladium Press (reprint), 1999, p. 114.
58. Brinkley, *The Wilderness Warrior*, p. 608.
59. Ibid., p. 613.
60. Roosevelt, *Outdoor Pastimes of an American Hunter*, pp. 71–72.
61. Charles "Buffalo" Jones had hunted the shaggy beasts on the Great Plains. He had a change of heart and established a buffalo farm near Yellowstone to help save the species. Theodore visited Jones's herd during his 1903 trip. Jones was appointed game warden of Yellowstone in July 1902.
62. The National Bison Range has a population of close to six hundred buffalo today.
63. In May 2016, President Obama signed into law a bill that designated the American buffalo as the official mammal of the United States.
64. Taft got his wish in 1921, when President Warren G. Harding nominated him as chief justice. Taft served until 1930, resigning due to health issues.

THE OLD LION'S AUTUMN

1. *Teddy Roosevelt: An American Lion*, Greystone Communications, Inc. / History Channel, 2002.
2. The expedition amassed a collection of 23,151 natural history specimens. The mammals alone numbered 5,013 specimens, including 9 lions, 13 rhinoceros, 20 zebras, 8 warthogs, and 4 hyenas. It took eight years to catalog all of the material.
3. The magazine paid Theodore a $50,000 fee for twelve articles. The articles, as well as additional material, would become his eighteenth book, *African Game Trails* (1910).
4. H. W. Brands, *T. R.: The Last Romantic*. New York: Basic Books, 1997, pp. 658–59.
5. Letter from Theodore Roosevelt to Seth Bullock, May 17, 1909. Theodore Roosevelt Collection. MS Am 1834 (94).
6. Brands, *T. R.: The Last Romantic*, p. 662.
7. Albert Bushnell Hart and Herbert Ronald Feleger, eds. *Theodore Roosevelt Cyclopedia*. Westport, CT: Theodore Roosevelt Association and Meckler Corporation, 1989, p. 387.
8. Letter from Theodore Roosevelt to Seth Bullock. May 17, 1909.
9. David A. Wolff, *Seth Bullock: Black Hills Lawman*. Pierre: South Dakota State Historical Society Press, 2009, p. 160.
10. Edmund Morris, *Colonel Roosevelt*. New York: Random House, 2010, pp. 82–85.
11. Ibid., p. 89.
12. Ibid., p. 170.
13. Brands, *T. R.: The Last Romantic*, p. 713.
14. Schrank was found guilty by reason of insanity. He was given a life sentence, and sent to the Central State Mental Hospital in Wisconsin, where he died in 1943 at the age of sixty-seven.
15. Morris, *Colonel Roosevelt*, p. 331.
16. Ibid., pp. 336–40.
17. Ibid., pp. 389–90.

18. Theodore had enlisted Seth Bullock to compile a list of men who would want to serve, much like his Rough Riders.

19. *Teddy Roosevelt: An American Lion.*

20. Ted Jr., Archie, and Kermit were wounded during the war, but survived.

21. Ted Jr. was buried in the World War II Normandy American Cemetery in Colleville-sur-Mer in France. In 1955, Quentin's remains were buried next to his older brother.

22. Rolf Sletten, *Medora: Boom, Bust, and Resurrection.* Medora, ND: Theodore Roosevelt Medora Foundation, 2013, p. 186.

23. Andrew Vietze, *Becoming Teddy Roosevelt: How a Maine Guide Inspired America's 26th President.* Lanham, MD: Down East, 2010, p. 151.

24. Ibid., p. 142.

25. Sletten, *Medora: Boom, Bust, and Resurrection,* p. 189.

26. Ibid., pp. 124–25, 148–49.

A LASTING MEMORIAL

1. The smaller park boundary would have been fourteen miles wide, extending ninety miles along the Little Missouri River from Marmarth to the eastern swing of the river south of Watford City. David Harmon, *At the Open Margin: The NPS's Administration of Theodore Roosevelt National Park.* Medora, ND: Theodore Roosevelt Nature and History Association, 1986, pp. 6–7.

2. Ibid., p. 13.

3. Ibid., p. 22.

4. The family that held the park concession for providing the trail rides retired in early 2015. As of this writing, there are no immediate plans to offer horseback rides through the park.

5. Birds that reside in the park year-round include golden eagles, wild turkeys, black-capped chickadees, white-breasted nuthatches, and great horned owls.

6. Highway 85 runs in a north-south direction on the western side of South and North Dakota. In 2012, this author saw a herd of a dozen pronghorns running alongside the highway in an open field. Driving at fifty-five miles per hour, the pronghorns were easily keeping up with the car.

7. Mike Thompson, *The Travels and Tribulations of Theodore Roosevelt's Cabin.* San Angelo, TX: Laughing Horse Publications, 2004, p. 57.

8. Ibid., pp. 38–40.

9. The Maltese Cross Ranch property is now privately owned. The owners have erected a sign marking the original site of Theodore's cabin.

10. H. Paul Jeffers, *The Bully Pulpit: A Teddy Roosevelt Book of Quotations.* Lanham, MD: Taylor Trade Publishing, 2002, p. 30.

11. "USGS Releases New Oil and Gas Assessment for Bakken and Three Forks Formations," US Department of the Interior, April 30, 2013.

12. A wellbore is the hole that forms a well, generally encased in steel or cement.

13. Ryan Howell, "North Dakota's Oil Boom Is a Blessing and a Curse," Governing.com, August 2011.

14. John McChesney, "Theodore Roosevelt's Elkhorn Ranch, the 'Walden Pond of the West,' Threatened by North Dakota's Oil Boom." Stanford University, Rural West Initiative, The Bill Lane Center for the American West, April 23, 2013.
15. "The Fight for the Elkhorn," *The Arena* (newsletter), Theodore Roosevelt Association, January/February 2015.
16. Jenny Buddenborg, interview with author, Denver, Colorado, February 18, 2015.
17. Jenny Buddenborg, "US Forest Service Approves Elkhorn Gravel Pit at Theodore Roosevelt's Elkhorn Ranch," National Trust for Historic Preservation (website), January 9, 2015.
18. Edmund Morris, "Bad News for the Badlands," *New York Times*, June 7, 2012.

THE ROMANCE OF HIS LIFE

1. H. Paul Jeffers, *The Bully Pulpit: A Teddy Roosevelt Book of Quotations*. Lanham, MD: Taylor Trade Publishing, 2002, p. 131.
2. John Burroughs, *Camping and Tramping with Roosevelt*. New York: Houghton Mifflin Company, 1907, pp. 12–14.
3. Douglas Brinkley, *The Wilderness Warrior: Theodore Roosevelt and the Crusade for America*. New York: HarperCollins Publishers, 2009, p. 641.
4. Clay S. Jenkinson, *A Free and Hardy Life: Theodore Roosevelt's Sojourn in the American West*. Washburn, ND: The Dakota Institute of the Lewis & Clark Fort Mandan Foundation, 2011, p. 11.

BIBLIOGRAPHY

BOOKS

Abbott, E. C. "Teddy Blue" and Helena Huntington Smith, *We Pointed Them North: Recollections of a Cowpuncher*. Norman: University of Oklahoma Press, 1955.

Abernathy, John R. *Catch 'em Alive Jack: The Life and Adventures of an American Pioneer*. Lincoln: University of Nebraska Press, 2006.

Blevins, Win. *Dictionary of the American West*. Seattle, WA: Sasquatch Books, 2001.

Brands, H. W. *The Selected Letters of Theodore Roosevelt*. New York: Cooper Square Press, 2001.

———. *T. R.: The Last Romantic*. New York: Basic Books, 1997.

Brinkley, Douglas. *The Wilderness Warrior: Theodore Roosevelt and the Crusade for America*. New York: HarperCollins, 2009.

Brooks, Chester L., and Ray H. Mattison. *Theodore Roosevelt and the Dakota Badlands*. Medora, ND: Theodore Roosevelt Nature and History Association, 1983.

Brown, Dee. *The American West*. New York: Touchstone / Simon & Schuster, 1994.

Brownlow, Kevin. *The War, the West, and the Wilderness*. New York: Alfred A. Knopf, 1978.

Burroughs, John. *Camping and Tramping with Roosevelt*. New York: Houghton Mifflin, 1907.

Cutright, Paul Russell. *Theodore Roosevelt: The Making of a Conservationist*. Chicago: University of Illinois Press, 1985.

DeArment, Robert K. *Gunfighter in Gotham: Bat Masterson's New York City Years*. Norman: University of Oklahoma Press, 2013.

DeArment, Robert K. and Jack DeMattos. *A Rough Ride to Redemption: The Ben Daniels Story*. Norman: University of Oklahoma Press, 2010.

DeMattos, Jack. *Garrett and Roosevelt*. College Station, TX: Creative Publishing Company, 1988.

———. *Masterson and Roosevelt*. College Station, TX: Creative Publishing Company, 1984.

de Quesada, Alejandro. *Roosevelt's Rough Riders*. New York: Osprey Publishing, 2009.

Di Silvestro, Roger L. *Theodore Roosevelt in the Badlands: A Young Politician's Quest for Recovery in the American West*. New York: Walker & Company, 2011.

Dresden, Donald. *The Marquis de Mores: Emperor of the Bad Lands*. Norman: University of Oklahoma Press, 1970.

Epting, Chris. *Teddy Roosevelt in California: The Whistle Stop Tour that Changed America*. Charleston, SC: The History Press, 2015.

Hagedorn, Hermann. *The Boy's Life of Theodore Roosevelt*. New York: Harpers, 1918.

———. *Roosevelt in the Badlands.* New York: Houghton Mifflin, 1921.

———. *The Theodore Roosevelt Treasury: A Self-Portrait from His Writings.* Norwalk, CT: Easton Press, 1988.

Harmon, David. *At the Open Margin: The NPS's Administration of Theodore Roosevelt National Park.* Medora, ND: Theodore Roosevelt Nature and History Association, 1986.

Hart, Albert Bushnell, and Herbert Ronald Feleger, eds. *Theodore Roosevelt Cyclopedia.* Westport, CT: Theodore Roosevelt Association and Meckler Corporation, 1989.

Jeffers, H. Paul. *The Bully Pulpit: A Teddy Roosevelt Book of Quotations.* Lanham, MD: Taylor Trade Publishing, 2002.

———. *Roosevelt the Explorer: Teddy Roosevelt's Amazing Adventures as a Naturalist, Conservationist, and Explorer.* Lanham, MD: Taylor Trade Publishing, 2003.

Jenkinson, Clay S. *A Free and Hardy Life: Theodore Roosevelt's Sojourn in the American West.* Washburn, ND: The Dakota Institute of the Lewis & Clark Fort Mandan Foundation, 2011.

———. *Theodore Roosevelt in the Dakota Badlands: A Historical Guide.* Dickinson, ND: Dickinson State University, 2008.

Kohn, Edward P., ed. *A Most Glorious Ride: The Diaries of Theodore Roosevelt, 1877–1886.* Albany, NY: Excelsior Editions, 2015.

Konstam, Angus. *San Juan Hill 1898: America's Emergence as a World Power.* Oxford, United Kingdom: Osprey Publishing, 1998.

Lamar, Howard, ed. *The New Encyclopedia of the American West.* New Haven, CT: Yale University Press, 1998.

Lang, Lincoln A. *Ranching with Roosevelt.* Philadelphia, PA: J. D. Lippincott, 1926.

Lott, Dale F. *American Bison: A Natural History.* Berkeley: University of California Press, 2002.

Mallard, Candice. *The River of Doubt: Theodore Roosevelt's Darkest Journey.* New York: Anchor Books, 2005.

McHugh, Tom. *The Time of the Buffalo.* New York: Alfred A Knopf, 1972.

Miller, Nathan. *Theodore Roosevelt: A Life.* New York: William Morrow and Company, 1992.

Morison, Elting E., ed. *The Letters of Theodore Roosevelt: The Years of Preparation, 1868–1898.* Cambridge, MA: Harvard University Press, 1951.

Morris, Edmund. *Colonel Roosevelt.* New York: New York: Random House, 2010.

———. *The Rise of Theodore Roosevelt.* New York: Random House, 1979.

———. *Theodore Rex.* New York: Random House, 2001.

Morris, Sylvia Jukes. *Edith Kermit Roosevelt.* New York: Modern Library, 2001.

Mullins, Linda. *The Teddy Bear Men: Theodore Roosevelt and Clifford Berryman.* Grantsville, MD: Hobby House Press, 1998.

Putnam, Carleton. *Theodore Roosevelt: The Formative Years, 1858–1886.* New York: Charles Scribner's Sons, 1958.

Robinson, Corrine Roosevelt. *My Brother Theodore Roosevelt.* New York: Charles Scribner's Sons, 1921.

Roosevelt, Theodore. *Hunting the Grisly and Other Sketches*. New York: G. P. Putnam's Sons, 1893.

———. *Hunting Trips of a Ranchman*. Birmingham, AL: Palladium Press (reprint), 1999.

———. Letters, Theodore Roosevelt Collection, Houghton Library, Harvard University.

———. *Outdoor Pastimes of an American Hunter*, Birmingham, AL: Palladium Press (reprint), 1999.

———. *Ranch Life and the Hunting-Trail*. Alexandria, VA: Time-Life Books (reprint), 1981.

———. *The Rough Riders*, New York: Fall River Press (reprint), 2014.

———. *Theodore Roosevelt: An Autobiography*. Norwalk, CT: Easton Press (reprint), 1996.

———. *The Wilderness Hunter*, New York: G. P. Putnam's Sons, 1893.

Shaw, Albert. *A Cartoon History of Roosevelt's Career*. New York: The Review of Reviews Company, 1910.

Sletten, Rolf. *Medora: Boom, Bust, and Resurrection*. Medora, ND: Theodore Roosevelt Medora Foundation, 2013.

———. *Roosevelt's Ranches: The Maltese Cross and the Elkhorn*. Medora, ND: Theodore Roosevelt Medora Foundation, 2015.

Tanner, Ogden. *The Old West: The Ranchers*. Alexandria, VA: Time-Life Books, 1977.

Thompson, Mike. *The Travels and Tribulations of Theodore Roosevelt's Cabin*. San Angelo, TX: Laughing Horse Publications, 2004.

Vietze, Andrew. *Becoming Teddy Roosevelt: How a Maine Guide Inspired America's 26th President*. Lanham, MD: Down East, 2010.

Vivian, James F. *The Romance of My Life: Theodore Roosevelt's Speeches in Dakota*. Fargo, ND: Prairie House / Theodore Roosevelt Medora Foundation, 1989.

Walker, Dale L. *The Boys of '98: Theodore Roosevelt and the Rough Riders*. New York: Forge Books, 1998.

Willis, Jack, with Horace Smith. *Roosevelt in the Rough*. New York: Ives Washburn, 1931.

Wolff, David A. *Seth Bullock: Black Hills Lawman*. Pierre, SD: South Dakota State Historical Society Press, 2009.

MAGAZINE, NEWSPAPER, AND INTERNET ARTICLES

Bad Lands Cow Boy (various articles). Theodore Roosevelt Center, Dickinson State University, Dickinson, North Dakota.

Bismarck Daily Tribune (various articles).

Brands, H. W. "Deliverance," *American History*, April 2013.

Buddenborg, Jenny. "US Forest Service Approves Elkhorn Gravel Pit at Theodore Roosevelt's Elkhorn Ranch," National Trust for Historic Preservation (website), January 9, 2015.

Denver Republican (February 2, 1904).

Edison Films, July 1901.

Eriksmoen, Curt, "How the Marquis de Morès Got Started in Medora," *Bismarck Tribune*, December 8, 2013.

———. "Marquis de Morès Worked Hard, But Efforts Failed," *Bismarck Tribune*, December 15, 2013.

———. "Marquis de Morès's Later Life Fueled by Hate," *Bismarck Tribune*, December 22, 2013.

———. "TR Had Three Good Friends in Dakota Territory," *Bismarck Tribune*, April 6, 2014.

———. "How TR Got Into the Cattle Business," *Bismarck Tribune*, April 13, 2014.

———. "TR's Friends Remained Loyal through Tough Times," *Bismarck Tribune*, April 20, 2014.

"The Fight for the Elkhorn," *The Arena* (newsletter), Theodore Roosevelt Association, January/February 2015, Vol. 95, Issue 1.

Frederick Enterprise (April 15, 1905).

Havig, Alan. "Presidential Images, History, and Homage: Memorializing Theodore Roosevelt, 1919–1967," *Theodore Roosevelt Association Journal* (Fall 2011).

Howell, Ryan. "North Dakota's Oil Boom Is a Blessing and a Curse," Governing.com, August 2011.

Kingseed, Wyatt. "Teddy Roosevelt's Frontier Justice," *American History*, February 2002.

McChesney, John. "Theodore Roosevelt's Elkhorn Ranch, the 'Walden Pond of the West,' Threatened by North Dakota's Oil Boom," Stanford University, Rural West Initiative (website), The Bill Lane Center for the American West, April 23, 2013.

Morris, Edmund. "Bad News for the Badlands," *New York Times*, June 7, 2012.

New York Daily Tribune (October 18, 1885).

New York Evening Telegraph (various articles).

New York Times (March 29, 1905).

Robinson III, Charles M. "The Cowboy President," *True West*, July 1993.

Variety, March 9, 1907.

Walker, Dale L. "Teddy's Terrors," *True West*, September 1998.

MANUSCRIPTS

Mattison, Ray H. "Roosevelt's Contemporaries Along the Little Missouri River," Theodore Roosevelt National Park, Theodore Roosevelt Digital Library, Dickinson State University, 1950.

Diaries of Theodore Roosevelt, Theodore Roosevelt Collection, Houghton Library, Harvard University.

Personal diaries of Theodore Roosevelt, Theodore Roosevelt Papers, Manuscript Division, Library of Congress.

DOCUMENTARIES

Teddy Roosevelt: An American Lion, Greystone Communications, Inc. / History Channel, 2002.

Theodore Roosevelt: A Cowboy's Ride to the White House, Dorgan Films, 2010.

The Roosevelts: An Intimate History, Florentine Films/WETA, 2014.

TR: The Story of Theodore Roosevelt, David Grubin Prods. / Public Broadcasting System, 1996.

Bibliography

INTERVIEWS

Jenny Buddenborg, Denver, Colorado, February 18, 2015.
Doug Ellison, Medora, North Dakota, September 16, 2014.
Robin McQuinn, Medora, North Dakota, September 16, 2014.

INDEX

ABOUT THE AUTHOR

MICHAEL F. BLAKE, A TWO-TIME EMMY AWARD–WINNING MAKEUP artist, has worked in the film and television industry for the past fifty-nine years.

As a child actor, Michael appeared in such television shows as *Adam-12*, *The Lucy Show*, *The Munsters*, *Bonanza*, *Kung Fu*, *The Red Skelton Show*, and *Marcus Welby, M.D.* At the age of twenty-one, he began his career as a makeup artist at Universal Studios. His credits include *Westworld*, *Spider-Man 3*, *Soapdish*, *X-Men: First Class*, *Domino*, *Independence Day*, *Tough Guys*, *Police Academy II*, *Strange Days*, *Magnum, P.I.*, and *Happy Days*.

A respected film scholar, with a master's degree from UCLA, Michael's three books on silent screen legend Lon Chaney are considered the definitive volumes on the actor. He has also written *Code of Honor: The Making of* High Noon, Shane, *and* The Searchers and *Hollywood and the O.K. Corral*, which are praised as important works about the Western genre.

A longtime admirer of Theodore Roosevelt, he spent three years traversing the Badlands on foot and on horseback, researching every aspect relating to TR's days in the Dakotas. Like the man he has written about, Michael has driven cattle, crossed rivers on horseback, and spent sunrise to sunset in the saddle, which gives him an authoritative voice relating to Roosevelt's days in the American West.

Michael lives in Los Angeles with his wife, Linda, and their dogs, Charli and Dobie. His two adopted mustangs, Theodore and Dillon, run free at the Black Hills Wild Horse Sanctuary.